〔美〕E·B·怀特 著 任溶溶 译

Charlotte's Web

·英汉双语珍藏本·

夏洛的网

Charlotte's Web

上海译文出版社

导读

好书

严　锋

有一本书，叫《夏洛的网》，是美国人E·B·怀特写的，在中国知道的人不算太多，喜欢的人却不少。

我第一次读到这本书是在一九七九年初夏的时候。那一年，我上初三，被升学考试压得昏头涨脑，有一天偶然到久违了的市图书馆去逛逛，发现那里竟然腾出一层楼面，新辟为“少年图书馆”，专为初中以下的读者服务。我头一热，就当场办了一张证进去了。这多少有点奇怪，因为我不太记得自己有什么少年儿童时期，从小学四年级开始，手头便拥有市图书馆的正式借书证，而且几乎从来不看“成人读物”以外的东西。根本就不屑看。偏偏在我行将告别少年的时候，会跑到一个姗姗来迟的“少年图书馆”，这实在要算是一种罕见的缘分，仿佛冥冥之中有一种指引，让我在“少年”的最后两个月里，终于读到了少年应该读的，并且可以读一辈子的东西。

印象当中，在“少年图书馆”里，大概前后就只借过这一本书。两个月以后我就读高中了，基本上和图书馆就断绝了来往。不过，套用一种我们比较习惯的说法，一本书可以顶一万本书。在我以后的有生之年里，大概过两三年我就要把这本书找得来看一遍，好像病人要定期吃药那样。有时候，生活中遇到一些额外不顺心的东西，像失恋啦，或是出国被人挤掉啦，那么就还会额外不定期地服用。服用之后便觉天高日丽，神完气足，心清肺明，好似用光了的蓄电池充足了电，又可以投入到人世间没完没了的损耗中去。

这实在是一本宝书。我觉得在一个理想的世界里，应该只有两种人存在：一种是读过《夏洛的网》的人；另一种是将要读《夏洛的网》的人。有时候，半夜里醒过来，摸摸胸口还在跳，就会很高兴，因为活着就意味着还能再把《夏洛的网》读一遍，而读《夏洛的网》就意味着还活着。

一天大清早，小姑娘弗恩看到他爸爸阿拉布尔手里拿着把斧头匆匆往外赶去，便问她妈妈这是怎么一回事。阿拉布尔太太告诉她，昨晚家里的老母猪生了一窝小猪，其中有一只必须被“杀掉”。小姑娘一听就急了，赶紧冲出去抢她爸爸的斧头。阿拉布尔先生告诉她，那只小猪先天不足，又瘦又小，恐怕是很难养大。这时，小姑娘说了一句非常精彩的话：“我也又瘦又小，难道也应该被杀掉？”

阿拉布尔先生让步了，弗恩独力喂养这只小猪，并为它取名威尔伯。可是弗恩还不算是这本书的主角。养到五个星期的时候，威尔伯已经太大，弗恩也养不了它了，于是听从阿拉布尔先生的劝告，六个美元把威尔伯卖到了附近农场的她舅舅朱克曼家的谷仓里，这样她还可以经常去看望它。

在朱克曼舅舅的谷仓里，威尔伯一天到晚吃吃喝喝，晒晒太阳，感到很满足。就当它开始变得膘肥体壮的时候，旁边的鹅、羊、马、牛以过来人的身份发出了盛世危言。它们明确地指出，威尔伯的未来就是圣诞节的火腿。威尔伯吓坏了，在大家的怂恿下，它盲目地进行了一次逃亡，结果当然是失败。它又被关回了谷仓，当夜晚来临的时候，威尔伯躺在烂泥里，闻着它熟悉而又喜爱的臭哄哄的味道，想着过去的幸福生活，想着迫在眉睫的悲惨结局，忍不住悲从中来，哭成了个泪人儿。“我不想死啊，我不想死啊！”可是又有谁能救得了它呢？猪的命运难道不就是那样吗？

就在恨意绵绵而又万念俱灰的一刹那，从谷仓的黑暗中传来了一个清朗的声音：“你不会死的。”

我真的记不得我看了多少遍《夏洛的网》了，我熟知那里的每一个细节。可是，每次当我再听到这个黑暗中的坚定的声音的时候，还是忍不住头皮发麻，热泪盈眶。这是（发生在谷仓里的）伟大的一瞬间，就像上帝在说：“要有光。”

但是这里却并没有什么上帝，而是一只叫作夏洛的蜘蛛。夏洛答应威尔伯，她一定会想办法拯救它的生命。夏洛说了一句我们每个人都应该记住的话：

“我可以做你的朋友，我喜欢你。睡觉吧。明天早晨你就看见我了。”

一开始，夏洛老实承认自己还没有具体的计划，但是它会在每天穿梭织网的时候不停地思考。最后，聪明的夏洛终于想出了一个绝妙的办法。亲爱的朋友，如果您是一只蜘蛛，如果您也想去拯救一头可爱的小猪，您会怎么做呢？您能有切实可行的计划吗？至于我，苦思冥想了很多年，所有想出来的办法都比不上夏洛的好。

朱克曼家的帮工勒维在早晨来到谷仓，倒完猪食后，他抬头一看，猪食槽上方有个大大的蜘蛛网，网上明确无误地结着几个大字：“王牌猪”(SOME PIG)。

消息顿时传遍了乡里，威尔伯成了一头名猪。来参观的人络绎不绝，朱克曼一家乐开了花。名气确实不是一件坏事情，至少对猪来说是如此，但是威尔伯的命运仍然在空中飘荡。在一个贪吃的老鼠坦普尔顿很不情愿的帮助下，夏洛用它的网上艺术对威尔伯的名声层层加码，连续推出“了不起”(TERRIFIC)、“光彩照人”(RADIANT) 等光辉字眼。最后，威尔伯参加了当地的农业博览会，在危急关头，已经衰老的夏洛，使尽全身的力气，用一个即兴发挥的“谦卑”(HUMBLE)把临阵怯场的威尔伯推上了金奖的宝座和名声的顶点，从而彻底地化解了威尔伯的性命问题。当胜利的消息传来，也是夏洛自觉衰老将亡的一刻，故事在此达到最高潮。

夏洛和威尔伯最后的对话简单中见真诚，感人至深：

“夏洛，”威尔伯停了一会儿说，“你为什么这样安静啊？”“我喜欢一动不动地坐着，”它说，“我一向就是十分安静。”“不过你今天好像特别安静，你没事吧？”“也许有点累，不过我觉得很平静。你今天上午在圆围栏里的成功，在很小的程度上也是我的成功。你的未来有保证了。你会活下去，安然无恙，威尔伯。现在没有什么能伤害你了。秋天的白昼要变短，天气要变冷。树叶要从树上飘落。圣诞节于是到了，接下来就下冬雪。你将活下来欣赏冰天雪地的美景，因为你对朱克曼先生来说太重要了，他怎么也不会伤害你。冬天会过去，白昼又变长，牧场池塘的冰要融化。北美歌雀将回来唱歌，青蛙将醒来，和暖的风又会吹起。所有这些景物、声音和香气都是供你享受的。威尔伯……噢，这个美好的世界，这些珍贵的日子……”夏洛说着说着停了下来。

夏洛缓慢而又安静地死去，但是在死以前，除了拯救威尔伯，实现了自己对朋友的承诺以外，它也完成了自己的一件最重大的作品，一只卵袋，里面安安稳稳地装着它的五百十四个未来的儿女。威尔伯想尽办法把卵袋带回了农场，到了来年春天，小夏洛们一个个地破囊而出，乘风而去，但还是有三个小蜘蛛愿意留下来陪伴威尔伯，继续它们的母亲和威尔伯的友谊。

一开始的时候，因为无知，我还以为作者怀特是个无名之辈，后来慢慢地收集了一些他的资料，才知道不那么简单。怀特写的儿童文学只有三部，除了《夏洛的网》以外，还有《精灵鼠小弟》和《吹小号的天鹅》，每一部都是不断再版的经典之作。这一发现着实令我欣喜若狂，但是也有莫名的失落，好像是突然发现自己偷偷暗恋的素面淡装的无名女孩竟然是当红的偶像明星。

从上世纪二十年代开始，怀特为《纽约客》（New Yorker）和后来的《哈珀斯》（Harpers）杂志撰写专栏散文，这些散文描写都市人情世态，名气也毫不在怀特的小说之下，至今还不断地结集再版。怀特的散文，一如其小说，朴素，明晰，隽永。这正是他在一九七九年修订的名著《风格的要素》中对文字的要求。

这也正是怀特的生活的风格。他迷恋简单素朴的农村生活。他的一生，有很大一部分光阴是在乡间渡过。怀特是养猪的好手，《夏洛的网》写的很大一部分就是他自己的生活，夏洛是真有其蛛，整个故事的源起也就在怀特拎着一桶猪食走向威尔伯的路上。在一篇谈自己创作的文章里，怀特写道："对一个喜爱动物的人来说，农场也是一个恼人的地方，因为绝大多数的牲畜的恩养者，同时也就是它们的谋杀者。牲口们平静地生活，却可怕地暴然死去，命运的不祥之音始终在它们耳际回荡。我养了一些猪，春天下的崽，我喂了它们一个夏天，一个秋天。这种情形令我苦恼。我和我的猪一天天地熟识，它们也一样。"最后，在《夏洛的网》里，怀特下决心要拯救一头小猪的性命。

拯救一头小猪的性命有意义吗？我想，和拯救大兵瑞恩的意义应该是一样的吧。

不过，从我第一次读《夏洛的网》到现在，已经有二十多年过去了，可是我一直都没能搞明白，这部“儿童文学”何以能够如此长久地令我着迷。这种着迷到最后已经成了一种偏执。我以传教般的热情把它推荐给自己所认识的每一个人，并且非常紧张地等待对方的反应，如果他们说好，我就会大大增加对他们的好感，如果对方反应平平，我就会掉头而去。我当然也记得我遇见的第一个自己在少年时期就读过《夏洛的网》的人，如今的著名学者包亚明先生。那还是刚上大学的时候，彼此还比较陌生，可是无意中谈及自己最喜爱的书，竟然都是《夏洛的网》，那种又惊又喜，相见恨晚的感觉，实在是难以言表。不用说，包君当场就成了我终身的朋友。

张炜在《柏慧》里提出了一个引起争议的看法，认为世界上所有的好人可能过去都是一个族里的，具有某种血缘的联系，后来因为某种原因而失散于世界各地。我觉得这种观点有点意思，想补充的是：这些好人们在联络的时候，会相互间说一些暗号，而《夏洛的网》就是暗号之一。就像《智取威虎山》里面对那种天王盖地虎式的切口一样，一个人说一声“王牌猪”，另一个人对一个“光彩照人”，相互就能够相视而笑，莫逆于心。

E.B. White

Charlotte's Web

Contents

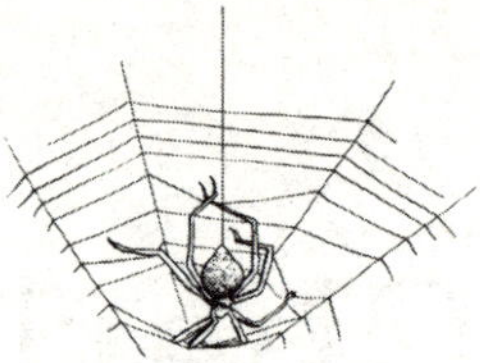

1. Before Breakfast / 3
2. Wilbur / 9
3. Escape / 14
4. Loneliness / 24
5. Charlotte / 30
6. Summer Days / 38
7. Bad News / 43
8. A Talk at Home / 46
9. Wilbur' s Boast / 49

10. An Explosion / 59
11. The Miracle / 68
12. A Meeting / 75
13. Good Progress / 80
14. Dr Dorian / 90
15. The Crickets / 97
16. Off to the Fair / 101
17. Uncle / 111
18. The Cool of the Evening / 117
19. The Egg Sac / 122
20. The Hour of Triumph / 132
21. Last Day / 139
22. A Warm Wind / 146

1.

Before Breakfast

'Where's Papa going with that axe?' said Fern to her mother as they were setting the table for breakfast.

'Out to the hoghouse,' replied Mrs Arable. 'Some pigs were born last night.'

'I don't see why he needs an axe,' continued Fern, who was only eight.

'Well,' said her mother, 'one of the pigs is a runt. It's very small and weak, and it will never amount to anything. So your father has decided to do away with it.'

'Do *away* with it?' shrieked Fern. 'You mean *kill* it? Just because it's smaller than the others?'

Mrs Arable put a pitcher of cream on the table. 'Don't yell, Fern!' she said. 'Your father is right. The pig would probably die anyway.'

Fern pushed a chair out of the way, and ran outdoors. The grass was wet and the earth smelled of springtime. Fern's sneakers were sopping by the time she caught up with her father.

'Please don't kill it!' she sobbed. 'It's unfair.'

Mr Arable stopped walking.

'Fern,' he said gently, 'you will have to learn to control yourself.'

'Control myself?' yelled Fern. 'This is a matter of life and death, and you talk about *controlling* myself.' Tears ran down her cheeks and she took hold of the axe and tried to pull it out of her father's hand.

'Fern,' said Mr Arable, 'I know more about raising a litter of pigs than you do. A weakling makes trouble. Now run along!'

'But it's unfair,' cried Fern. 'The pig couldn't help being born small, could it? If *I* had been very small at birth, would you have killed *me*?'

Mr Arable smiled. 'Certainly not,' he said, looking down at his daughter with love. 'But this is different. A little girl is one thing, a little runty pig is another.'

'I see no difference,' replied Fern, still hanging on to the axe. 'This is the most terrible case of injustice I ever heard of.'

A queer look came over John Arable's face. He seemed almost ready to cry himself.

'All right,' he said. 'You go back to the house and I will bring the runt when I come in. I'll let you raise it on a bottle, like a baby. Then you'll see what trouble a pig can be.'

When Mr Arable returned to the house half an hour later, he carried a carton under his arm. Fern was upstairs changing her sneakers. The kitchen table was set for breakfast, and the room smelt of coffee, bacon, damp plaster, and wood-smoke from the stove.

'Put it on her chair!' said Mrs Arable. Mr Arable set the carton down at Fern's place. Then he walked to the sink and washed his hands and dried them on the roller towel.

Fern came slowly down the stairs. Her eyes were red from crying. As she approached her chair, the carton wobbled, and there was a scratching noise. Fern looked at her father. Then she lifted the lid of the carton. There, inside, looking up at her, was the newborn pig. It was a white one. The morning light shone through its ears, turning them pink.

'He's yours,' said Mr Arable. 'Saved from an untimely death. And may the good Lord forgive me for this foolishness.'

Fern couldn't take her eyes off the tiny pig. 'Oh,' she whispered. 'Oh, *look* at him! He's absolutely perfect.'

She closed the carton carefully. First she kissed her father, then she kissed her mother. Then she opened the lid again, lifted the pig out, and held it against her cheek. At this moment her brother Avery came into the room. Avery was ten. He was heavily armed — an air rifle in one hand, a wooden dagger in the other.

'What's that?' he demanded. 'What's Fern got?'

'She's got a guest for breakfast,' said Mrs Arable. 'Wash your hands and face, Avery!'

'Let's see it!' said Avery, setting his gun down. 'You call that miserable thing a pig? That's a *fine* specimen of a pig — it's no bigger than a white rat.'

'Wash up and eat your breakfast, Avery!' said his mother. 'The school bus will be along in half an hour.'

'Can I have a pig too, Pop?' asked Avery.

'No, I only distribute pigs to early risers,' said Mr Arable. 'Fern was up at daylight, trying to rid the world of injustice. As a result, she now has a pig. A small one, to be sure, but nevertheless a pig. It just shows what can happen if a person gets out of bed promptly. Let's eat!'

But Fern couldn't eat until her pig had had a drink of milk. Mrs Arable found a baby's nursing bottle and a rubber nipple. She poured warm milk into the bottle, fitted the nipple over the top, and handed it to Fern. 'Give him his breakfast!' she said.

A minute later, Fern was seated on the floor in the corner of the kitchen with her infant between her knees, teaching it to suck from the bottle. The pig, although tiny, had a good appetite and caught on quickly.

The school bus honked from the road.

'Run!' commanded Mrs Arable, taking the pig from Fern and slipping a doughnut into her hand. Avery grabbed his gun and another doughnut.

The children ran out to the road and climbed into the bus. Fern took no notice of the others in the bus. She just sat and stared out of the window, thinking what a blissful world it was and how lucky she was to have entire charge of a pig. By the time the bus reached school, Fern had named her pet, selecting the most beautiful name she could think of.

'Its name is Wilbur,' she whispered to herself.

She was still thinking about the pig when the teacher said: 'Fern, what is the capital of Pennsylvania?'

'Wilbur,' replied Fern, dreamily. The pupils giggled. Fern blushed.

2.

Wilbur

Fern loved Wilbur more than anything. She loved to stroke him, to feed him, to put him to bed. Every morning, as soon as she got up, she warmed his milk, tied his bib on, and held the bottle for him. Every afternoon, when the school bus stopped in front of her house, she jumped out and ran to the kitchen to fix another bottle for him. She fed him again at suppertime, and again just before going to bed. Mrs Arable gave him a feeding around noontime each day, when Fern was away in school. Wilbur loved his milk, and he was never happier than when Fern was warming up a bottle for him. He would stand and gaze up at her with adoring eyes.

For the first few days of his life, Wilbur was allowed to live in a box near the stove in the kitchen. Then, when Mrs Arable complained, he was moved to a bigger box in the woodshed. At two weeks of age, he was moved outdoors. It was apple-blossom time, and the days were getting warmer. Mr Arable fixed a small yard specially for Wilbur under an apple tree, and gave him a large wooden box full of straw, with a doorway cut in it so he could walk in and out as he pleased.

‘Won’ t he be cold at night?’ asked Fern.

‘No,’ said her father. ‘You watch and see what he does.’

Carrying a bottle of milk, Fern sat down under the apple tree inside the yard. Wilbur ran to her and she held the bottle for him while he sucked. When he had finished the last drop, he grunted

and walked sleepily into the box. Fern peered through the door. Wilbur was poking the straw with his snout. In a short time he had dug a tunnel in the straw. He crawled into the tunnel and disappeared from sight, completely covered with straw. Fern was enchanted. It relieved her mind to know that her baby would sleep covered up, and would stay warm.

Every morning after breakfast, Wilbur walked out to the road with Fern and waited with her till the bus came. She would wave good-bye to him, and he would stand and watch the bus until it

vanished round a turn. While Fern was in school, Wilbur was shut up inside his yard. But as soon as she got home in the afternoon, she would take him out and he would follow her round the place. If she went into the house, Wilbur went too. If she went upstairs, Wilbur would wait at the bottom step until she came down again. If she took her doll for a walk in the doll carriage, Wilbur followed along. Sometimes, on these journeys, Wilbur would get tired, and Fern would pick him up and put him in the carriage alongside the doll. He liked this. And if he was *very* tired, he would close his eyes and go to sleep under the doll's blanket. He looked cute when his eyes were closed, because his lashes were so long. The doll would close her eyes, too, and Fern would wheel the carriage very slowly and smoothly so as not to wake her infants.

One warm afternoon, Fern and Avery put on bathing suits and went down to the brook for a swim. Wilbur tagged along at Fern's heels. When she waded into the brook, Wilbur waded in with her. He found the water quite cold—too cold for his liking. So while the children swam and played and splashed water at each other, Wilbur amused himself in the mud along the edge of the brook, where it was warm and moist and delightfully sticky and oozy.

Every day was a happy day, and every night was peaceful.

Wilbur was what farmers call a spring pig, which simply means that he was born in springtime. When he was five weeks old, Mr Arable said he was now big enough to sell, and would have to be sold. Fern broke down and wept. But her father was firm about it.

Wilbur's appetite had increased; he was beginning to eat scraps of food in addition to milk. Mr Arable was not willing to provide for him any longer. He had already sold Wilbur's ten brothers and sisters.

'He's got to go, Fern,' he said. 'You have had your fun raising a baby pig, but Wilbur is not a baby any longer and he has got to be sold.'

'Call up the Zuckermans,' suggested Mrs Arable to Fern. 'Your Uncle Homer sometimes raises a pig. And if Wilbur goes there to live, you can walk down the road and visit him as often as you like.'

'How much money should I ask for him?' Fern wanted to know.

'Well,' said her father, 'he's a runt. Tell your Uncle Homer you've got a pig you'll sell for six dollars, and see what he says.'

It was soon arranged. Fern phoned and got her Aunt Edith, and her Aunt Edith hollered for Uncle Homer and Uncle Homer came in from the barn and talked to Fern. When he heard that the price was only six dollars, he said he would buy the pig. Next day Wilbur was taken from his home under the apple tree and went to live in a manure pile in the cellar of Zuckerman's barn.

3.

Escape

The barn was very large. It was very old. It smelled of hay and it smelled of manure. It smelled of the perspiration of tired horses and the wonderful sweet breath of patient cows. It often had a sort of peaceful smell—as though nothing bad could happen ever again in the world. It smelled of grain and of harness dressing and of axle grease and of rubber boots and of new rope. And whenever the cat was given a fishhead to eat, the barn would smell of fish. But mostly it smelled of hay, for there was always hay in the great loft up overhead. And there was always hay being pitched down to the cows and the horses and the sheep.

The barn was pleasantly warm in winter when the animals spent most of their time indoors, and it was pleasantly cool in summer when the big doors stood wide open to the breeze. The barn had stalls on the main floor for the work horses, tie-ups on the main floor for the cows, a sheepfold down below for the sheep, a pigpen down below for Wilbur, and it was full of all sorts of things that you find in barns: ladders, grindstones, pitch forks, monkey wrenches, scythes, lawn mowers, snow shovels, axe handles, milk pails, water buckets, empty grain sacks, and rusty rat traps. It was the kind of barn that swallows like to build their nests in. It was the kind of barn that children like to play in. And the whole thing was owned by Fern's uncle, Mr Homer L. Zuckerman.

Wilbur's new home was in the lower part of the barn, directly underneath the cows. Mr Zuckerman knew that a manure pile is a good place to keep a young pig. Pigs needed warmth, and it was warm and comfortable down there in the barn cellar on the south side.

Fern came almost every day, to visit him. She found an old milking stool that had been discarded, and she placed the stool in the sheepfold next to Wilbur's pen. Here she sat quietly during the long afternoons, thinking and listening and watching Wilbur. The sheep soon got to know her and trust her. So did the geese, who lived with the sheep. All the animals trusted her, she was so quiet and friendly. Mr Zuckerman did not allow her to take Wilbur out, and he did not allow her to get into the pigpen. But he told Fern that she could sit on the stool and watch Wilbur as long as she wanted to. It made her happy just to be near the pig, and it made Wilbur happy to know that she was sitting there, right outside his pen. But he never had any fun—no walks, no rides, no swims.

One afternoon in June, when Wilbur was almost two months old, he wandered out into his small yard outside the barn. Fern had not arrived for her usual visit. Wilbur stood in the sun feeling lonely and bored.

'There's never anything to do round here,' he thought. He walked slowly to his food trough and sniffed to see if anything

had been overlooked at lunch. He found a small strip of potato skin and ate it. His back itched, so he leaned against the fence and rubbed against the boards. When he tired of this, he walked indoors, climbed to the top of the manure pile , and sat down. He didn't feel like going to sleep, he didn't feel like digging, he was tired of standing still, tired of lying down. 'I' m less than two months old and I' m tired of living,' he said. He walked out to the yard again.

'When I'm out here,' he said, 'there's no place to go but in. When I' m indoors, there' s no place to go but out in the yard.'

'That's where you're wrong, my friend, my friend,' said a voice.

Wilbur looked through the fence and saw the goose standing

there.

'You don't have to stay in that dirty–little dirty–little dirty–little yard,' said the goose, who talked rather fast. 'One of the boards is loose. Push on it, push–push–push on it, and come on out!'

'What?' said Wilbur. 'Say it slower!'

'At–at–at, at the risk of repeating myself,' said the goose, 'I suggest that you come on out. It' s wonderful out here.'

'Did you say a board was loose?'

'That I did, that I did,' said the goose.

Wilbur walked up to the fence and saw that the goose was right —one board was loose. He put his head down, shut his eyes, and pushed. The board gave way. In a minute he had squeezed through the fence and was standing in the long grass outside his yard. The goose chuckled.

'How does it feel to be free?' she asked.

'I like it,' said Wilbur. 'That is, I *guess* I like it.' Actually, Wilbur felt queer to be outside his fence, with nothing between him and the big world.

'Where do you think I'd better go?'

'Anywhere you like, anywhere you like,' said the goose. 'Go down through the orchard, root up the sod! Go down through the garden, dig up the radishes! Root up everything! Eat grass! Look for corn! Look for oats! Run all over! Skip and dance, jump and prance! Go down through the orchard and stroll in the woods! The world is a wonderful place when you' re young.'

'I can see that,' replied Wilbur. He gave a jump in the air, twirled, ran a few steps, stopped, looked all round, sniffed the smells of afternoon, and then set off walking down through the orchard. Pausing in the shade of an apple tree, he put his strong snout into the ground and began pushing, digging, and rooting. He felt very happy. He had ploughed up quite a piece of ground before anyone noticed him. Mrs Zuckerman was the first to see him. She saw him from the kitchen window, and she immediately shouted for the men.

'Ho–*mer*!' she cried. 'Pig's out! Lurvy! Pig's out! Homer! Lurvy! Pig's out. He's down there under that apple tree.'

'Now the trouble starts,' thought Wilbur. 'Now I'll catch it.'

The goose heard the racket and she, too, started hollering. 'Run–run–run downhill, make for the woods, the woods!' she shouted to Wilbur. 'They'll never–never–never catch you in the woods.'

The cocker spaniel heard the commotion and he ran out from the barn to join in the chase. Mr Zuckerman heard, and he came out of the machine shed where he was mending a tool. Lurvy, the hired man, heard the noise and came up from the asparagus patch where he was pulling weeds. Everybody walked towards Wilbur and Wilbur didn't know what to do. The woods seemed a long way off, and anyway, he had never been down there in the woods, and wasn't sure he would like it.

'Get round behind him, Lurvy,' said Mr Zuckerman, 'and drive him towards the barn! And take it easy — don't rush him!

I'll go and get a bucket of slops.'

The news of Wilbur's escape spread rapidly among the animals on the place. Whenever any creature broke loose on Zuckerman's farm, the event was of great interest to the others. The goose shouted to the nearest cow that Wilbur was free, and soon all the cows knew. Then one of the cows told one of the sheep, and soon all the sheep knew. The lambs learned about it from their mothers. The horses, in their stalls in the barn, pricked up their ears when they heard the goose hollering; and soon the horses had caught on to what was happening. 'Wilbur's out,' they said. Every animal stirred its head and became excited to know that one of its friends had got free and was no longer penned up or tied fast.

Wilbur didn't know what to do or which way to run. It seemed as though everybody was after him. 'If this is what it's like to be free,' he thought, 'I believe I'd rather be penned up in my own yard.'

The cocker spaniel was sneaking up on him from one side. Lurvy the hired man was sneaking up on him from the other side. Mrs Zuckerman stood ready to head him off if he started for the garden, and now Mr Zuckerman was coming down towards him carrying a pail. 'This is really awful,' thought Wilbur. 'Why doesn't Fern come?' He began to cry.

The goose took command and began to give orders.

'Don't just stand there, Wilbur! Dodge about, dodge about!' cried the goose. 'Skip around, run towards me, slip in and out, in and out, in and out! Make for the woods! Twist and turn!'

The cocker spaniel sprang for Wilbur's hind leg. Wilbur jumped and ran. Lurvy reached out and grabbed. Mrs Zuckerman screamed at Lurvy. The goose cheered for Wilbur. Wilbur dodged between Lurvy's legs. Lurvy missed Wilbur and grabbed the spaniel instead. 'Nicely done, nicely done!' cried the goose. 'Try it again, try it again!'

'Run downhill!' suggested the cows.

'Run towards me!' yelled the gander.

'Run uphill!' cried the sheep.

'Turn and twist!' honked the goose.

'Jump and dance!' said the rooster.

'Look out for Lurvy!' called the cows.

'Look out for Zuckerman!' yelled the gander.

'Watch out for the dog!' cried the sheep.

'Listen to me, listen to me!' screamed the goose.

Poor Wilbur was dazed and frightened by this hullabaloo. He didn't like being the centre of all this fuss. He tried to follow the instructions his friends were giving him, but he couldn't run downhill and uphill at the same time, and he couldn't turn and twist when he was jumping and dancing, and he was crying so hard he could barely see anything that was happening. After all, Wilbur was a very young pig — not much more than a baby, really. He wished Fern were here to take him in her arms and comfort him. When he looked up and saw Mr Zuckerman standing quite close to him, holding a pail of warm slops, he felt relieved. He lifted his nose and sniffed. The smell was delicious — warm

milk, potato skins, wheat middlings, toasted corn flakes, and a popover left from the Zuckermans' breakfast.

'Come, pig!' said Mr Zuckerman, tapping the pail. 'Come pig!'

Wilbur took a step towards the pail.

'No–no–no!' said the goose. 'It's the old pail trick, Wilbur. Don't fall for it, don't fall for it! He's trying to lure you back into captivity–ivity. He's appealing to your stomach.'

Wilbur didn't care. The food smelled appetizing. He took another step towards the pail.

'Pig, pig!' said Mr Zuckerman in a kind voice, and began walking slowly towards the barnyard, looking all about him

innocently, as if he didn't know that a little white pig was following along behind him.

'You'll be sorry–sorry–sorry,' called the goose.

Wilbur didn't care. He kept walking towards the pail of slops.

'You'll miss your freedom,' honked the goose. 'An hour of freedom is worth a barrel of slops.'

Wilbur didn't care.

When Mr Zuckerman reached the pigpen, he climbed over the fence and poured the slops into the trough. Then he pulled the loose board away from the fence, so that there was a wide hole for

Wilbur to walk through.

'Reconsider, reconsider!' cried the goose.

Wilbur paid no attention. He stepped through the fence into his yard. He walked to the trough and took a long drink of slops, sucking in the milk hungrily and chewing the popover. It was good to be home again.

While Wilbur ate, Lurvy fetched a hammer and some eight-penny nails and nailed the board in place. Then he and Mr Zuckerman leaned lazily on the fence and Mr Zuckerman scratched Wilbur's back with a stick.

'He's quite a pig,' said Lurvy.

'Yes, he'll make a good pig,' said Mr Zuckerman. Wilbur heard the words of praise. He felt the warm milk inside his stomach. He felt the pleasant rubbing of the stick along his itchy back. He felt peaceful and happy and sleepy. This had been a tiring afternoon. It was still only about four o'clock but Wilbur was ready for bed.

'I'm really too young to go out into the world alone,' he thought as he lay down.

4.

Loneliness

The next day was rainy and dark. Rain fell on the roof of the barn and dripped steadily from the eaves. Rain fell in the barnyard and ran in crooked courses down into the lane where thistles and pigweed grew. Rain spattered against Mrs Zuckerman's kitchen windows and came gushing out of the downspouts. Rain fell on the backs of the sheep as they grazed in the meadow. When the sheep tired of standing in the rain, they walked slowly up the lane and into the fold.

Rain upset Wilbur's plans. Wilbur had planned to go out, this day, and dig a new hole in his yard. He had other plans, too. His plans for the day went something like this:

Breakfast at six-thirty. Skim milk, crusts, middlings, bits of doughnuts, wheat cakes with drops of maple syrup sticking to them, potato skins, left-over custard pudding with raisins, and bits of Shredded Wheat.

Breakfast would be finished at seven.

From seven to eight, Wilbur planned to have a talk with Templeton, the rat that lived under his trough. Talking with Templeton was not the most interesting occupation in the world but it was better than nothing.

From eight to nine, Wilbur planned to take a nap outdoors in the sun.

From nine to eleven, he planned to dig a hole, or trench, and possibly find something good to eat buried in the dirt.

From eleven to twelve, he planned to stand still and watch flies on the boards, watch bees in the clover, and watch swallows in the air.

Twelve o'clock — lunchtime. Middlings, warm water, apple parings, meat gravy, carrot scrapings, meat scraps, stale hominy, and the wrapper off a package of cheese. Lunch would be over at one.

From one to two, Wilbur planned to sleep.

From two to three, he planned to scratch itchy places by rubbing against the fence.

From three to four, he planned to stand perfectly still and think of what it was like to be alive, and to wait for Fern.

At four would come supper. Skim milk, provender, left-over sandwich from Lurvy's lunchbox, prune skins, a morsel of this, a bit of that, fried potatoes, marmalade drippings, a little more of this, a little more of that, a piece of baked apple, a scrap of upside-down cake.

Wilbur had gone to sleep thinking about these plans. He awoke at six and saw the rain, and it seemed as though he couldn't bear it.

'I get everything all beautifully planned out and it has to go and rain,' he said.

For a while he stood gloomily indoors. Then he walked to the door and looked out. Drops of rain struck his face. His yard was cold and wet. His trough had an inch of rain water in it. Templeton was nowhere to be seen.

'Are you out there, Templeton?' called Wilbur. There was no answer. Suddenly Wilbur felt lonely and friendless.

'One day just like another,' he groaned. 'I'm very young, I have no real friend here in the barn, it's going to rain all morning and all afternoon, and Fern won't come in such bad weather. Oh, *honestly*!' And Wilbur was crying again, for the second time in two days.

At six-thirty Wilbur heard the banging of a pail. Lurvy was standing outside in the rain, stirring up breakfast.

'C'mon, pig!' said Lurvy.

Wilbur did not budge. Lurvy dumped the slops, scraped the pail, and walked away. He noticed that something was wrong with the pig.

Wilbur didn't want food, he wanted love. He wanted a friend —someone who would play with him. He mentioned this to the goose, who was sitting quietly in a corner of the sheepfold.

'Will you come over and play with me?' he asked.

'Sorry, sonny, sorry,' said the goose. 'I'm sitting-sitting on my eggs. Eight of them. Got to keep them toasty-oasty-oasty warm. I have to stay right here, I'm no flibberty-ibberty-gibbet. I do not play when there are eggs to hatch. I'm expecting goslings.'

'Well, I didn't think you were expecting woodpeckers,' said Wilbur bitterly.

Wilbur next tried one of the lambs.

'Will you please play with me?' he asked.

'Certainly not,' said the lamb. 'In the first place, I cannot get into your pen, as I am not old enough to jump over the fence. In the second place, I am not interested in pigs. Pigs mean less than nothing to me.'

'What do you mean, *less* than nothing?' replied Wilbur. 'I don't think there is any such thing as less than nothing. Nothing is absolutely the limit of nothingness. It's the lowest you can go. It's the end of the line. How can something be less than nothing? If there were something that was less than nothing, then nothing would not be nothing, it would be something — even though it's just a very little bit of something. But if nothing is *nothing*, then nothing has nothing that is less than *it* is.'

'Oh, be quiet!' said the lamb. 'Go play by yourself! I don't play with pigs.'

Sadly, Wilbur lay down and listened to the rain. Soon he saw the rat climbing down a slanting board that he used as a stairway.

'Will you play with me, Templeton?' asked Wilbur.

'Play?' said Templeton, twirling his whiskers. 'Play? I hardly know the meaning of the word.'

'Well,' said Wilbur, 'it means to have fun, to frolic, to run and skip and make merry.'

'I never do those things if I can avoid them,' replied the rat, sourly. 'I prefer to spend my time eating, gnawing, spying, and hiding. I am a glutton but not a merrymaker. Right now I am on my way to your trough to eat your breakfast, since you haven't got sense enough to eat it yourself.' And Templeton, the rat, crept stealthily along the wall and disappeared into a private tunnel that he had dug between the door and the trough in Wilbur's yard. Templeton was a crafty rat, and he had things pretty much his own way. The tunnel was an example of his skill and cunning. The tunnel enabled him to get from the barn to his hiding-place under the pig trough without coming out into the open. He had tunnels and runways all over Mr Zuckerman's farm and could get from one place to another without being seen. Usually he slept during the daytime and was abroad only after dark.

Wilbur watched him disappear into his tunnel. In a moment he saw the rat's sharp nose poke out from underneath the wooden trough. Cautiously Templeton pulled himself up over the edge of the trough. This was almost more than Wilbur could stand: on this dreary, rainy day to see his breakfast being eaten by somebody else. He knew Templeton was getting soaked, out there in the pouring rain, but even that didn't comfort him. Friendless, dejected, and hungry, he threw himself down in the manure and sobbed.

Late that afternoon, Lurvy went to Mr Zuckerman. 'I think there's something wrong with that pig of yours. He hasn't touched his food.'

'Give him two spoonfuls of sulphur and a little molasses,'

said Mr Zuckerman.

Wilbur couldn't believe what was happening to him when Lurvy caught him and forced the medicine down his throat. This was certainly the worst day of his life. He didnt know whether he could endure the awful loneliness any more.

Darkness settled over everything. Soon there were only shadows and the noises of the sheep chewing their cuds, and occasionally the rattle of a cow-chain up overhead. You can imagine Wilbur's surprise when, out of the darkness, came a small voice he had never heard before. It sounded rather thin, but pleasant. 'Do you want a friend, Wilbur?' it said. 'I'll be a friend to you. I've watched you all day and I like you.'

'But I can't see you,' said Wilbur, jumping to his feet. 'Where are you? And *who* are you?'

'I'm right up here,' said the voice. 'Go to sleep. You'll see me in the morning.'

5.

Charlotte

The night seemed long. Wilbur's stomach was empty and his mind was full. And when your stomach is empty and your mind is full, it's always hard to sleep.

A dozen times during the night Wilbur woke and stared into the blackness, listening to the sounds and trying to figure out what time it was. A barn is never perfectly quiet. Even at midnight there is usually something stirring.

The first time he woke, he heard Templeton gnawing a hole in the grain bin. Templeton's teeth scraped loudly against the wood and made quite a racket. 'That crazy rat!' thought Wilbur. 'Why does he have to stay up all night, grinding his clashers and destroying people's property? Why can't he go to sleep, like any decent animal?'

The second time Wilbur woke, he heard the goose turning on her nest and chuckling to herself.

'What time is it?' whispered Wilbur to the goose.

'Probably-obably-obably about halfpast eleven,' said the goose, 'Why aren't you asleep, Wilbur?'

'Too many things on my mind,' said Wilbur.

'Well,' said the goose, 'that's not *my* trouble. I have nothing at all on my mind, but I've too many things under my behind. Have you ever tried to sleep while sitting on eight eggs?'

'No,' replied Wilbur. 'I suppose it *is* uncomfortable. How long does it take a goose egg to hatch?'

'Approximately-oximately thirty days, all told,' answered the goose. 'But I cheat a little. On warm afternoons, I just pull a little straw over the eggs and go out for a walk.'

Wilbur yawned and went back to sleep. In his dreams he heard again the voice saying, 'I'll be a friend to you. Go to sleep — you'll see me in the morning.'

About half an hour before dawn, Wilbur woke and listened. The barn was still dark. The sheep lay motionless. Even the goose was quiet. Overhead, on the main floor, nothing stirred: the cows were resting, the horses dozed. Templeton had quit work and gone off somewhere on an errand. The only sound was a slight scraping noise from the rooftop, where the weathervane swung back and forth. Wilbur loved the barn when it was like this — calm and quiet, waiting for light.

'Day is almost here,' he thought.

Through a small window, a faint gleam appeared.One by one the stars went out. Wilbur could see the goose a few feet away. She sat with head tucked under a wing. Then he could see the sheep and the lambs. The sky lightened.

'Oh, beautiful day, it is here at last! Today I shall find my friend.'

Wilbur looked everywhere. He searched his pen thoroughly. He examined the window ledge, stared up at the ceiling. But he saw nothing new. Finally he decided he would have to speak up. He hated to break the lovely stillness of dawn by using his voice, but he couldn't think of any other way to locate the mysterious new friend who was nowhere to be seen. So Wilbur cleared his throat.

'Attention, please!' he said in a loud, firm voice. 'Will the party who addressed me at bedtime last night kindly make himself or herself known by giving an appropriate sign or signal!'

Wilbur paused and listened. All the other animals lifted their heads and stared at him. Wilbur blushed. But he was determined to get in touch with his unknown friend.

'Attention, please!' he said. 'I will repeat the message. Will the party who addressed me at bedtime last night kindly speak up. Please tell me where you are, if you are my friend!'

The sheep looked at each other in disgust.

'Stop your nonsense, Wilbur!' said the oldest sheep. 'If you have a new freind here, you are probably disturbing his rest; and the quickest way to spoil a friendship is to wake somebody up in the morning before he is ready. How can you be sure your friend is an early riser?'

'I beg everyone's pardon,' whispered Wilbur. 'I didn't mean to be objectionable.'

He lay down meekly in the manure, facing the door. He did not know it, but his friend was very near. And the old sheep was right — the friend was still asleep.

Soon Lurvy appeared with slops for breakfast. Wilbur rushed out, ate everything in a hurry, and licked the trough. The sheep moved off down the lane, the gander waddled along behind them, pulling grass. And then, just as Wilbur was settling down for his morning nap, he heard again the thin voice that had addressed him the night before.

'Salutations!' said the voice.

Wilbur jumped to his feet. 'Salu-*what*?' he cried.

'Salutations!' repeated the voice.

'What are *they*, and where are *you*?' screamed Wilbur. 'Please, please, tell me where you are. And what are salutations?'

'Salutations are greetings,' said the voice. 'When I say "salutations", it's just my fancy way of saying hello or good morning. Actually, it's a silly expression, and I am surprised that I used it at all. As for my whereabouts, that's easy. Look up here in the corner of the doorway! Here I am. Look, I'm waving!'

At last Wilbur saw the creature that had spoken to him in such a kindly way. Stretched across the upper part of the doorway was a big spider's web, and hanging from the top of the web, head down, was a large grey spider. She was about the size of a gumdrop. She had eight legs, and she was waving one of them at Wilbur in friendly greeting. 'See me now?' she asked.

'Oh, yes indeed,' said Wilbur. 'Yes indeed! How are you? Good morning! Salutations! Very pleased to meet you. What is your name, please? May I have your name?'

'My name,' said the spider, 'is Charlotte.'

'Charlotte what?' asked Wilbur, eagerly.

'Charlotte A. Cavatica. But just call me Charlotte.'

'I think you're beautiful,' said Wilbur.

'Well, I am pretty,' replied Charlotte. 'There's no denying that. Almost all spiders are rather nice-looking. I'm not as flashy as some, but I'll do. I wish I could see you, Wilbur, as clearly as you can see me.'

'Why can't you?' asked the pig. 'I'm right here.'

'Yes, but I'm near-sighted,' replied Charlotte. 'I've always been dreadfully near-sighted. It's good in some ways, not so good in others. Watch me wrap up this fly.'

A fly that had been crawling along Wilbur's trough had flown up and blundered into the lower part of Charlotte's web and was tangled in the sticky threads. The fly was beating its wings furiously, trying to break loose and free itself.

'First,' said Charlotte, 'I dive at him.' She plunged head-first towards the fly. As she dropped, a tiny silken thread unwound from her rear end.

'Next, I wrap him up.' She grabbed the fly, threw a few jets of silk round it, and rolled it over and over, wrapping it so that it couldn't move. Wilbur watched in horror. He could hardly believe what he was seeing, and although he detested flies he was sorry for this one.

'There!' said Charlotte. 'Now I knock him out, so he'll be more comfortable.' She bit the fly. 'He can't feel a thing now,'

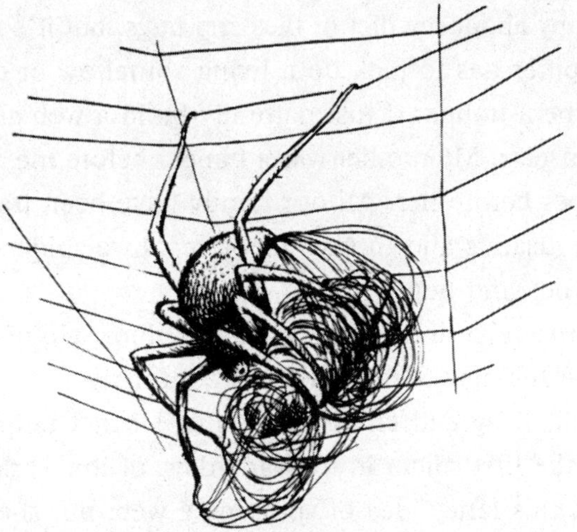

she remarked. 'He'll make a perfect breakfast for me.'

'You mean you *eat* flies?' gasped Wilbur.

'Certainly. Flies, bugs, grasshoppers, choice beetles, moths, butterflies, tasty cockroaches, gnats, midgets, daddy-long-legs, centipedes, mosquitoes, crickets—anything that is careless enough to get caught in my web. I have to live, don't I?'

'Why, yes, of course,' said Wilbur. 'Do they taste good?'

'Delicious. Of course, I don't really eat them. I drink them—drink their blood. I love blood,' said Charlotte, and her pleasant, thin voice grew even thinner and more pleasant.

'Don't say that!' groaned Wilbur. 'Please don't say things like that!'

'Why not ? It's true, and I have to say what is true. I am not entirely happy about my diet of flies and bugs, but it' s the way I'm made. A spider has to pick up a living somehow or other, and I happen to be a trapper. I just naturally build a web and trap flies and other insects. My mother was a trapper before me. Her mother was a trapper before her. All our family have been trappers. Way back for thousands and thousands of years we spiders have been laying for flies and bugs.'

'It's a miserable inheritance,' said Wilbur, gloomily. He was sad because his new friend was so bloodthirsty.

'Yes, it is,' agreed charlotte. 'But I can't help it. I don't know how the first spider in the early days of the world happened to think up this fancy idea of spinning a web, but she did, and it was clever of her, too. And since then, all of us spiders have had to work the same trick. It's not a bad pitch, on the whole.'

'It's cruel,' replied Wilbur, who did not intend to be argued out of his position.

'Well, *you* can't talk,' said Charlotte. '*You* have your meals brought to you in a pail. Nobody feeds me. I have to get my own living. I live by my wits. I have to be sharp and clever, lest I go hungry. I have to think things out, catch what I can, take what comes. And it just so happens, my friend, that what comes is flies and insects and bugs. And *furthermore*,' said Charlotte, shaking one of her legs, 'do you realize that if I didn't catch bugs and eat them, bugs would increase and multiply and get so numerous that they' d destroy the earth, wipe out everything?'

'Really?' said Wilbur. 'I wouldn't want *that* to happen. Perhaps your web is a good thing after all.'

The goose had been listening to this conversation and chuckling to herself. 'There are a lot of things Wilbur doesn't know about life,' she thought. 'He's really a very innocent little pig. He doesn't even know what's going to happen to him around Christmastime; he has no idea that Mr Zuckerman and Lurvy are plotting to kill him.' And the goose raised herself a bit and poked her eggs a little farther under her so that they would receive the full heat from her warm body and soft feathers.

Charlotte stood quietly over the fly, preparing to eat it. Wilbur lay down and closed his eyes. He was tired from his wakeful night and from the excitement of meeting someone for the first time. A breeze brought him the smell of clover—the sweet-smelling world beyond his fence. 'Well,' he thought, 'I've got a new friend, all right. But what a gamble friendship is! Charlotte is fierce, brutal, scheming, bloodthirsty—everything I don't like. How can I learn to like her, even though she is pretty and, of course, clever?'

Wilbur was merely suffering the doubts and fears that often go with finding a new friend. In good time he was to discover that he was mistaken about Charlotte. Underneath her rather bold and cruel exterior, she had a kind heart, and she was to prove loyal and true to the very end.

6.

Summer Days

The early summer days on a farm are the happiest and fairest days of the year. Lilacs bloom and make the air sweet, and then fade. Apple blossoms come with the lilacs, and the bees visit round among the apple trees. The days grow warm and soft. School ends, and children have time to play and to fish for trout in the brook. Avery often brought a trout home in his pocket, warm and stiff and ready to be fried for supper.

Now that school was over, Fern visited the barn almost every day, to sit quietly on her stool. The animals treated her as an equal. The sheep lay calmly at her feet.

Around the first of July, the work horses were hitched to the mowing machine, and Mr Zuckerman climbed into the seat and drove into the field. All morning you could hear the rattle of the machine as it went round and round, while the tall grass fell down behind the cutter bar in long green swathes. Next day, if there was no thunder shower, all hands would help rake and pitch and load, and the hay would be carried to the barn in the high hay wagon, with Fern and Avery riding at the top of the load. Then the hay would be hoisted, sweet and warm, into the big loft, until the whole barn seemed like a wonderful bed of timothy and clover. It was fine to jump in, and perfect to hide in. And sometimes Avery would find a little grass snake in the hay, and would add it to the other things in his pocket.

Early summer days are a jubilee time for birds. In the fields, around the house, in the barn, in the woods, in the swamp — everywhere love and songs and nests and eggs. From the edge of the woods, the white-throated sparrow (which must come all the way from Boston) calls, 'Oh, Peabody, Peabody, Peabody!' On an apple bough, the phoebe teeters and wags its tail and says, 'Phoebe, phoe-bee!' The song sparrow, who knows how brief and lovely life is, says, 'Sweet, sweet, sweet interlude; sweet, sweet, sweet interlude.' If you enter the barn, the swallows swoop down from their nests and scold. 'Cheeky, cheeky!' they say.

In early summer there are plenty of things for a child to eat and drink and suck and chew. Dandelion stems are full of milk, clover heads are loaded with nectar, the Frigidaire is full of ice-cold drinks. Everywhere you look is life; even the little ball of spit on the weed stalk, if you poke it apart, has a green worm inside it. And on the underside of the leaf of the potato vine are the bright orange eggs of the potato bug.

It was on a day in early summer that the goose eggs hatched. This was an important event in the barn cellar. Fern was there, sitting on her stool, when it happened.

Except for the goose herself, Charlotte was the first to know that the goslings had at last arrived. The goose knew a day in advance that they were coming—she could hear their weak voices calling from inside the egg. She knew that they were in a desperately cramped position inside the shell and were most anxious to break through and get out. So she sat quite still, and talked less than usual.

When the first gosling poked its grey-green head through the goose's feathers and looked around, Charlotte spied it and made the announcement.

'I am sure,' she said, 'that every one of us here will be gratified to learn that after four weeks of unremitting effort and patience on the part of our friend the goose, she now has something to show for it. The goslings have arrived. May I offer my sincere congratulations!'

'Thank you, thank you, thank you!' said the goose, nodding and bowing shamelessly.

'Thank you,' said the gander.

'Congratulations!' shouted Wilbur. 'How many goslings are there? I can only see one.'

'There are seven,' said the goose.

'Fine!' said Charlotte. 'Seven is a lucky number.'

'Luck had nothing to do with this,' said the goose. 'It was good management and hard work.'

At this point, Templeton showed his nose from his hiding-place under Wilbur' s trough. He glanced at Fern, then crept cautiously towards the goose, keeping close to the wall. Everyone watched him, for he was not well liked, not trusted.

'Look,' he began in his sharp voice, 'you say you have seven goslings. There were eight eggs. What happened to the other egg? Why didn't it hatch?'

'It's a dud, I guess,' said the goose.

'What are you going to do with it?' continued Templeton, his little round beady eyes fixed on the goose.

'You can have it,' replied the goose. 'Roll it away and add it to that nasty collection of yours.' (Templeton had a habit of picking up unusual objects round the farm and storing them in his home. He saved everything.)

'Certainly–ertainly–ertainly,' said the gander. 'You may have the egg. But I'll tell you one thing, Templeton, if I ever catch you poking–oking–oking your ugly nose around our goslings, I'll give you the worst pounding a rat ever took.' And the gander opened his strong wings and beat the air with them to show his power. He was strong and brave, but, the truth is, both the goose and the gander were worried about Templeton. And with good reason. The rat had no morals, no conscience, no scruples, no consideration, no decency, no milk of rodent kindness, no compunctions, no higher feeling, no friendliness, no anything. He would kill a gosling if he could get away with it — the goose knew that. Everybody knew it.

With her broad bill the goose pushed the unhatched egg out of the nest, and the entire company watched in disgust while the rat rolled it away. Even Wilbur, who could eat almost anything, was appalled. 'Imagine wanting a junky old rotten egg!' he muttered.

'A rat is a rat,' said Charlotte. She laughed a tinkling little laugh. 'But, my friends, if that ancient egg ever breaks, this barn will be untenable.'

'What's that mean?' asked Wilbur.

'It means nobody will be able to live here on account of the smell. A rotten egg is a regular stink bomb.'

'I won't break it,' snarled Templeton. 'I know what I'm doing. I handle stuff like this all the time.'

He disappeared into his tunnel, pushing the goose egg in front of him. He pushed and nudged till he succeeded in rolling it to his lair under the trough.

That afternoon, when the wind had died down and the barnyard was quiet and warm, the grey goose led her seven goslings off the nest and out into the world. Mr Zuckerman spied them when he came with Wilbur's supper.

'Well, hello there!' he said, smiling all over. 'Let's see... one, two, three, four, five, six, seven. Seven baby geese. Now isn't that lovely!'

7.

Bad News

Wilbur liked Charlotte better and better each day. Her campaign against insects seemed sensible and useful. Hardly anybody around the farm had a good word to say for a fly. Flies spent their time pestering others. The cows hated them. The horses detested them. The sheep loathed them. Mr and Mrs Zuckerman were always complaining about them, and putting up screens.

Wilbur admired the way Charlotte managed. He was particularly glad that she always put her victim to sleep before eating it.

'It's real thoughtful of you to do that, Charlotte,' he said.

'Yes,' she replied in her sweet, musical voice, 'I always give them an anaesthetic so they won't feel pain. It's a little service *I* throw in.'

As the days went by, Wilbur grew and grew. He ate three big meals a day. He spent long hours lying on his side, half asleep, dreaming pleasant dreams. He enjoyed good health and he gained a lot of weight. One afternoon, when Fern was sitting on her stool, the oldest sheep walked into the barn, and stopped to pay a call on Wilbur.

'Hello!' she said. 'Seems to me you're putting on weight.'

'Yes, I guess I am,' replied Wilbur. 'At my age it's a good idea to keep gaining.'

'Just the same, I don't envy you,' said the old sheep. 'You know why they're fattening you up, don't you?'

'No,' said Wilbur.

'Well, I don't like to spread bad news,' said the sheep, 'but they're fattening you up because they're going to kill you, that's why.'

'They're going to *what*?' screamed Wilbur. Fern grew rigid on her stool.

'Kill you. Turn you into smoked bacon and ham,' continued the old sheep. 'Almost all young pigs get murdered by the farmer as soon as the real cold weather sets in. There's a regular conspiracy around here to kill you at Christmastime. Everybody is in the plot — Lurvy, Zuckerman, even John Arable.'

'Mr Arable?' sobbed Wilbur. 'Fern's father?'

'Certainly. When a pig is to be butchered, everybody helps. I'm an old sheep and I see the same thing, same old business, year after year. Arable arrives with his .22, shoots the...'

'Stop!' screamed Wilbur. 'I don't want to die! Save me, somebody! Save me!' Fern was just about to jump up when a voice was heard.

'Be quiet, Wilbur!' said Charlotte, who had been listening to this awful conversation.

'I can't be quiet,' screamed Wilbur, racing up and down. 'I

don' t want to be killed. I don' t want to die. Is it true what the old sheep says, Charlotte? Is it true they are going to kill me when the cold weather comes?'

'Well,' said the spider, plucking thoughtfully at her web, 'the old sheep has been around this barn a long time. She has seen many a spring pig come and go. If she says they plan to kill you, I'm sure it's true. It's also the dirtiest trick I ever heard of. What people don' t think of !'

Wilbur burst into tears. 'I don't *want* to die,' he moaned. 'I want to stay alive, right here in my comfortable manure pile with all my friends. I want to breathe the beautiful air and lie in the beautiful sun.'

'You're certainly making a beautiful noise,' snapped the old sheep.

'I don't want to die!' screamed Wilbur, throwing himself to the ground.

'You shall not die,' said Charlotte, briskly.

'What? Really?' cried Wilbur. 'Who' s going to save me?'

'I am,' said Charlotte.

'How?' asked Wilbur.

'That remains to be seen. But I am going to save you, and I want you to quiet down immediately. You' re carrying on in a childish way. Stop your crying! I can' t stand hysterics.'

8.

A Talk at Home

On Sunday morning Mr and Mrs Arable and Fern were sitting at breakfast in the kitchen. Avery had finished and was upstairs looking for his sling shot.

'Did you know that Uncle Homer' s goslings had hatched?' asked Fern.

'How many?' asked Mr Arable.

'Seven,' replied Fern. 'There were eight eggs but one egg didn' t hatch and the goose told Templeton she didn' t want it any more, so he took it away.'

'The goose did what?' asked Mrs Arable, gazing at her daughter with a queer, worried look.

'Told Templeton she didn't want the egg any more,' repeated Fern.

'Who is Templeton?' asked Mrs Arable.

'He' s the rat,' replied Fern. 'None of us like him much.'

'Who is "us"?' asked Mr Arable.

'Oh, everybody in the barn cellar. Wilbur and the sheep and the lambs and the goose and the gander and the goslings and Charlotte and me.'

'Charlotte?' said Mrs Arable. 'Who's Charlotte?'

'She's Wilbur's best friend. She's terribly clever.'

'What does she look like?' asked Mrs Arable.

'Well–l,' said Fern, thoughtfully, 'she has eight legs. All spiders do, I guess.'

'Charlotte is a spider?' asked Fern's mother.

Fern nodded. 'A big grey one. She has a web across the top of Wilbur's doorway. She catches flies and sucks their blood. Wilbur adores her.'

'Does he really?' said Mrs Arable, rather vaguely. She was staring at Fern with a worried expression on her face.

'Oh, yes, Wilbur adores Charlotte,' said Fern. 'Do you know what Charlotte said when the goslings hatched?'

'I haven't the faintest idea,' said Mr Arable. 'Tell us.'

'Well, when the first gosling stuck its little head out from under the goose, I was sitting on my stool in the corner and Charlotte was on her web. She made a speech. She said: "I am sure that every one of us here in the barn cellar will be gratified to learn that after four weeks of unremitting effort and patience on the part of the goose, she now has something to show for it." Don't you think that was a pleasant thing for her to say?'

'Yes, I do,' said Mrs Arable. 'And now, Fern, it's time to get ready for Sunday School And tell Avery to get ready. And this afternoon you can tell me more about what goes on in Uncle Homer's barn. Aren't you spending quite a lot of time there? You go there almost every afternoon, don't you?'

'I like it there,' replied Fern. She wiped her mouth and ran upstairs. After she had left the room, Mrs Arable spoke in a low voice to her husband.

'I worry about Fern,' she said. 'Did you hear the way she rambled on about the animals, pretending that they talked?'

Mr Arable chuckled. 'Maybe they do talk,' he said. 'I've sometimes wondered. At any rate, don't worry about Fern — she's just got a lively imagination. Kids think they hear all sorts of things.'

'Just the same, I *do* worry about her,' replied Mrs Arable. 'I think I shall ask Dr Dorian about her the next time I see him. He loves Fern almost as much as we do, and I want him to know how queerly she is acting about that pig and everything. I don't think it's normal. You know perfectly well animals don't talk.'

Mr Arable grinned. 'Maybe our ears aren't as sharp as Fern's,' he said.

9.

Wilbur's Boast

A spider' s web is stronger than it looks. Although it is made of thin, delicate strands, the web is not easily broken. However, a web gets torn every day by the insects that kick around in it, and a spider must rebuild it when it gets full of holes. Charlotte liked to do her weaving during the late afternoon, and Fern liked to sit nearby and watch. One afternoon she heard a most interesting conversation and witnessed a strange event.

'You have awfully hairy legs, Charlotte,' said Wilbur, as the spider busily worked at her task.

'My legs are hairy for a good reason,' replied Charlotte. 'Furthermore, each leg of mine has seven sections — the coxa, the trochanter, the femur, the patella, the tibia, the metatarsus, and the tarsus.'

Wilbur sat bolt upright, 'You' re kidding,' he said.

'No, I' m not, either.'

'Say those names again, I didn' t catch them the first time.'

'Coxa, trochanter, femur, patella, tibia, metatarsus, and tarsus.'

'Goodness!' said Wilbur, looking down at his own chubby legs. 'I don' t think *my* legs have seven sections.'

'Well,' said Charlotte, 'you and I lead different lives. You don't have to spin a web. That takes real legwork.'

'I could spin a web if I tried,' said Wilbur, boasting. 'I've just never tried.'

'Let's see you do it,' said Charlotte. Fern chuckled softly, and her eyes grew wide with love for the pig.

'OK,' replied Wilbur. 'You coach me and I'll spin one. It must be a lot of fun to spin a web. How do I start?'

'Take a deep breath!' said Charlotte, smiling. Wilbur breathed deeply. 'Now climb to the highest place you can get to, like this.' Charlotte raced up to the top of the doorway. Wilbur scrambled to the top of the manure pile.

'Very good!' said Charlotte. 'Now make an attachment with your spinnerets, hurl yourself into space, and let out a dragline as you go down!'

Wilbur hesitated a moment, then jumped out into the air. He glanced hastily behind to see if a piece of rope was following him to check his fall, but nothing seemed to be happening in his rear, and the next thing he knew he landed with a thump. 'Ooomp!' he grunted

Charlotte laughed so hard her web began to sway.

'What did I do wrong?' asked the pig, when he recovered from his bump.

'Nothing,' said Charlotte. 'It was a nice try.'

'I think I'll try again,' said Wilbur, cheerfully. 'I believe what I need is a little piece of string to hold me.'

The pig walked out to his yard. 'You there, Templeton?' he called. The rat poked his head out from under the trough.

'Got a little piece of string I could borrow?' asked Wilbur. 'I need it to spin a web.'

'Yes, indeed,' replied Templeton, who saved string. 'No trouble at all. Anything to oblige.' He crept down into his hole, pushed the goose egg out of the way, and returned with an old piece of dirty white string. Wilbur examined it.

'That's just the thing,' he said. 'Tie one end to my tail, will you, Templeton?'

Wilbur crouched low, with his thin, curly tail towards the rat. Templeton seized the string, passed it round the end of the pig's tail, and tied two half hitches. Charlotte watched in delight. Like Fern, she was truly fond of Wilbur, whose smelly pen and stale food attracted the flies that she needed, and she was proud to see that he was not a quitter and was willing to try again to spin a web.

While the rat and the spider and the little girl watched, Wilbur climbed again to the top of the manure pile, full of energy and hope.

'Everybody watch!' he cried. And summoning all his strength, he threw himself into the air, head-first. The string trailed behind him. But as he had neglected to fasten the other end to anything, it didn't really do any good, and Wilbur landed with a thud, crushed and hurt. Tears came to his eyes. Templeton grinned. Charlotte just sat quietly. After a bit she spoke.

'You can't spin a web, Wilbur, and I advise you to put the idea out of your mind. You lack two things needed for spinning a web.'

'What are they?' asked Wilbur, sadly.

'You lack a set of spinnerets, and you lack know-how. But cheer up, you don't need a web. Zuckerman supplies you with three big meals a day. Why should you worry about trapping food?'

Wilbur sighed. 'You're ever so much cleverer and brighter than I am, Charlotte. I guess I was just trying to show off. Serves me right.'

Templeton untied his string and took it back to his home. Charlotte returned to her weaving.

'You needn't feel too badly, Wilbur,' she said. 'Not many creatures can spin webs. Even men aren't as good at it as spiders, although they *think* they're pretty good, and they'll *try* anything. Did you ever hear of the Queensborough Bridge?'

Wilbur shook his head. 'Is it a web?'

'Sort of,' replied Charlotte. 'But do you know how long it took men to build it? Eight whole years. My goodness, I would have starved to death waiting that long. I can make a web in a single evening.'

'What do people catch in the Queensborough Bridge—bugs?' asked Wilbur.

'No,' said Charlotte. 'They don't catch anything. They just keep trotting back and forth across the bridge thinking there is

something better on the other side. If they' d hang head–down at the top of the thing and wait quietly, maybe something good would come along. But no — with men it' s rush, rush, rush, every minute. I' m glad I' m a sedentary spider.'

'What does sedentary mean?' asked Wilbur.

'Means I sit still a good part of the time and don't go wandering all over creation. I know a good thing when I see it, and my web is a good thing. I stay put and wait for what comes. Gives me a chance to think.'

'Well, I' m sort of sedentary myself, I guess,' said the pig. 'I have to hang around here whether I want to or not. You know where I' d really like to be this evening?'

'Where?'

'In a forest looking for beech nuts and truffles and delectable roots, pushing leaves aside with my wonderful strong nose, searching and sniffing along the ground, smelling, smelling, smelling...'

'You smell just the way you are,' remarked a lamb who had just walked in. I can smell you from here. You' re the smelliest creature in the place.'

Wilbur hung his head. His eyes grew wet with tears. Charlotte noticed his embarrassment and she spoke sharply to the lamb.

'Let Wilbur alone!' she said. 'He has a perfect right to smell, considering his surroundings. You' re no bundle of sweet peas yourself. Furthermore, you are interrupting a very pleasant conversation. What were we talking about, Wilbur, when we were so rudely interrupted?'

'Oh, I don't remember,' said Wilbur. 'It doesn't make any difference. Let's not talk any more for a while, Charlotte. I'm getting sleepy. You go ahead and finish fixing your web and I'll just lie here and watch you. It's a lovely evening.' Wilbur stretched out on his side and sighed a long sigh.

Twilight settled over Zuckerman's barn, and a feeling of peace. Fern knew it was almost suppertime but she couldn't bear to leave. Swallows passed on silent wings, in and out of the doorways, bringing food to their young ones. From across the road a bird sang 'Whippoorwill, whippoorwill!' Lurvy sat down under an apple tree and lit his pipe: the animals sniffed the familiar smell of strong tobacco. Wilbur heard the trill of the tree toad and the occasional slamming of the kitchen door. All these sounds made him comfortable and happy, for he loved life and loved to be a part of the world on a summer evening. But as he lay there he remembered what the old sheep had told him. The thought of death came to him and he began to tremble with fear.

'Charlotte?' he said, softly.

'Yes, Wilbur?'

'I don't want to die.'

'Of course you don't,' said Charlotte in a comforting voice.

'I just love it here in the barn,' said Wilbur. 'I love everything about this place.'

'Of course you do,' said Charlotte. 'We all do.'

The goose appeared, followed by her seven goslings. They thrust their little necks out and kept up a musical whistling, like a tiny troupe of pipers. Wilbur listened to the sound with love in his heart.

'Charlotte?' he said.

'Yes?' said the spider.

'Were you serious when you promised you would keep them from killing me?'

'I was never more serious in my life. I am not going to let you die, Wilbur.'

'How are you going to save me?' asked Wilbur, whose curiosity was very strong on this point.

'Well,' said Charlotte, vaguely, 'I don't really know. But I'm working on a plan.'

'That's wonderful,' said Wilbur. 'How is the plan coming, Charlotte? Have you got very far with it? Is it coming along pretty well?' Wilbur was trembling again, but Charlotte was cool and collected.

'Oh, it's coming all right,' she said, lightly. 'The plan is still in its early stages and hasn't completely shaped up yet, but I'm working on it.

'When do you work on it?' begged Wilbur.

'When I'm hanging head-down at the top of my web. That's when I do my thinking, because then all the blood is in my head.'

'I'd be only too glad to help in any way I can.'

'Oh, I'll work it out alone,' said Charlotte. 'I can think

better if I think alone.'

'All right,' said Wilbur. 'But don't fail to let me know if there's anything I can do to help, no matter how slight.'

'Well,' replied Charlotte, 'you must try to build yourself up. I want you to get plenty of sleep, and stop worrying. Never hurry and never worry! Chew your food thoroughly and eat every bit of it, except you must leave just enough for Templeton. Gain weight and stay well — that's the way you can help. Keep fit, and don't lose your nerve. Do you think you understand?'

'Yes, I understand,' said Wilbur.

'Go along to bed then,' said Charlotte. 'Sleep is important.'

Wilbur trotted over to the darkest corner of his pen and threw himself down. He closed his eyes. In another minute he spoke.

'Charlotte?' he said.

'Yes, Wilbur?'

'May I go out to my trough and see if I left any of my supper? I think I left just a tiny bit of mashed potato.'

'Very well,' said Charlotte. 'But I want you in bed again without delay.'

Wilbur started to race out to his yard.

'Slowly, slowly!' said Charlotte. 'Never hurry and never worry!'

Wilbur checked himself and crept slowly to his trough. He found a bit of potato, chewed it carefully, swallowed it, and walked back to bed. He closed his eyes and was silent for a while.

'Charlotte?' he said, in a whisper.

'Yes?'

'May I get a drink of milk? I think there are a few drops of milk left in my trough.'

'No, the trough is dry, and I want you to go to sleep. No more talking! Close your eyes and go to sleep!'

Wilbur shut his eyes. Fern got up from her stool and started for home, her mind full of everything she had seen and heard.

'Good night, Charlotte!' said Wilbur.

'Good night, Wilbur!'

There was a pause.

'Good night, Charlotte!'

'Good night, Wilbur!'

'Good night!'

'Good night!'

10.

An Explosion

Day after day the spider waited, head–down, for an idea to come to her. Hour by hour she sat motionless, deep in thought. Having promised Wilbur that she would save his life, she was determined to keep her promise.

Charlotte was naturally patient. She knew from experience that if she waited long enough, a fly would come to her web; and she felt sure that if she thought long enough about Wilbur' s problem, an idea would come to her mind.

Finally, one morning towards the middle of July, the idea came. 'Why, how perfectly simple!' she said to herself. 'The way to save Wilbur' s life is to play a trick on Zuckerman. If I can fool a bug,' thought Charlotte, 'I can surely fool a man. People are not as smart as bugs.'

Wilbur walked into his yard just at that moment.

'What are you thinking about, Charlotte?' he asked.

'I was just thinking,' said the spider, 'that people are very gullible.'

'What does "gullible" mean?'

'Easy to fool,' said Charlotte.

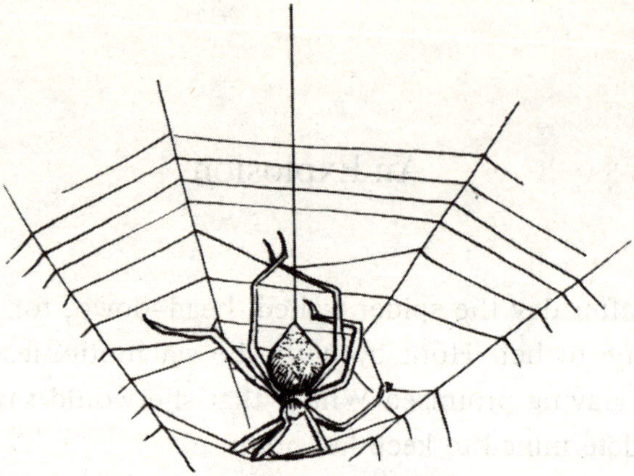

'That's a mercy,' replied Wilbur, and he lay down in the shade of his fence and went fast asleep. The spider, however, stayed wide awake, gazing affectionately at him and making plans for his future. Summer was half gone. She knew she didn't have much time.

That morning, just as Wilbur fell asleep, Avery Arable wandered into the Zuckermans' front yard, followed by Fern. Avery carried a live frog in his hand. Fern had a crown of daisies in her hair. The children ran for the kitchen.

'Just in time for a piece of blueberry pie,' said Mrs Zuckerman.

'Look at my frog!' said Avery, placing the frog on the drainboard and holding out his hand for pie.

'Take that thing out of here!' said Mrs Zuckerman.

'He's hot,' said Fern. 'He's almost dead, that frog.'

'He is not,' said Avery. 'He lets me scratch him between the eyes.' The frog jumped and landed in Mrs Zuckerman's dishpan full of soapy water.

'You're getting your pie on you,' said Fern. 'Can I look for eggs in the henhouse, Aunt Edith?'

'Run outdoors, both of you! And don't bother the hens!'

'It's getting all over everything,' shouted Fern. 'His pie is all over his front.'

'Come on, frog!' cried Avery. He scooped up his frog. The fog kicked, splashing soapy water onto the blueberry pie.

'Another crisis!' groaned Fern.

'Let's swing in the swing!' said Avery.

The children ran to the barn.

Mr Zuckerman had the best swing in the county. It was a single long piece of heavy rope tied to the beam over the north doorway. At the bottom end of the rope was a fat knot to sit on. It was arranged so that you could swing without being pushed. You climbed a ladder to the hayloft. Then, holding the rope, you stood at the edge and looked down, and were scared and dizzy. Then you straddled the knot, so that it acted as a seat. Then you got up all your nerve, took a deep breath, and jumped. For a second you seemed to be falling to the barn floor far below, but then suddenly the rope would begin to catch you, and you would sail through the barn door going a mile a minute, with the wind whistling in your eyes and ears and hair. Then you would zoom upwards into the sky, and look up at the clouds, and the rope would twist and you would twist and turn with the rope. Then you would drop down, down, down out of the sky and come sailing back into the barn almost into the hayloft, then sail out again (not quite so far this time), then in again (not quite so high), then out again, then in again, then out, then in; and then you' d jump off and fall down and let somebody else try it.

Mothers for miles around worried about Zuckerman' s swing. They feared some child would fall off. But no child ever did. Children almost always hang on to things tighter than their parents think they will.

Avery put the frog in his pocket and climbed to the hayloft. 'The last time I swang in this swing, I almost crashed into a barn swallow,' he yelled.

'Take that frog out!' ordered Fern.

Avery straddled the rope and jumped. He sailed out through the door, frog and all, and into the sky, frog and all. Then he sailed back into the barn.

'Your tongue is purple!' screamed Fern.

'So is yours!' cried Avery, sailing out again with the frog.

'I have hay inside my dress! It itches!' called Fern.

'Scratch it!' yelled Avery, as he sailed back.

'It' s my turn,' said Fern. 'Jump off!'

'Fern' s got the itch!' sang Avery.

When he jumped off, he threw the swing up to his sister. She shut her eyes tight and jumped. She felt the dizzy drop, then the

supporting lift of the swing. When she opened her eyes she was looking up into the blue sky and was about to fly back through the door.

They took turns for an hour.

When the children grew tired of swinging, they went down towards the pasture and picked wild raspberries and ate them. Their tongues turned from purple to red. Fern bit into a raspberry that had a bad-tasting bug inside it, and got discouraged. Avery found an empty candy box and put his frog in it. The frog seemed tired after his morning in the swing. The children walked slowly up towards the barn. They, too, were tired and hardly had energy enough to walk.

'Let's build a tree house,' suggested Avery. 'I want to live in a tree, with my frog.'

'I'm going to visit Wilbur,' Fern announced.

They climbed the fence into the lane and walked lazily towards the pigpen. Wilbur heard them coming and got up.

Avery noticed the spider web, and, coming closer, he saw Charlotte.

'Hey, look at that big spider!' he said. 'It's tremenjus.'

'Leave it alone!' commanded Fern. 'You've got a frog — isn't that enough?'

'That's a fine spider and I'm going to capture it,' said Avery. He took the cover off the candy box. Then he picked up a stick. 'I'm going to knock that ol' spider into this box,' he said.

Wilbur's heart almost stopped when he saw what was going

on. This might be the end of Charlotte if the boy succeeded in catching her.

'You stop it, Avery!' cried Fern.

Avery put one leg over the fence of the pigpen. He was just about to raise his stick to hit Charlotte when he lost his balance. He swayed and toppled and landed on the edge of Wilbur's trough. The trough tipped up and then came down with a slap. The goose egg was right underneath. There was a dull explosion as the egg broke, and then a horrible smell.

Fern screamed. Avery jumped to his feet. The air was filled with the terrible gases and smells from the rotten egg. Templeton, who had been resting in his home, scuttled away into the barn.

'Good *night*!' screamed Avery. 'Good *night*! What a stink! Let's get out of here!'

Fern was crying. She held her nose and ran towards the house. Avery ran after her, holding his nose. Charlotte felt greatly relieved to see him go. It had been a narrow escape.

Later on that morning, the animals came up from the pasture — the sheep, the lambs, the gander, the goose, and the seven goslings. There were many complaints about the awful smell, and Wilbur had to tell the story over and over again, of how the Arable boy had tried to capture Charlotte, and how the smell of the broken egg drove him away just in time. 'It was that rotten goose egg that saved charlotte's life,' said Wilbur.

The goose was proud of her share in the adventure. 'I'm delighted that the egg never hatched,' she gabbled.

Templeton, of course, was miserable over the loss of his beloved egg. But he couldn't resist boasting. 'It pays to save things,' he said in his surly voice. 'A rat never knows when something is going to come in handy. I never throw anything away.'

'Well,' said one of the lambs, 'this whole business is all well and good for Charlotte, but what about the rest of us? The smell is unbearable. Who wants to live in a barn that is perfumed with rotten egg?'

'Don't worry, you'll get used to it,' said Templeton. He sat up and pulled wisely at his long whiskers, then crept away to pay a visit to the dump.

When Lurvy showed up at lunchtime carrying a pail of food for Wilbur, he stopped short a few paces from the pigpen. He sniffed the air and made a face.

'What in thunder?' he said. Setting the pail down, he picked up the stick that Avery had dropped and pried the trough up. 'Rats!' he said. 'Phew! I might a'known a rat would make a nest under this trough. How I hate a rat!'

And Lurvy dragged Wilbur's trough across the yard and kicked some dirt into the rat's nest, burying the broken egg and all Templeton's other possessions. Then he picked up the pail. Wilbur stood in the trough, drooling with hunger. Lurvy poured. The slops ran creamily down around the pig's eyes and ears. Wilbur grunted. He gulped and sucked, and sucked and gulped, making swishing and swooshing noises, anxious to get everything at once. It was a delicious meal — skim milk, wheat middlings, left-over pancakes, half a doughnut, the rind of a summer squash, two pieces of stale toast, a third of a ginger snap, a fish tail, one orange peel, several noodles from a noodle soup, the skin off a cup of cocoa, an ancient jelly roll, a strip of paper from the lining of the garbage pail, and a spoonful of raspberry jelly.

Wilbur ate heartily. He planned to leave half a noodle and a few drops of milk for Templeton. Then he remembered that the rat had been useful in saving Charlotte' s life, and that Charlotte was trying to save *his* life. So he left a whole noodle, instead of a half.

Now that the broken egg was buried, the air cleared and the barn smelt good again. The afternoon passed, and evening came. Shadows lengthened. The cool and kindly breath of evening entered through doors and windows. Astride her web, Charlotte sat moodily eating a horse–fly and thinking about the future. After a while she bestirred herself.

She descended to the center of the web and there she began to cut some of her lines. She worked slowly but steadily while the other creatures drowsed. None of the others, not even the goose, noticed that she was at work. Deep in his soft bed, Wilbur snoozed. Over in their favourite corner, the goslings whistled a night song.

Charlotte tore quite a section out of her web, leaving an open space in the middle. Then she started weaving something to take the place of the threads she had removed. When Templeton got back from the dump, around midnight, the spider was still at work.

11.

The Miracle

The next day was foggy. Everything on the farm was dripping wet. The grass looked like a magic carpet. The asparagus patch looked like a silver forest.

On foggy mornings, Charlotte's web was truly a thing of beauty. This morning each thin strand was decorated with dozens of tiny beads of water. The web glistened in the light and made a pattern of loveliness and mystery, like a delicate veil. Even Lurvy, who wasn't particularly interested in beauty, noticed the web when he came with the pig's breakfast. He noted how clearly it showed up and he noted how big and carefully built it was. And then he took another look and he saw something that made him set his pail down. There, in the center of the web, neatly woven in block letters, was a message. It said:

SOME PIG

Lurvy felt weak. He brushed his hand across his eyes and stared harder at Charlotte's web.

'I'm seeing things,' he whispered. He dropped to his knees

and uttered a short prayer. Then, forgetting all about Wilbur's breakfast, he walked back to the house and called Mr Zuckerman.

'I think you'd better come down to the pigpen,' he said.

'What's the trouble?' asked Mr Zuckerman. 'Anything wrong with the pig?'

'N—not exactly,' said Lurvy. 'Come and see for yourself.'

The two men walked silently down to Wilbur's yard. Lurvy pointed to the spider's web. 'Do you see what I see?' he asked.

Zuckerman stared at the writing on the web. Then he murmured the words 'Some Pig'. Then he looked at Lurvy. Then they both began to tremble. Charlotte, sleepy after her night's exertions, smiled as she watched. Wilbur came and stood directly under the web.

'Some pig!' muttered Lurvy in a low voice.

'Some pig!' whispered Mr Zuckerman. They stared and stared for a long time at Wilbur. Then they stared at Charlotte.

'You don't suppose that that spider . . . ' began Mr Zuckerman —but he shook his head and didn't finish the sentence. Instead, he walked solemnly back up to the house and spoke to his wife. 'Edith, something has happened,' he said, in a weak voice. He went into the living-room and sat down, and Mrs Zuckerman followed.

'I've got something to tell you, Edith,' he said. 'You better sit down.'

Mrs Zuckerman sank into a chair. She looked pale and frightened.

'Edith,' he said, trying to keep his voice steady, 'I think you had best be told that we have a very unusual pig.'

A look of complete bewilderment came over Mrs Zuckerman's face. 'Homer Zuckerman, what in the world are you talking about?' she said.

'This is a very serious thing, Edith,' he replied. 'Our pig is completely out of the ordinary.'

'What's unusual about the pig?' asked Mrs Zuckerman, who was beginning to recover from her scare.

'Well, I don't really know yet,' said Mr Zuckerman. 'But we

have received a sign, Edith — a mysterious sign. A miracle has happened on this farm. There is a large spider's web in the doorway of the barn cellar, right over the pigpen, and when Lurvy went to feed the pig this morning, he noticed the web because it was foggy, and you know how a spider's web looks very distinct in a fog. And right spang in the middle of the web there were the words "Some Pig." The words were woven right into the web. They were actually part of the web, Edith. I know, because I have been down there and seen them. It says, "Some Pig," just as clear as clear can be. There can be no mistake about it. A miracle has happened and a sign has occurred here on earth, right on our farm, and we have no ordinary pig.'

'Well,' said Mrs Zuckerman, 'it seems to me you're a little off. It seems to me we have no ordinary *spider*.'

'Oh, no,' said Zuckerman. 'It's the pig that's unusual. It says so, right there in the middle of the web.'

'Maybe so,' said Mrs Zuckerman. 'Just the same, I intend to have a look at that spider.'

'It's just a common grey spider,' said Zuckerman.

They got up, and together they walked down to Wilbur's yard. 'You see, Edith? It's just a common grey spider.'

Wilbur was pleased to receive so much attention. Lurvy was still standing there, and Mr And Mrs Zuckerman, all three, stood for about an hour, reading the words on the web over and over, and watching Wilbur.

Charlotte was delighted with the way her trick was working.

She sat without moving a muscle, and listened to the conversation of the people. When a small fly blundered into the web, just beyond the word 'pig', Charlotte dropped quickly down, rolled the fly up, and carried it out of the way.

After a while the fog lifted. The web dried off and the words didn't show up so plainly. The Zuckermans and Lurvy walked back to the house. Just before they left the pigpen, Mr Zuckerman took one last look at Wilbur.

'You know,' he said, in an important voice, 'I've thought all along that that pig of ours was an extra good one. He's a solid pig. That pig is as solid as they come. You notice how solid he is around the shoulders, Lurvy?'

'Sure, sure I do,' said Lurvy. 'I've always noticed that pig. He's quite a pig.'

'He's long, and he's smooth,' said Zuckerman.

'That's right,' agreed Lurvy. 'He's as smooth as they come. He's some pig.'

When Mr Zuckerman got back to the house, he took off his work clothes and put on his best suit. Then he got into his car and drove to the minister's house. He stayed for an hour and explained to the minister that a miracle had happened on the farm.

'So far,' said Zuckerman, 'only four people on earth know about this miracle—myself, my wife Edith, my hired man Lurvy, and you.'

'Don't tell anybody else,' said the minister. 'We don't know what it means yet, but perhaps if I give thought to it, I can explain it in my sermon next Sunday. There can be no doubt that you have a most unusual pig. I intend to speak about it in my sermon and point out the fact that this community has been visited with a wondrous animal. By the way, does the pig have a name?'

'Why, yes,' said Mr Zuckerman. 'My little niece calls him Wilbur. She's rather queer child—full of notions. She raised the pig on a bottle and I bought him from her when he was a month old.'

He shook hands with the minister, and left.

Secrets are hard to keep. Long before Sunday came, the news spread all over the county. Everybody knew that a sign had appeared in a spider's web on the Zuckerman place. Everybody knew that the Zuckermans had a wondrous pig. People came from miles around to look at Wilbur and to read the words on Charlotte's web. The Zuckermans' driveway was full of cars and trucks from morning till night — Fords and Chevvies and Buick roadmasters and GMC pickups and Plymouths and Studebakers and Packards and De Sotos with gyromatic transmissions and Oldsmobiles with rocket engines and Jeep station wagons and Pontiacs. The news of the wonderful pig spread clear up into the hills, and farmers came rattling down in buggies and buckboards, to stand hour after hour at Wilbur's pen admiring the miraculous animal. All said they had never seen such a pig before in their lives.

When Fern told her mother that Avery had tried to hit the Zuckermans'spider with a stick, Mrs Arable was so shocked that she sent Avery to bed without any supper, as punishment.

In the days that followed, Mr Zuckerman was so busy entertaining visitors that he neglected his farm work. He wore his good clothes all the time now—got right into them when he got up in the morning. Mrs Zuckerman prepared special meals for Wilbur. Lurvy shaved and got a haircut; and his principal farm duty was to feed the pig while people looked on.

Mr Zuckerman ordered Lurvy to increase Wilbur's feedings from three meals a day to four meals a day. The Zuckermans were so busy with visitors they forgot about other things on the farm. The blackberries got ripe, and Mrs Zuckerman never put up any blackberry jam. The corn needed hoeing, and Lurvy didn't find time to hoe it.

On Sunday the church was full. The minister explained the miracle. He said that the words on the spider's web proved that human beings must always be on the watch for the coming of wonders.

All in all, the Zuckermans' pigpen was the center of attraction. Fern was happy, for she felt that Charlotte's trick was working and that Wilbur's life would be saved. But she found that the barn was not nearly so pleasant—too many people. She liked it better when she could be all alone with her friends the animals.

12.

A Meeting

One evening, a few days after the writing had appeared in Charlotte' s web, the spider called a meeting of all the animals in the barn cellar.

'I shall begin by calling the roll. Wilbur?'

'Here!' said the pig.

'Gander?'

'Here, here, here!' said the gander.

'You sound like three ganders,' muttered Charlotte. 'Why can' t you just say "here"? Why do you have to repeat everything?'

'It' s my idio–idio–idiosyncrasy,' replied the gander.

'Goose?' said Charlotte.

'Here, here, here!' said the goose. Charlotte glared at her.

'Goslings, one through seven?'

'Bee–bee–bee!' 'Bee–bee–bee!' 'Bee–bee–bee!' 'Bee–bee–bee!' 'Bee–bee–bee!' 'Bee–bee–bee!' 'Bee–bee–bee!' said the goslings.

'This is getting to be quite a meeting,' said Charlotte. 'Anybody would think we had three ganders, three geese, and twenty-one goslings. Sheep?'

'He–aa–aa!' answered the sheep all together.

'Lambs?'

'He–aa–aa!' answered the lambs all together.

'Templeton?'

No answer.

'Templeton?'

No answer.

'Well, we are all here except the rat,' said Charlotte. 'I guess we can proceed without him. Now, all of you must have noticed what's been going on around here the last few days. The message I wrote in my web, praising Wilbur, has been received. The Zuckermans have fallen for it, and so has everybody else. Zuckerman thinks Wilbur is an unusual pig, and therefore he won' t want to kill him and eat him. I dare say my trick will work and Wilbur' s life can be saved.

'Hurray!' cried everybody.

'Thank you very much,' said Charlotte. 'Now I called this meeting in order to get suggestions. I need new ideas for the web. People are already getting sick of reading the words "SOME PIG!" If anybody can think of another message, or remark, I' ll be glad to weave it into the web. Any suggestions for a new slogan?'

'How about "Pig Supreme"?' asked one of the lambs.

'No good,' said Charlotte. 'It sounds like a rich dessert.'

'How about "Terrific, terrific, terrific"?' asked the goose.

'Cut that down to one "terrific" and it will do very nicely,' said Charlotte. 'I think "terrific" might impress Zuckerman.'

'But, Charlotte,' said Wilbur, 'I' m not terrific.'

'That doesn' t make a particle of difference,' replied Charlotte. 'Not a particle. People believe almost anything they see in print. Does anybody here know how to spell "terrific"?'

'I think,' said the gander, 'it's tee double ee double rr double rr double eye double ff double eye double see see see see see.'

'What kind of an acrobat do you think I am?' said Charlotte in disgust. 'I would have to have St Vitus's Dance to weave a word like that into my web.'

'Sorry, sorry, sorry,' said the gander.

Then the oldest sheep spoke up. 'I agree that there should be something new written in the web if Wilbur's life is to be saved. And if Charlotte needs help in finding words, I think she can get it from our friend Templeton. The rat visits the dump regularly and has access to old magazines. He can tear out bits of advertisements and bring them up here to the barn cellar, so that Charlotte can have something to copy.'

'Good idea,' said Charlotte. 'But I'm not sure Templeton will be willing to help. You know how he is—always looking out for himself, never thinking of the other fellow.'

'I bet I can get him to help,' said the old sheep. 'I'll appeal to his baser instincts, of which he has plenty. Here he comes now. Everybody keep quiet while I put the matter up to him!'

The rat entered the barn the way he always did — creeping along close to the wall.

'What's up?' he asked, seeing the animals assembled.

'We're holding a directors' meeting,' replied the old sheep.

'Well, break it up!' said Templeton. 'Meetings bore me.' And the rat began to climb a rope that hung against the wall.

'Look,' said the old sheep, 'next time you go to the dump, Templeton, bring back a clipping from a magazine. Charlotte needs new ideas so she can write messages in her web and save Wilbur's life.'

'Let him die,' said the rat. 'I should worry.'

'You'll worry all right when next winter comes,' said the sheep. 'You'll worry all right on a zero morning next January when Wilbur is dead and nobody comes down here with a nice pail of warm slops to pour into the trough. Wilbur's left-over food is your chief source of supply, Templeton. *You* know that. Wilbur's food is your food; therefore Wilbur's destiny and your destiny are closely linked. If Wilbur is killed and his trough stands empty day after day, you'll grow so thin we can look right through your stomach and see objects on the other side.'

Templeton's whiskers quivered.

'Maybe you're right,' he said gruffly. 'I'm making a trip to the dump tomorrow afternoon. I'll bring back a magazine clipping if I can find one.'

'Thanks,' said Charlotte. 'The meeting is now adjourned. I have a busy evening ahead of me. I've got to tear my web apart and write TERRIFIC.'

Wilbur blushed. 'But I'm not terrific, Charlotte. I'm just about average for a pig.'

'You're terrific as far as *I'm* concerned,' replied Charlotte, sweetly, 'and that's what counts. You're my best friend, and *I* think you're sensational. Now stop arguing and go get some sleep!'

13.

Good Progress

Far into the night, while the other creatures slept, Charlotte worked on her web. First she ripped out a few of the orb lines near the center. She left the radial lines alone, as they were needed for support. As she worked, her eight legs were a great help to her. So were her teeth. She loved to weave and she was an expert at it. When she had finished ripping things out, her web looked something like this

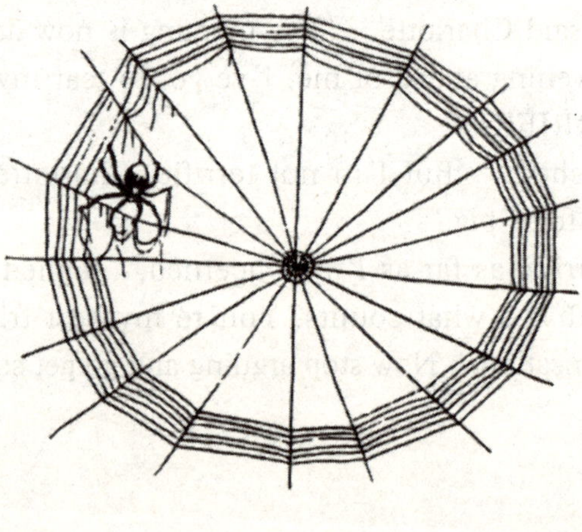

A spider can produce several kinds of thread. She uses a dry, tough thread for foundation lines, and she uses a sticky thread for snare lines — the ones that catch and hold insects. Charlotte decided to use her dry thread for writing the new message.

'If I write the word TERRIFIC with sticky thread,' she thought, 'every bug that comes along will get stuck in it and spoil the effect.'

'Now let' s see, the first letter is T.'

Charlotte climbed to a point at the top of the left-hand side of the web. Swinging her spinnerets into position, she attached her thread and then dropped down. As she dropped, her spinning tubes went into action and she let out thread. At the bottom, she attached the thread. This formed the upright part of the letter T. Charlotte was not satisfied, however. She climbed up and made another attachment, right next to the first. Then she carried the line down, so that she had a double line instead of a single line. 'It will show up better if I make the whole thing with double lines.'

She climbed back up, moved over about an inch to the left, touched her spinnerets to the web, and then carried a line across to the right, forming the top of the T. She repeated this, making it double. Her eight legs were very busy helping.

'Now for the E!'

Charlotte got so interested in her work, she began to talk to herself, as though to cheer herself on. If you had been sitting quietly in the barn cellar that evening, you would have heard something like this:

'Now for the R! Up we go! Attach! Descend! Pay out line! Whoa! Attach! Good! Up you go! Repeat! Attach! Descend! Pay out line. Whoa, girl! Steady now! Attach! Climb! Attach! Over to the right! Pay out line! Attach! Now right and down and swing that loop and around and around! Now in to the left! Attach! Climb! Repeat! OK! Easy, keep those lines together! Now, then, out and down for the leg of the R! Pay out line! Whoa! Attach! Ascend! Repeat! Good girl!'

And so, talking to herself, the spider worked at her difficult task. When it was completed, she felt hungry. She ate a small bug that she had been saving. Then she slept.

Next morning, Wilbur arose and stood beneath the web. He breathed the morning air into his lungs. Drops of dew, catching the sun, made the web stand out clearly. When Lurvy arrived with breakfast, there was the handsome pig, and over him, woven neatly in block letters, was the word TERRIFIC. Another miracle.

Lurvy rushed and called Mr Zuckerman. Mr Zuckerman rushed and called Mrs Zuckerman. Mrs Zuckerman ran to the phone and called the Arables. The Arables climbed into their truck and hurried over. Everybody stood at the pigpen and stared at the web and read the word, over and over, while Wilbur, who really *felt* terrific, stood quietly swelling out his chest and swinging his snout from side to side.

'Terrific!' breathed Zuckerman, in joyful admiration. 'Edith, you better phone the reporter on the *Weekly Chronicle* and tell

him what has happened. He will want to know about this. He may want to bring a photographer. There isn't a pig in the whole state that is as terrific as our pig.'

The news spread. People who had journeyed to see Wilbur

when he was 'some pig' came back again to see him now that he was 'terrific'.

That afternoon, when Mr Zuckerman went to milk the cows and clean out the tie-ups, he was still thinking about what a wondrous pig he owned.

'Lurvy!' he called. 'There is to be no more cow manure thrown down into that pigpen. I have a terrific pig. I want that pig to have clean, bright straw every day for his bedding. Understand?'

'Yes, sir,' said Lurvy.

'Furthermore,' said Mr Zuckerman, 'I want you to start building a crate for Wilbur. I have decided to take the pig to the County Fair on September sixth. Make the crate large and paint it green with gold letters!'

'What will the letters say?' asked Lurvy.

'They should say *Zuckerman's Famous Pig*.'

Lurvy picked up a pitchfork and walked away to get some clean straw. Having such an important pig was going to mean plenty of extra work, he could see that.

Below the apple orchard, at the end of a path, was the dump where Mr Zuckerman threw all sorts of trash and stuff that nobody wanted any more. Here, in a small clearing hidden by young alders and wild raspberry bushes, was an astonishing pile of old bottles and empty tin cans and dirty rags and bits of metal and broken bottles and broken hinges and broken springs and dead batteries and last month's magazines and old discarded dishmops and tattered overalls and rusty spikes and leaky pails and forgotten stoppers and useless junk of all kinds, including a wrong-size crank for a broken ice-cream freezer.

Templeton knew the dump and liked it. There were good hiding-places there — excellent cover for a rat. And there was usually a tin can with food still clinging to the inside.

Templeton was down there now, rummaging around. When he returned to the barn, he carried in his mouth an advertisement he had torn from a crumpled magazine.

'How's this?' he asked, showing the ad. to Charlotte. 'It says CRUNCHY. "Crunchy" would be a good word to write in your web.'

'Just the wrong idea,' replied Charlotte. 'Couldn't be worse. We don't want Zuckerman to think Wilbur is crunchy. He might start thinking about crisp, crunchy bacon and tasty ham. That would put ideas into his head. We must advertise Wilbur's noble qualities, not his tastiness. Go get another word, please, Templeton!'

The rat looked disgusted. But he sneaked away to the dump and was back in a while with a strip of cotton cloth. 'How's this?' he asked. 'It's a label off an old shirt.'

Charlotte examined the label. It said PRESHRUNK.

'I'm sorry, Templeton,' she said, 'but PRESHRUNK is out of the question. We want Zuckerman to think Wilbur is nicely filled out, not all shrunk up. I'll have to ask you to try again.'

'What do you think I am, a messenger boy?' grumbled the rat. 'I'm not going to spend all my time chasing down to the dump after advertising material.'

'Just once more—please!' said Charlotte.

'I'll tell you what I'll do,' said Templeton. 'I know where there's a package of soap flakes in the woodshed. It has writing on it. I'll bring you a piece of the package.'

He climbed the rope that hung on the wall and disappeared through a hole in the ceiling. When he came back he had a strip of blue-and-white cardboard in his teeth.

'There!' he said, triumphantly. 'How's that?'

Charlotte read the words: 'With New Radiant Action.'

'What does it mean?' asked Charlotte, who had never used any soap flakes in her life.

'How should I know?' said Templeton. 'You asked for words and I brought them. I suppose the next thing you'll want me to fetch is a dictionary.'

Together they studied the soap ad. 'With new radiant action,' repeated Charlotte, slowly. 'Wilbur!' she called.

Wilbur, who was asleep in the straw, jumped up.

'Run around!' commanded Charlotte. 'I want to see you in action, to see if you are radiant.'

Wilbur raced to the end of his yard.

'Now back again, faster!' said Charlotte.

Wilbur galloped back. His skin shone. His tail had a fine, tight curl in it.

'Jump into the air!' cried Charlotte.

Wilbur jumped as high as he could.

'Keep your knees straight and touch the ground with your ears!' called Charlotte.

Wilbur obeyed.

'Do a back flip with a half twist in it!' cried Charlotte.

Wilbur went over backwards, writhing and twisting as he went.

'OK, Wilbur,' said Charlotte. 'You can go back to sleep. OK, Templeton, the soap ad. will do, I guess. I' m not sure Wilbur' s action is exactly radiant, but it' s interesting.'

'Actually,' said Wilbur, 'I feel radiant.'

'Do you?' said Charlotte, looking at him with affection. 'Well, you' re a good little pig, and radiant you shall be. I' m in this thing pretty deep now — I might as well go the limit.'

Tired from his romp, Wilbur lay down in the clean straw. He closed his eyes. The straw seemed scratchy—not as comfortable as the cow manure, which was always delightfully soft to lie in. So he pushed the straw to one side and stretched out in the manure. Wilbur sighed. It had been a busy day—his first day of being terrific. Dozens of people had visited his yard during the afternoon, and he had had to stand and pose, looking as terrific as he could. Now he was tired. Fern had arrived and seated herself quietly on her stool in the corner.

'Tell me a story, Charlotte!' said Wilbur, as he lay waiting for sleep to come. 'Tell me a story!'

So Charlotte, although she, too, was tired, did what Wilbur wanted.

'Once upon a time,' she began, 'I had a beautiful cousin who managed to build her web across a small stream. One day a tiny fish leaped into the air and got tangled in the web. My cousin was very much surprised, of course. The fish was thrashing wildly. My cousin hardly dared tackle it. But she did. She swooped down and threw great masses of wrapping material around the fish and fought bravely to capture it.'

'Did she succeed?' asked Wilbur.

'It was a never-to-be-forgotten battle,' said Charlotte. 'There was the fish, caught only by one fin, and its tail wildly thrashing and shining in the sun. There was the web, sagging dangerously under the weight of the fish.'

'How much did the fish weigh?' asked Wilbur eagerly.

'I don't know,' said Charlotte. 'There was my cousin, slipping in, dodging out, beaten mercilessly over the head by the wildly thrashing fish, dancing in, dancing out, throwing her threads and fighting hard. First she threw a left around the tail. The fish lashed back. Then a left to the tail and a right to the mid-section. Then a left to the tail and a right to the mid-section. The fish lashed back. Then she dodged to one side and threw a right, and another right to the fin. Then a hard left to the head, while the web swayed and stretched.'

'Then what happened?' asked Wilbur.

'Nothing,' said Charlotte. 'The fish lost the fight. My cousin wrapped it up so tight it conldn't budge.'

'Then what happened?' asked Wilbur.

'Nothing,' said Charlotte. 'My cousin kept the fish for a while, and then, when she got good and ready, she ate it.'

'Tell me another story!' begged Wilbur.

So Charlotte told him about another cousin of hers who was an aeronaut.

'What is an aeronaut?' asked Wilbur.

'A balloonist,' said Charlotte. 'My cousin used to stand on her head and let out enough thread to form a balloon. Then she'd let go and be lifted into the air and carried upwards on the warm wind.'

'Is that true?' asked Wilbur. 'Or are you just making it up?'

'It's true,' replied Charlotte. 'I have some very remarkable cousins. And now, Wilbur, it's time you went to sleep.'

'Sing something!' begged Wilbur, closing his eyes.

So Charlotte sang a lullaby, while crickets chirped in the grass and the barn grew dark. This was the song she sang:

'Sleep, sleep, my love, my only,
Deep, deep, in the dung and the dark;
Be not afraid and be not lonely!
This is the hour when frogs and thrushes
Praise the world from the woods and the woods and rushes.
Rest form care, my one and only,
Deep in the dung and the dark!'

But Wilbur was already asleep. When the song ended, Fern got up and went home.

14.

Dr Dorian

The next day was Saturday. Fern stood at the kitchen sink drying the breakfast dishes as her mother washed them. Mrs Arable worked silently. She hoped Fern would go out and play with other children, instead of heading for the Zuckermans' barn to sit and watch animals.

'Charlotte is the best storyteller I ever heard,' said Fern, poking her dish towel into a cereal bowl.

'Fern,' said her mother sternly, 'you must not invent things. You know spiders don't tell stories. Spiders can't talk.'

'Charlotte can,' replied Fern. 'She doesn't talk very loud, but she talks.'

'What kind of story did she tell?' asked Mrs Arable.

'Well,' began Fern, 'she told me about a cousin of hers who caught a fish in her web. Don't you think that's fascinating?'

'Fern, dear, how would a fish get in a spider's web?' said Mrs Arable. 'You know it couldn't happen. You're making this up.'

'Oh, it happened all right,' replied Fern. 'Charlotte never fibs. This cousin of hers built a web across a stream. One day she was hanging around on the web and a tiny fish leaped into the air and got tangled in the web. The fish was caught by one fin, Mother; its tail was wildly thrashing and shining in the sun. Can't you just see the web, sagging dangerously under the weight of the fish? Charlotte's cousin kept slipping in, dodging out, and she was beaten mercilessly over the head by the wildly thrashing fish, dancing in, dancing out, throwing...'

'Fern!' snapped her mother. 'Stop it! Stop inventing these wild tales!'

'I'm not inventing,' said Fern. 'I'm just telling you the facts.'

'What finally happened?' asked her mother, whose curiosity began to get the better of her.

'Charlotte's cousin won. She wrapped the fish up, then she ate him when she got good and ready. Spiders have to eat, the same as the rest of us.'

'Yes, I suppose they do,' said Mrs Arable, vaguely.

'Charlotte has another cousin who is a balloonist. She stands on her head, lets out a lot of line, and is carried aloft on the wind. Mother, wouldn't you simply love to do that?'

'Yes, I would, come to think of it,' replied Mrs Arable. 'But Fern, darling, I wish you would play outdoors today instead of going to Uncle Homer's barn. Find some of your playmates and do something nice outdoors. You're spending too much time in that barn — it isn't good for you to be alone so much.'

'Alone?' said Fern. 'Alone? My best friends are in the barn cellar. It is a very sociable place. Not at all lonely.'

Fern disappeared after a while, walking down the road towards

Zuckermans. Her mother dusted the sitting-room. As she worked she kept thinking about Fern. It didn't seem natural for a little girl to be so interested in animals. Finally Mrs Arable made up her mind she would pay a call on old Dr Dorian and ask his advice. She got in the car and drove to his office in the village.

Dr Dorian had a thick beard. He was glad to see Mrs Arable and gave her a comfortable chair.

'It's about Fern,' she explained. 'Fern spends entirely too much time in the Zuckermans' barn. It doesn't seem normal. She sits on a milk stool in a corner of the barn cellar, near the pigpen, and watches animals, hour after hour. She just sits and listens.'

Dr Dorian leaned back and closed his eyes.

'How enchanting!' he said. 'It must be real nice and quiet down there. Homer has some sheep, hasn't he?'

'Yes,' said Mrs Arable. 'But it all started with that pig we let Fern raise on a bottle. She calls him Wilbur. Homer bought the pig, and ever since it left our place Fern has been going to her uncle's to be near it.'

'I've been hearing things about that pig,' said Dr Dorian, opening his eyes. 'They say he's quite a pig.'

'Have you heard about the words that appeared in the spider's web?' asked Mrs Arable nervously.

'Yes,' replied the doctor.

'Well, do you understand it?' asked Mrs Arable.

'Understand what?'

'Do you understand how there could be any writing in a spider' s web?'

'Oh, no,' said Dr Dorian. 'I don't understand it. But for that matter I don't understand how a spider learned to spin a web in the first place. When the words appeared, everyone said they were a miracle. But nobody pointed out that the web itself is a miracle.'

'What's miraculous about a spider's web?' said Mrs Arable. 'I don't see why you say a web is a miracle — it' s just a web.'

'Ever try to spin one?' asked Dr Dorian.

Mrs Arable shifted uneasily in her chair. 'No,' she replied. 'But I can crochet a doily and I can knit a sock.'

'Sure,' said the doctor. 'But somebody taught you, didn't they?'

'My mother taught me.'

'Well, who taught a spider? A young spider knows how to spin a web without any instructions from anybody. Don't you regard that as a miracle?'

'I suppose so,' said Mrs Arable. 'I never looked at it that way before. Still, I don't understand it, and I don't like what I can't understand.'

'None of us do,' said Dr Dorian, sighing. 'I'm a doctor. Doctors are supposed to understand everything. But I don't understand everything, and I don't intend to let it worry me.'

Mrs Arable fidgeted. 'Fern says the animals talk to each other. Dr Dorian, do you believe animals talk?'

'I never heard one say anything,' he replied. 'But that proves nothing. It is quite possible that an animal has spoken civilly to me and that I didn't catch the remark because I wasn't paying attention. Children pay better attention than grown-ups. If Fern says that the animals in Zuckerman's barn talk, I'm quite ready to believe her. Perhaps if people talked less, animals would talk more. People are incessant talkers — I can give you my word on that.'

'Well, I feel better about Fern,' said Mrs Arable. 'You don't think I need worry about her?'

'Does she look well?' asked the doctor.

'Oh, yes.'

'Appetite good?'

'Oh, yes, she's always hungry.'

'Sleep well at night?'

'Oh, yes.'

'Then don't worry,' said the doctor.

'Do you think she'll ever start thinking about something besides pigs and sheep and geese and spiders?

'How old is Fern? '

'She's eight.'

'Well,' said Dr Dorian, 'I think she will always love animals. But I doubt that she spends her entire life in Homer Zuckerman's barn cellar. How about boys — does she know any boys?'

'She knows Henry Fussy,' said Mrs Arable brightly.

Dr Dorian closed his eyes again and went into deep thought. 'Henry Fussy,' he mumbled. 'Hmm. Remarkable. Well, I don't think you have anything to worry about. Let Fern associate with her friends in the barn if she wants to. I would say, offhand, that spiders and pigs were fully as interesting as Henry Fussy. Yet I predict that the day will come when even Henry will drop some chance remark that catches Fern's attention. It's amazing how children change from year to year. How's Avery?' he asked, opening his eyes wide.

'Oh, Avery,' chuckled Mrs Arable. 'Avery is always fine. Of course, he gets into poison ivy and gets stung by wasps and bees and brings frogs and snakes home and breaks everything he lays his hands on. He's fine.'

'Good!' said the doctor.

Mrs Arable said good-bye and thanked Dr Dorian very much for his advice. She felt greatly relieved.

15.

The Crickets

The crickets sang in the grasses. They sang the song of summer's ending, a sad, monotonous song. 'Summer is over and gone,' they sang. 'Over and gone, over and gone. Summer is dying, dying.'

The crickets felt it was their duty to warn everybody that summertime cannot last for ever. Even on the most beautiful days in the whole year—the days when summer is changing into autumn — the crickets spread the rumor of sadness and change.

Everybody heard the song of the crickets. Avery and Fern Arable heard it as they walked the dusty road. They knew that school would soon begin again. The young geese heard it and knew that they would never be little goslings again. Charlotte heard it and knew that she hadn't much time left. Mrs Zuckerman, at work in the kitchen, heard the crickets, and a sadness came over her, too. 'Another summer gone,' she sighed. Lurvy, at work building a crate for Wilbur, heard the song and knew it was time to dig potatoes.

'Summer is over and gone,' repeated the crickets. 'How many nights till frost?' said the crickets. 'Good-bye, summer, good-bye, good-bye!'

The sheep heard the crickets, and they felt so uneasy they broke a hole in the pasture fence and wandered up into the field across the road. The gander discovered the hole and led his family through, and they walked to the orchard and ate the apples that were lying on the ground. A little maple tree in the swamp heard the cricket song and turned bright red with anxiety.

Wilbur was now the center of attraction on the farm. Good food and regular hours were showing results: Wilbur was a pig any man would be proud of. One day more than a hundred people came to stand at his yard and admire him. Charlotte had written the word RADIANT, and Wilbur really looked radiant as he stood in the golden sunlight. Ever since the spider had befriended him, he had done his best to live up to his reputation. When Charlotte' s web said SOME PIG, Wilbur had tried hard to look like some pig. When Charlotte's web said TERRIFIC, Wilbur had tried to look terrific. And now that the web said RADIANT, he did everything possible to make himself glow.

It is not easy to look radiant, but Wilbur threw himself into it with a will. He would turn his head slightly and blink his long eye-lashes. Then he would breathe deeply. And when his audience grew bored, he would spring into the air and do a back flip with a half twist. At this the crowd would yell and cheer. 'How's that for a pig?' Mr Zuckerman would ask, well pleased with himself. 'That pig is radiant.'

Some of Wilbur's friends in the barn worried for fear all this attention would go to his head and make him stuck up. But it never did. Wilbur was modest; fame did not spoil him. He still worried some about the future, as he could hardly believe that a mere spider would be able to save his life. Sometimes at night he would have a bad dream. He would dream that men were coming to get him with knives and guns. But that was only a dream. In the daytime, Wilbur usually felt happy and confident. No pig ever had truer friends, and he realized that friendship is one of the most satisfying things in the world. Even the song of the crickets did not make Wilbur too sad. He knew it was almost time for the County Fair, and he was looking forward to the trip. If he could distinguish himself at the Fair, and maybe win some prize money, he was sure Zuckerman would let him live.

Charlotte had worries of her own, but she kept quiet about them. One morning Wilbur asked her about the Fair.

'You're going *with* me, aren't you, Charlotte?' he said.

'Well, I don't know,' replied Charlotte. 'The Fair comes at a bad time for me. I shall find it inconvenient to leave home, even for a few days.'

'Why?' asked Wilbur.

'Oh, I just don't feel like leaving my web. Too much going on around here.'

'*Please* come with me!' begged Wilbur. 'I need you, Charlotte. I can't stand going to the Fair without you. You've just *got* to come.'

'No,' said charlotte, 'I believe I'd better stay home and see if I can't get some work done.'

'What kind of work?' asked Wilbur.

'Egg laying. It's time I made an egg sac and filled it with eggs.'

'I didn't know you could lay eggs,' said Wilbur in amazement.

'Oh, sure,' said the spider. 'I'm versatile.'

'What does "versatile" mean—full of eggs?' asked Wilbur.

'Certainly not,' said Charlotte. '"Versatile" means I can turn with ease from one thing to another. It means I don't have to limit my activities to spinning and trapping and stunts like that.'

'Why don't you come with me to the Fair Grounds and lay your eggs there?' pleaded Wilbur. 'It would be wonderful fun.'

Charlotte gave her web a twitch and moodily watched it sway. 'I'm afraid not,' she said. 'You don't know the first thing about egg laying, Wilbur. I can't arrange my family duties to suit the management of the County Fair. When I get ready to lay eggs, I have to lay eggs, Fair or no Fair. However, I don't want you to worry about it—you might lose weight. We'll leave it this way: I'll come to the Fair if I possibly can.'

'Oh, good!' said Wilbur. 'I knew you wouldn't forsake me just when I need you most.'

All that day Wilbur stayed inside, taking life easy in the straw. Charlotte rested and ate a grasshopper. She knew that she couldn't help Wilbur much longer. In a few days she would have to drop everything and build the beautiful little sac that would hold her eggs.

16.

Off to the Fair

The night before the County Fair, everybody went to bed early. Fern and Avery were in bed by eight. Avery lay dreaming that the Ferris wheel had stopped and that he was in the top car. Fern lay dreaming that she was getting sick in the swings.

Lurvy was in bed by eight-thirty. He lay dreaming that he was throwing baseballs at a cloth cat and winning a genuine Navajo blanket. Mr and Mrs Zuckerman were in bed by nine. Mrs Zuckerman lay dreaming about a deep-freeze unit. Mr Zuckerman lay dreaming about Wilbur. He dreamt that Wilbur had grown until he was one hundred and sixteen feet long and ninety-two feet high and that he had won all the prizes at the Fair and was covered with blue ribbons and even had a blue ribbon tied to the end of his tail.

Down in the barn cellar, the animals, too, went to sleep early, all except Charlotte. Tomorrow would be Fair Day. Every creature planned to get up early to see Wilbur off on his great adventure.

When morning came, everybody got up at daylight. The day was hot. Up the road at the Arables' house, Fern lugged a pail of hot water to her room and took a sponge bath. Then she put on her prettiest dress because she knew she would see boys at the Fair. Mrs Arable scrubbed the back of Avery's neck, and wet his hair, and parted it, and brushed it down hard till it stuck to the top of his head — all but about six hairs that stood straight up. Avery put on clean underwear, clean blue jeans, and a clean jersey. Mr Arable dressed, ate breakfast, and then went out and polished his truck. He had offered to drive everybody to the Fair, including Wilbur.

Bright and early, Lurvy put clean straw in Wilbur's crate and lifted it into the pigpen. The crate was green. In gold letters it said:

ZUCKERMAN'S FAMOUS PIG

Charlotte had her web looking fine for the occasion. Wilbur ate his breakfast slowly. He tried to look radiant without getting food in his ears.

In the kitchen, Mrs Zuckerman suddenly made an announcement.

'Homer,' she said to her husband, 'I am going to give that pig a buttermilk bath.'

'A what?' said Mr Zuckerman.

'A buttermilk bath. My grandmother used to bathe her pig with buttermilk when it got dirty — I just remembered.'

'Wilbur's not dirty,' said Mr Zuckerman proudly.

'He's filthy behind the ears,' said Mrs Zuckerman. 'Every

time Lurvy slops him, the food runs down around the ears. Then it dries and forms a crust. He also has a smudge on one side where he lays in the manure.'

'He lays in clean straw,' corrected Mr Zuckerman.

'Well, he's dirty, and he's going to have a bath.'

Mr Zuckerman sat down weakly and ate a doughnut. His wife went to the woodshed. When she returned, she wore rubber boots and an old raincoat, and she carried a bucket of buttermilk and a small wooden paddle.

'Edith, you're crazy,' mumbled Zuckerman.

But she paid no attention to him. Together they walked to the pigpen. Mrs Zuckerman wasted no time. She climbed in with Wilbur and went to work. Dipping her paddle in the buttermilk, she rubbed him all over. The geese gathered around to see the fun, and so did the sheep and lambs. Even Templeton poked his head out cautiously, to watch Wilbur get a buttermilk bath. Charlotte got so interested, she lowered herself on a dragline so she could see better. Wilbur stood still and closed his eyes. He could feel the buttermilk trickling down his sides. He opened his mouth and some buttermilk ran in. It was delicious. He felt radiant and happy. When Mrs Zuckerman got through and rubbed him dry, he was the cleanest, prettiest pig you ever saw. He was pure white, pink around the ears and snout, and smooth as silk.

The Zuckermans went up to change into their best clothes. Lurvy went to shave and put on his plaid shirt and his purple necktie. The animals were left to themselves in the barn.

The seven goslings paraded round and round their mother.

'Please, please, please take us to the Fair!' begged a gosling. Then all seven began teasing to go.

'Please, please, please, please, please, please...' They made quite a racket.

'Children!' snapped the goose. 'We're staying quietly–ietly–ietly at home. Only Wilbur–ilbur–ilbur is going to the Fair.'

Just then Charlotte interrupted.

'I shall go, too,' she said, softly. 'I have decided to go with Wilbur. He may need me. We can't tell what may happen at the Fair Grounds. Somebody's got to go along who knows how to write. And I think Templeton better come, too — I might need somebody to run errands and do general work.'

'I'm staying right here,' grumbled the rat. 'I haven't the slightest interest in fairs.'

'That's because you've never been to one,' remarked the old sheep. 'A fair is a rat's paradise. Everybody spills food at a fair. A rat can creep out late at night and have a feast. In the horse barn you will find oats that the trotters and pacers have spilled. In the trampled grass of the in-field you will find old discarded lunchboxes containing the foul remains of peanut butter sandwiches, hard-boiled eggs, cracker crumbs, bits of doughnuts, and particles of cheese. In the hard-packed dirt of the midway, after the glaring lights are out and the people have gone home to bed, you will find a veritable treasure of popcorn fragments, frozen custard dribblings, candied apples abandoned by tired children, sugar fluff crystals, salted almonds, popsicles, partially gnawed ice cream cones, and the wooden sticks of lollypops. Everywhere is loot for a rat — in tents, in booths, in hay lofts — why, a fair has enough disgusting left-over food to satisfy a whole army of rats.'

Templeton's eyes were blazing.

'Is this true?' he asked. 'Is this appetizing yarn of yours true? I like high living, and what you say tempts me.'

'It is true,' said the old sheep. 'Go to the Fair, Templeton. You will find that the conditions at a fair will surpass your wildest dreams. Buckets with sour mash sticking to them, tin cans containing particles of tuna fish, greasy paper bags stuffed with rotten...'

'That's enough!' cried Templeton. 'Don't tell me any more. I'm going.'

'Good,' said Charlotte, winking at the old sheep. 'Now then —there is no time to be lost. Wilbur will soon be put into the crate. Templeton and I must get in the crate right now and hide ourselves.'

The rat didn't waste a minute. He scampered over to the crate, crawled between the slats, and pulled straw up over him so he was hidden from sight.

'All right,' said Charlotte, 'I'm next.' She sailed into the air, let out a dragline, and dropped gently to the ground. Then she climbed the side of the crate and hid herself inside a knothole in the top board.

The old sheep nodded. 'What a cargo!' she said. 'That sign ought to say "Zuckerman's Famous Pig and Two Stowaways".'

'Look out, the people are coming–oming–oming!' shouted the gander. 'Cheese it, cheese it, cheese it!'

The big truck with Mr Arable at the wheel backed slowly down towards the barnyard. Lurvy and Mr Zuckerman walked alongside. Fern and Avery were standing in the body of the truck hanging on to the sideboards.

'Listen to me,' whispered the old sheep to Wilbur. 'When they open the crate and try to put you in, struggle! Don't go without a struggle. Pigs always resist when they are being loaded.'

'If I struggle I'll get dirty,' said Wilbur.

'Never mind that—do as I say! Struggle! If you were to walk into the crate without resisting, Zuckerman might think you were bewitched. He'd be scared to go to the Fair.'

Templeton poked his head up through the straw. 'Struggle if you must,' said he, 'but kindly remember that I'm hiding down here in this crate and I don't want to be stepped on, or kicked in the face, or pummelled, or crushed in any way, or squashed, or buffeted about, or bruised, or lacerated, or scarred, or biffed. Just watch what you're doing, Mr Radiant, when they get shoving you in!'

'Be quiet, Templeton!' said the sheep. 'Pull in your head — they're coming. Look radiant, Wilbur! Lay low, Charlotte! Talk it up, geese!'

The truck backed slowly to the pigpen and stopped. Mr Arable cut the motor, got out, walked round to the rear, and lowered the tailgate. The geese cheered. Mrs Arable got out of the truck. Fern and Avery jumped to the ground. Mrs Zuckerman came walking down from the house. Everybody lined up at the fence and stood for a moment admiring Wilbur and the beautiful green crate. Nobody realized that the crate already contained a rat and a spider.

'That's some pig!' said Mrs Arable.

'He's terrific,' said Lurvy.

'He's very radiant,' said Fern, remembering the day he was born.

'Well,' said Mrs Zuckerman, 'he's clean, anyway. The buttermilk certainly helped.'

Mr Arable studied Wilbur carefully. 'Yes, he's a wonderful pig,' he said. 'It's hard to believe that he was the runt of the litter. You'll get some extra good ham and bacon, Homer, when it comes time to kill that pig.'

Wilbur heard these words and his heart almost stopped. 'I think I'm going to faint,' he whispered to the old sheep, who was watching.

'Kneel down!' whispered the old sheep. 'Let the blood rush to your head!'

Wilbur sank to his knees, all radiance gone. His eyes closed.

'Look!' screamed Fern. 'He's fading away!'

'Hey, watch me!' yelled Avery, crawling on all fours into the crate. 'I'm a pig! I'm a pig!'

Avery's foot touched Templeton under the straw. 'What a mess!' thought the rat. 'What fantastic creatures boys are! Why did I let myself in for this?'

The geese saw Avery in the crate and cheered.

'Avery, you get out of that crate this instant!' commanded his mother. 'What do you think you are?'

'I'm a pig!' cried Avery, tossing handfuls of straw into the air. 'Oink, oink, oink!'

'The truck is rolling away, Papa,' said Fern.

The truck, with no one at the wheel, had started to roll downhill. Mr Arable dashed to the driver's seat and pulled on the emergency brake. The truck stopped. The geese cheered. Charlotte crouched and made herself as small as possible in the knothole, so Avery wouldn't see her.

'Come out at once!' cried Mrs Arable. Avery crawled out of the crate on hands and knees, making faces at Wilbur. Wilbur fainted away.

'The pig has passed out,' said Mrs Zuckerman. 'Throw water on him!'

'Throw buttermilk!' suggested Avery.

The geese cheered.

Lurvy ran for a pail of water. Fern climbed into the pen and knelt by Wilbur' s side.

'It' s sunstroke,' said Zuckerman. 'The heat is too much for him.'

'Maybe he' s dead,' said Avery,

'Come out of that pigpen *immediately*!' cried Mrs Arable. Avery obeyed his mother and climbed into the back of the truck so he could see better. Lurvy returned with cold water and dashed it on Wilbur.

'Throw some on me!' cried Avery. 'I' m hot, too.'

'Oh, keep quiet!' hollered Fern. 'Keep *qui*–ut!' Her eyes were

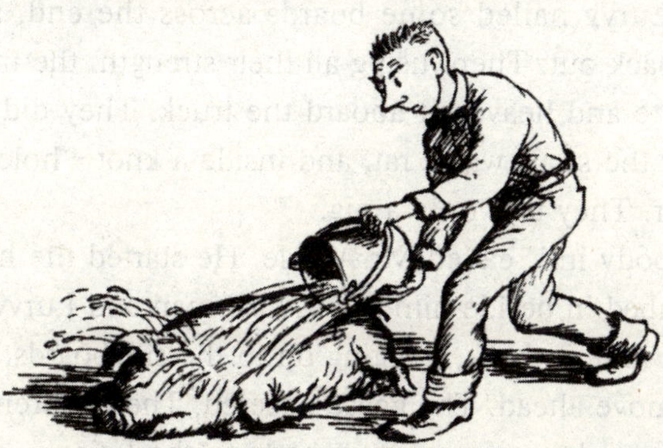

brimming with tears.

Wilbur, feeling the cold water, came to. He rose slowly to his feet, while the geese cheered.

He's up!' said Mr Arable. 'I guess there's nothing wrong with him.'

'I'm hungry,' said Avery. 'I want a candied apple.'

'Wilbur's all right now,' said Fern. 'We can start. I want to take a ride in the Ferris wheel.'

Mr Zuckerman and Mr Arable and Lurvy grabbed the pig and pushed him head-first towards the crate. Wilbur began to struggle. The harder the men pushed, the harder he held back. Avery jumped down and joined the men. Wilbur kicked and thrashed and grunted. 'Nothing wrong with *this* pig,' said Mr Zuckerman cheerfully, pressing his knee against Wilbur's behind. 'All together, now, boys! Shove!'

With a final heave they jammed him into the crate. The geese cheered. Lurvy nailed some boards across the end, so Wilbur couldn't back out. Then, using all their strength, the men picked up the crate and heaved it aboard the truck. They did not know that under the straw was a rat, and inside a knot-hole was a big grey spider. They saw only a pig.

'Everybody in!' called Mr Arable. He started the motor. The ladies climbed in beside him. Mr Zuckerman and Lurvy and Fern and Avery rode in back, hanging on to the sideboards. The truck began to move ahead. The geese cheered. The children answered their cheer, and away went everybody to the Fair.

17.

Uncle

When they pulled into the Fair Grounds, they could hear music and see the Ferris wheel turning in the sky. They could smell the dust of the race–track where the sprinkling cart had moistened it; and they could smell hamburgers frying and see balloons aloft. They could hear sheep blatting in their pens. An enormous voice over the loudspeaker said: 'Attention, please! Will the owner of a Pontiac car, licence number H–2439, please move your car away from the fireworks shed!'

'Can I have some money?' asked Fern.

'Can I, too?' asked Avery.

'I'm going to win a doll by spinning a wheel and it will stop at the right number,' said Fern.

'I'm going to steer a jet plane and make it bump into another one.'

'Can I have a balloon?' asked Fern.

'Can I have a frozen custard and a cheeseburger and some raspberry soda pop?' asked Avery.

'You children be quiet till we get the pig unloaded,' said Mrs Arable.

'Let's let the children go off by themselves,' suggested Mr Arable. 'The Fair only comes once a year.' Mr Arable gave Fern two quarters and tow dimes. He gave Avery five dimes and four nickels. 'Now run along!' he said. 'And remember, the money has to last *all day*. Don't spend it all the first few minutes. And be back here at the truck at noontime so we can all have lunch together. And don't eat a lot of stuff that's going to make you sick to your stomachs.'

'And if you go in those swings,' said Mrs Arable, 'you hang on tight! You hang on *very* tight. Hear me?'

'And don't get lost!' said Mrs Zuckerman.

'And don't get dirty!'

'Don't get overheated!' said their mother.

'Watch out for pickpockets!' cautioned their father.

'And don't cross the race-track when the horses are coming!' cried Mrs Zuckerman.

The children grabbed each other by the hand and danced off in the direction of the merry-go-round, towards the wonderful music and the wonderful adventure and the wonderful excitement, into the wonderful midway where there would be no parents to guard them and guide them, and where they could be happy and free and do as they pleased. Mrs Arable stood quietly and watched them go. Then she sighed. Then she blew her nose.

'Do you really think it's all right?' she asked.

'Well, they've got to grow up some time,' said Mr Arable. 'And a fair is a good place to start, I guess.'

While Wilbur was being unloaded and taken out of his crate and into his new pigpen, crowds gathered to watch. They stared at the sign ZUCKERMAN'S FAMOUS PIG. Wilbur stared back and tried to look extra good. He was pleased with his new home. The pen was grassy, and it was shaded from the sun by a shed roof.

Charlotte, watching her chance, scrambled out of the crate and climbed a post to the under side of the roof. Nobody noticed her.

Templeton, not wishing to come out in broad daylight, stayed quietly under the straw at the bottom of the crate. Mr Zuckerman poured some skim milk into Wilbur's trough, pitched clean straw into his pen, and then he and Mrs Zuckerman and the Arables walked away towards the cattle barn to look at purebred cows and to see the sights. Mr Zuckerman particularly wanted to look at tractors. Mrs Zuckerman wanted to see a deep freeze. Lurvy wandered off by himself, hoping to meet friends and have some fun on the midway.

As soon as the people were gone, Charlotte spoke to Wilbur.

'It's a good thing you can't see what *I* see,' she said.

'What do you see?' asked Wilbur.

'There's a pig in the next pen and he's enormous. I'm afraid he's much bigger than you are.'

'Maybe he's older than I am, and has had more time to grow,' suggested Wilbur. Tears began to come to his eyes.

'I'll drop down and have a closer look,' Charlotte said. Then she crawled along a beam till she was directly over the next pen.

She let herself down on a dragline until she hung in the air just in front of the big pig's snout.

'May I have your name?' she asked, politely.

The pig stared at her. 'No name,' he said in a big, hearty voice. 'Just call me Uncle.'

'Very well, Uncle,' replied Charlotte. 'What is the date of your birth? Are you a spring pig?'

'Sure I'm a spring pig,' replied Uncle. 'What did you think I was, a spring chicken? Haw, haw—that's a good one, eh, sister?'

'Mildly funny,' said Charlotte. 'I've heard funnier ones, though. Glad to have met you, and now I must be going.'

She ascended slowly and returned to Wilbur's pen.

'He claims he's a spring pig,' reported Charlotte, 'and perhaps he is. One thing is certain, he has a most unattractive personality. He is too familiar, too noisy, and he cracks weak jokes. Also, he's not anywhere near as clean as you are, nor as pleasant. I took quite a dislike to him in our brief interview. He's going to be a hard pig to beat, though, Wilbur, on account of his size and weight. But with me helping you, it can be done.'

'When are you going to spin a web?' asked Wilbur.

'This afternoon, late, if I'm not too tired,' said Charlotte. 'The least thing tires me these days. I don't seem to have the energy I once had. My age, I guess.'

Wilbur looked at his friend. She looked rather swollen and seemed listless.

'I'm awfully sorry to hear that you're feeling poorly, Charlotte,'

he said. 'Perhaps if you spin a web and catch a couple of flies you' ll feel better.'

'Perhaps,' she said, wearily. 'But I feel like the end of a long day.' Clinging upside down to the ceiling, she settled down for a nap, leaving Wilbur very much worried.

All morning people wandered past Wilbur's pen. Dozens and dozens of strangers stopped to stare at him and to admire his silky white coat, his curly tail, his kind and radiant expression. Then they would move on to the next pen where the bigger pig lay. Wilbur heard several people make favorable remarks about Uncle's great size. He couldn't help overhearing these remarks,and he couldn't help worrying. 'And now, with Charlotte not feeling well ...' he thought. 'Oh, dear!'

All morning Templeton slept quietly under the straw. The day grew fiercely hot. At noon the Zuckermans and the Arables returned to the pigpen. Then, a few minutes later, Fern and Avery showed up. Fern had a monkey doll in her arms and was eating Kracker–jack. Avery had a balloon tied to his ear and was chewing a candied apple. The children were hot and dirty.

'Isn't it hot?' said Mrs Zuckerman.

'It's *terribly* hot,' said Mrs Arable, fanning herself with an advertisement of a deep freeze.

One by one they climbed into the truck and opened lunch–boxes. The sun beat down on everything. Nobody seemed hungry.

'When are the judges going to decide about Wilbur?' asked Mrs Zuckerman.

'Not till tomorrow,' said Mr Zuckerman.

Lurvy appeared, carrying an Indian blanket that he had won.

'That's just what we need,' said Avery. 'A blanket.'

'Of course it is,' replied Lurvy. And he spread the blanket across the sideboards of the truck so that it was like a little tent. The children sat in the shade, under the blanket, and felt better.

After lunch, they stretched out and fell asleep.

18.

The Cool of the Evening

In the cool of the evening, when shadows darkened the Fair Grounds, Templeton crept from the crate and looked around. Wilbur lay asleep in the straw. Charlotte was building a web. Templeton's keen nose detected many fine smells in the air. The rat was hungry and thirsty. He decided to go exploring. Without saying anything to anybody, he started off.

'Bring me back a word!' Charlotte called after him. 'I shall be writing tonight for the last time.'

The rat mumbled something to himself and disappeared into the shadows. He did not like being treated like a messenger boy.

After the heat of the day, the evening came as a welcome relief to all. The Ferris wheel was lighted now. It went round and round in the sky and seemed twice as high as by day. There were lights on the midway, and you could hear the crackle of the gambling machines and the music of the merry-go-round and the voice of the man in the beano booth calling numbers.

The children felt refreshed after their nap. Fern met her friend Henry Fussy, and he invited her to ride with him in the Ferris wheel. He even bought a ticket for her, so it didn't cost her anything. When Mrs Arable happened to look up into the starry sky and saw her little daughter sitting with Henry Fussy and going higher and higher into the air, and saw how happy Fern looked, she just shook her head. 'My, my!' she said. 'Henry Fussy. Think of that!'

Templeton kept out of sight. In the tall grass behind the cattle barn he found a folded newspaper. Inside it were left–overs from somebody's lunch: a devilled ham sandwich, a piece of Swiss cheese, part of a hard–boiled egg, and the core of a wormy apple. The rat crawled in and ate everything. Then he tore a word out of the paper, rolled it up, and started back to Wilbur's pen.

Charlotte had her web almost finished when Templeton returned, carrying the newspaper clipping. She had left a space in the middle of the web. At this hour, no people were round the pigpen, so the rat and the spider and the pig were by themselves.

'I hope you brought a good one,' Charlotte said. 'It's the last word I shall ever write.'

'Here,' said Templeton, unrolling the paper.

'What does it say?' asked Charlotte. 'You'll have to read it for me.'

'It says HUMBLE,' replied the rat.

'Humble?' said Charlotte. '"Humble" has two meanings. It means "not proud" and it means "near the ground". That's Wilbur all over. He's not proud and he's near the ground.'

'Well, I hope you're satisfied,' sneered the rat. 'I'm not going to spend all my time fetching and carrying. I came to this Fair to enjoy myself, not to deliver papers.'

'You've been very helpful,' Charlotte said. 'Run along, if you want to see more of the Fair.'

The rat grinned. 'I'm going to make a night of it,' he said. 'The old sheep was right — this Fair is a rat's paradise. What eating! And what drinking! And everywhere good hiding and good hunting. Bye-bye, my humble Wilbur! Fare thee well, Charlotte, you old schemer! This will be a night to remember in a rat's life.'

He vanished into the shadows.

Charlotte went back to her work. It was quite dark now. In the distance, fireworks began going off—rockets, scattering fiery balls in the sky. By the time the Arables and the Zuckermans and Lurvy returned from the grandstand, Charlotte had finished her web. The word HUMBLE was woven neatly in the center. Nobody noticed it in the darkness. Everyone was tired and happy.

Fern and Avery climbed into the truck and lay down. They pulled the Indian blanket over them. Lurvy gave Wilbur a forkful of fresh straw. Mr Arable patted him. 'Time for us to go home,' he said to the pig. 'See you tomorrow.'

The grown-ups climbed slowly into the truck and Wilbur heard the engine start and then heard the truck moving away in low speed. He would have felt lonely and homesick, had Charlotte not been with him. He never felt lonely when she was near. In the distance he could still hear the music of the merry-go-round.

As he was dropping off to sleep he spoke to Charlotte.

'Sing me that song again, about the dung and the dark,' he

begged.

'Not tonight,' she said in a low voice. 'I'm too tired.' Her voice didn't seem to come from her web.

'Where are you?' asked Wilbur. 'I can't see you. Are you on your web?'

'I'm back here,' she answered. 'Up in this back corner.'

'Why aren't you on your web?' asked Wilbur. 'You almost *never* leave your web.'

'I've left it tonight,' she said.

Wilbur closed his eyes. 'Charlotte,' he said, after a while, 'do you really think Zuckerman will let me live and not kill me when the cold weather comes? Do you really think so?'

'Of course,' said Charlotte. 'You are a famous pig and you are a good pig. Tomorrow you will probably win a prize. The whole world will hear about you. Zuckerman will be proud and happy to own such a pig. You have nothing to fear, Wilbur—nothing to worry about. Maybe you'll live for ever—who knows?

And now, go to sleep.'

For a while there was no sound. Then Wilbur's voice:

'What are you doing up there, Charlotte?'

'Oh, making something,' she said. 'Making something, as usual.'

'Is it something for me?' asked Wilbur.

'No,' said Charlotte. 'It's something for *me*, for a change.'

'Please tell me what it is,' begged Wilbur.

'I'll tell you in the morning,' she said. 'When the first light comes into the sky and the sparrows stir and the cows rattle their chains, when the rooster crows and the stars fade, when early cars whisper along the highway, you look up here and I'll show you something. I will show you my masterpiece.'

Before she finished the sentence, Wilbur was asleep. She could tell by the sound of his breathing that he was sleeping peacefully, deep in the straw.

Miles away, at the Arables' house, the men sat around the kitchen table eating a dish of canned peaches and talking over the events of the day. Upstairs, Avery was already in bed and asleep. Mrs Arable was tucking Fern into bed.

'Did you have a good time at the Fair?' she asked as she kissed her daughter.

Fern nodded. 'I had the best time I have ever had anywhere or any time in all of my whole life.'

'Well!' said Mrs. Arable. 'Isn't that nice.'

19.

The Egg Sac

Next morning when the first light came into the sky and the sparrows stirred in the trees, when the cows rattled their chains and the rooster crowed and the early automobiles went whispering along the road, Wilbur awoke and looked for Charlotte. He saw her up overhead in a corner near the back of his pen. She was very quiet. Her eight legs were spread wide. She seemed to have shrunk during the night. Next to her, attached to the ceiling, Wilbur saw a curious object. It was a sort of sac, or cocoon. It was peach-colored and looked as though it were made of cotton candy.

'Are you awake, Charlotte?' he said softly.

'Yes,' came the answer.

'What is that nifty little thing? Did you make it?'

'I did indeed,' replied Charlotte in a weak voice.

'Is it a plaything?'

'Plaything? I should say not. It is my egg sac, my *magnum opus*.'

'I don't know what a *magnum opus* is,' said Wilbur.

'That's Latin,' explained Charlotte. 'It means "great work." This egg sac is my great work—the finest thing I have ever made.'

'What's inside it?' asked Wilbur. 'Eggs?'

'Five hundred and fourteen of them,' she replied.

'Five *hundred* and *fourteen*? said Wilbur. 'You're kidding.'

'No, I'm not. I counted them. I got started counting, so I kept on — just to keep my mind occupied.'

'It's a perfectly beautiful egg sac,' said Wilbur, feeling as happy as though he had constructed it himself.

'Yes, it *is* pretty,' replied Charlotte, patting the sac with her two front legs. 'Anyway, I can guarantee that it is strong. It's made out of the toughest material I have. It is also waterproof. The eggs are inside and will be warm and dry.'

'Charlotte,' said Wilbur dreamily, 'are you really going to have five hundred and fourteen children?'

'If nothing happens, yes,' she said. 'Of course, they won't

show up till next spring.' Wilbur noticed that Charlotte's voice sounded sad.

'What makes you sound so down-hearted? I should think you'd be terribly happy about this.'

'Oh, don't pay any attention to me,' said Charlotte. 'I just don't have much pep any more. I guess I feel sad because I won't ever see my children.'

'What do you mean you won't see your children! Of *course* you will. We'll *all* see them. It's going to be simply wonderful next spring in the barn cellar with five hundred and fourteen baby spiders running around all over the place. And the geese will have a new set of goslings, and the sheep will have their new lambs ...'

'Maybe,' said Charlotte quietly. 'However, I have a feeling I'm not going to see the results of last night's efforts. I don't feel good at all. I think I'm languishing, to tell you the truth.'

Wilbur didn't understand the word 'languish' and he hated to bother Charlotte by asking her to explain. But he was so worried he felt he had to ask.

'What does "languishing" mean?'

'It means I'm slowing up, feeling my age. I'm not young any more, Wilbur. But I don't want you to worry about me. This is your big day today. Look at my web — doesn't it show up well with the dew on it?'

Charlotte's web never looked more beautiful than it looked this morning. Each strand held dozens of bright drops of early morning dew. The light from the east struck it and made it plain and clear. It was a perfect piece of designing and building. In another hour or two, a steady stream of people would pass by, admiring it, and reading it, and looking at Wilbur, and marveling at the miracle.

As Wilbur was studying the web, a pair of whiskers and a sharp face appeared. Slowly Templeton dragged himself across the pen and threw himself down in a corner.

'I'm back,' he said in a husky voice. 'What a night!'

The rat was swollen to twice his normal size. His stomach was as big round as a jelly jar.

'What a night!' he repeated, hoarsely. 'What feasting and carousing! A real gorge! I must have eaten the remains of thirty lunches. Never have I seen such leavings, and everything well

ripened and seasoned with the passage of time and the heat of the day. Oh, it was rich, my friends, rich!'

'You ought to be ashamed of yourself,' said Charlotte in disgust. 'It would serve you right if you had an acute attack of indigestion.'

'Don't worry about my stomach,' snarled Templeton. 'It can handle anything. And by the way, I've got some bad news. As I came past that pig next door – the one that calls himself Uncle —I noticed a blue tag on the front of his pen. That means he has won first prize. I guess you're licked, Wilbur. You might as well relax—nobody is going to hang any medal on *you*. Furthermore, I wouldn't be surprised if Zuckerman changes his mind about you. Wait till he gets hankering for some fresh pork and smoked ham and crisp bacon! He'll take the knife to you, my boy.'

'Be still, Templeton!' said Charlotte. 'You're too stuffed and bloated to know what you're saying. Don't pay any attention to him, Wilbur!'

Wilbur tried not to think about what the rat had just said. He decided to change the subject.

'Templeton,' said Wilbur, 'if you weren't so dopey, you would have noticed that Charlotte has made an egg sac. She is going to become a mother. For your information, there are five hundred and fourteen eggs in that peachy little sac.'

'Is this true?' asked the rat, eyeing the sac suspiciously.

'Yes, it's true,' sighed Charlotte.

'Congratulations!' murmured Templeton. 'This *has* been a

night!' He closed his eyes, pulled some straw over himself, and dropped off into a deep sleep. Wilbur and Charlotte were glad to be rid of him for a while.

At nine o'clock, Mr Arable's truck rolled into the Fair Grounds and came to a stop at Wilbur's pen. Everybody climbed out.

'Look!' cried Fern. 'Look at Charlotte's web! Look what it says!'

The grown–ups and the children joined hands and stood there, studying the new sign.

'HUMBLE,' said Mr Zuckerman. 'Now isn't that just the word for Wilbur!'

Everyone rejoiced to find that the miracle of the web had been repeated. Wilbur gazed up lovingly into their faces. He looked very humble and very grateful. Fern winked at Charlotte. Lurvy soon got busy. He poured a bucket of warm slops into the trough, and while Wilbur ate his breakfast Lurvy scratched him gently with a smooth stick.

'Wait a minute!' cried Avery. 'Look at this!' He pointed to the blue tag on Uncle's pen. 'This pig has won first prize already.'

The Zuckermans and the Arables stared at the tag. Mrs Zuckerman began to cry. Nobody said a word. They just stared at the tag. Then they stared at Uncle. Then they stared at the tag again. Lurvy took out an enormous handkerchief and blew his nose very loud — so loud, in fact, that the noise was heard by stableboys over at the horse barn.

'Can I have some money?' asked Fern. 'I want to go out on the midway.'

'You stay right where you are!' said her mother. Tears came to Fern's eyes.

'What's everybody crying about?' asked Mr Zuckerman. 'Let's get busy! Edith, bring the buttermilk!'

Mrs Zuckerman wiped her eyes with her handkerchief. She went to the truck and came back with a gallon jar of buttermilk.

'Bath time!' said Zuckerman, cheerfully. He and Mrs Zuckerman and Avery climbed into Wilbur's pen. Avery slowly poured buttermilk on Wilbur's head and back, and as it trickled down his sides and cheeks, Mr and Mrs Zuckerman rubbed it into his hair and skin. Passers-by stopped to watch. Pretty soon quite a crowd had gathered. Wilbur grew beautifully white and smooth. The morning sun shone through his pink ears.

'He isn't as big as that pig next door,' remarked one bystander, 'but he's cleaner. That's what I like.'

'So do I,' said another man.

'He's humble, too,' said a woman, reading the sign on the web.

Everybody who visited the pigpen had a good word to say about Wilbur. Everyone admired the web. And of course nobody noticed Charlotte.

Suddenly a voice was heard on the loudspeaker.

'Attention, please!' it said. 'Will Mr Homer Zuckerman bring his famous pig to the judges' booth in front of the grandstand. A special award will be made there in twenty minutes.Everyone is invited to attend. Crate your pig, please, Mr Zuckerman,and report to the judges' booth promptly!'

For a moment after this announcement, the Arables and the Zuckermans were unable to speak or move. Then Avery picked up a handful of straw and threw it high in the air and gave a loud yell. The straw fluttered down like confetti into Fern' s hair. Mr Zuckerman hugged Mrs Zuckerman. Mr Arable kissed Mrs Arable. Avery kissed Wilbur. Lurvy shook hands with everybody. Fern hugged her mother. Avery hugged Fern. Mrs Arable hugged Mrs Zuckerman.

Up overhead, in the shadows of the ceiling, Charlotte crouched unseen, her front legs encircling her egg sac. Her heart was not beating as strongly as usual and she felt weary and old, but she was sure at last that she had saved Wilbur' s life, and she felt peaceful and contented.

'We have no time to lose!' shouted Mr Zuckerman. 'Lurvy, help with the crate!'

'Can I have some money?' asked Fern.

'You *wait*!' said Mrs Arable. 'Can't you see everybody is busy?'

'Put that empty buttermilk jar into the truck!' commanded Mr Arable. Avery grabbed the jar and rushed to the truck.

'Does my hair look all right?' asked Mrs Zuckerman.

'Looks fine,' snapped Mr Zuckerman, as he and Lurvy set the crate down in front of Wilbur.

'You didn' t even *look* at my hair!' said Mrs Zuckerman.

'You're all right, Edith,' said Mrs Arable. 'Just keep calm.'

Templeton, asleep in the straw, heard the commotion and awoke. He didn't know exactly what was going on, but when he saw the men shoving Wilbur into the crate he made up his mind to go along. He watched his chance and, when no one was looking, he crept into the crate and buried himself in the straw at the bottom.

'All ready, boys!' cried Mr Zuckerman. 'Let's go!' He and Mr Arable and Lurvy and Avery grabbed the crate and boosted it over the side of the pen and up into the truck. Fern jumped aboard and sat on top of the crate. She still had straw in her hair and looked very pretty and excited. Mr Arable started the motor. Everyone climbed in, and off they drove to the judges' booth in front of the grandstand.

As they passed the Ferris wheel, Fern gazed up at it and wished she were in the topmost car with Henry Fussy at her side.

20.

The Hour of Triumph

'Special announcement!' said the loudspeaker in a pompous voice. 'The management of the Fair takes great pleasure in presenting Mr Homer L. Zuckerman and his famous pig. The truck bearing this extraordinary animal is now approaching the infield. Kindly stand back and give the truck room to proceed! In a few moments the pig will be unloaded in the special judging ring in front of the grandstand, where a special award will be made. Will the crowd please make way and let the truck pass. Thank you.'

Wilbur trembled when he heard this speech. He felt happy but dizzy. The truck crept along slowly in low speed. Crowds of people surrounded it, and Mr Arable had to drive very carefully in order not to run over anybody. At last he managed to reach the judges' stand. Avery jumped out and lowered the tailgate.

'I'm scared to death,' whispered Mrs Zuckerman. 'Hundreds of people are looking at us.'

'Cheer up,' replied Mrs Arable, 'this is fun.'

'Unload your pig, please!' said the loudspeaker.

'Altogether, now, boys!' said Mr Zuckerman. Several men

stepped forward from the crowd to help lift the crate. Avery was the busiest helper of all.

'Tuck your shirt in, Avery!' cried Mrs Zuckerman. 'And tighten your belt. Your pants are coming down.'

'Can't you see I'm busy?' replied Avery in disgust.

'Look!' cried Fern, pointing. 'There's Henry!'

'Don't shout, Fern!' said her mother. 'And don't point!'

'Can't I *please* have some money?' asked Fern. 'Henry invited me to go on the Ferris wheel again, only I don't think he has any money left. He ran out of money.'

Mrs Arable opened her handbag. 'Here,' she said. 'Here is forty cents. Now don't get lost! And be back at our regular meeting-place by the pigpen very soon!'

Fern raced off, ducking and dodging through the crowd, in search of Henry.

'The Zuckerman pig is now being taken from his crate,' boomed the voice of the loudspeaker. 'Stand by for an announcement!'

Templeton crouched under the straw at the bottom of the crate. 'What a lot of nonsense!' muttered the rat. 'What a lot of fuss about nothing!'

Over in the pigpen, silent and alone, Charlotte rested. Her two front legs embraced the egg sac. Charlotte could hear everything that was said on the loudspeaker. The words gave her courage. This was her hour of triumph.

As Wilbur came out of the crate, the crowd clapped and

cheered. Mr Zuckerman took off his cap and bowed. Lurvy pulled his big handkerchief from his pocket and wiped the sweat from the back of his neck. Avery knelt in the dirt by Wilbur's side, busily stroking him and showing off. Mrs Zuckerman and Mrs Arable stood on the running board of the truck.

'Ladeez and gentlemen,' said the loudspeaker, 'we now present Mr Homer L. Zuckerman's distinguished pig. The fame of this unique animal has spread to the far corners of the earth, attracting many valuable tourists to our great State. Many of you will recall that never–to–be–forgotten day last summer when the writing appeared mysteriously on the spider's web in Mr Zuckerman's barn, calling the attention of all and sundry to the fact that this pig was completely out of the ordinary. This miracle has never been fully explained, although learned men have visited the Zuckerman pigpen to study and observe the phenomenon. In the last analysis, we simply know that we are dealing with supernatural forces here, and we should all feel proud and grateful. In the words of the spider's web, ladies and gentlemen, this is some pig.'

Wilbur blushed. He stood perfectly still and tried to look his best.

'This magnificent animal,' continued the loudspeaker, 'is truly terrific. Look at him, ladies and gentlemen! Note the smoothness and whiteness of the coat, observe the spotless skin, the healthy pink glow of ears and snout.'

'It's the buttermilk,' whispered Mrs Arable to Mrs Zuckerman.

'Note the general radiance of this animal! Then remember the day when the word "radiant" appeared clearly on the web. Whence came this mysterious writing? Not from the spider, we can rest assured of that. Spiders are very clever at weaving their webs, but needless to say spiders cannot write.'

'Oh, they can't, can't they?' murmured Charlotte to herself.

'Ladeez and gentlemen,' continued the loudspeaker, 'I must not take any more of your valuable time. On behalf of the governors of the Fair, I have the honour of awarding a special prize of twenty-five dollars to Mr Zuckerman, together with a handsome bronze medal suitably engraved, in token of our appreciation of the part played by this pig—this radiant, this terrific, this humble pig — in attracting so many visitors to our great County Fair.'

Wilbur had been feeling dizzier and dizzier through this long, complimentary speech. When he heard the crowd begin to cheer and clap again, he suddenly fainted away. His legs collapsed, his mind went blank, and he fell to the ground, unconscious.

'What's wrong?' asked the loudspeaker. 'What's going on, Zuckerman? What's the trouble with your pig?'

Avery was kneeling by Wilbur's head, stroking him. Mr Zuckerman was dancing about, fanning him with his cap.

'He's all right,' cried Mr Zuckerman. 'He gets these spells. He's modest and can't stand praise.'

'Well, we can't give a prize to a *dead* pig,' said the loudspeaker. 'It's never been done.'

'He isn't dead,' hollered Zuckerman. 'He's fainted. He gets

embarrassed easily. Run for some water, Lurvy!'

Lurvy sprang from the judges' ring and disappeared.

Templeton poked his head from the straw. He noticed that the end of Wilbur's tail was within reach. Templeton grinned. 'I'll tend to this,' he chuckled. He took Wilbur's tail in his mouth and bit it, just as hard as he could bite. The pain revived Wilbur. In a flash he was back on his feet.

'Ouch!' he screamed.

'Hoorray!' yelled the crowd. 'He's up! The pig's up! Good word, Zuckerman! That's some pig!'Everyone was delighted. Mr Zuckerman was the most pleased of all. He sighed with relief. Nobody had seen Templeton. The rat had done his work well.

And now one of the judges climbed into the ring with the prizes. He handed Mr Zuckerman two ten-dollar bills and a five-dollar bill. Then he tied the medal around Wilbur's neck. Then he shook hands with Mr Zuckerman while Wilbur blushed. Avery put out his hand and the judge shook hands with him, too. The crowd cheered. A photographer took Wilbur's picture.

A great feeling of happiness swept over the Zuckermans and the Arables. This was the greatest moment in Mr Zuckerman's life. It is deeply satisfying to win a prize in front of a lot of people.

As Wilbur was being shoved back into the crate, Lurvy came charging through the crowd carrying a pail of water. His eyes had a wild look. Without hesitating a second, he dashed the water at Wilbur. In his excitement he missed his aim, and the water splashed all over Mr Zuckerman and Avery. They got soaking wet.

'For goodness'sake!' bellowed Mr Zuckerman, who was really drenched. 'What ails you, Lurvy? Can't you see the pig is all right?'

'You asked for water,' said Lurvy meekly.

'I didn't ask for a shower bath,' said Mr Zuckerman. The crowd roared with laughter. Finally Mr Zuckerman had to laugh, too. And of course Avery was tickled to find himself so wet, and he immediately started to act like a clown. He pretended he was taking a shower bath; he made faces and danced around and rubbed imaginary soap under his armpits. Then he dried himself with an imaginary towel.

'Avery, stop it!' cried his mother. 'Stop showing off!'

But the crowd loved it. Avery heard nothing but the applause. He liked being a clown in a ring, with everybody watching, in front of a grandstand. When he discovered there was still a little water left in the bottom of the pail, he raised the pail high in the air and dumped the water on himself and made faces. The children in the grandstand screamed with appreciation.

At last things calmed down. Wilbur was loaded into the truck. Avery was led from the ring by his mother and placed on the seat of the truck to dry off. The truck, driven by Mr Arable, crawled slowly back to the pigpen. Avery's wet trousers made a big wet spot on the seat.

21.

Last Day

Charlotte and Wilbur were alone. The families had gone to look for Fern. Templeton was asleep. Wilbur lay resting after the excitement and strain of the ceremony. His medal still hung from his neck; by looking out of the corner of his eye he could see it.

'Charlotte,' said Wilbur after a while, 'why are you so quiet?'

'I like to sit still,' she said. 'I've always been rather quiet.'

'Yes, but you seem specially so today. Do you feel all right?'

'A little tired, perhaps. But I feel peaceful. Your success in the ring this morning was, to a small degree, *my* success. Your future is assured. You will live, secure and safe, Wilbur. Nothing can harm you now. These autumn days will shorten and grow cold. The leaves will shake loose from the trees and fall. Christmas will come, then the snows of winter. You will live to enjoy the beauty of the frozen world, for you mean a great deal to Zuckerman and he will not harm you, ever. Winter will pass, the days will lengthen, the ice will melt in the pasture pond. Then song sparrow will return and sing, the frogs will awake, the warm wind will blow again. All these sights and sounds and smells will be yours to enjoy, Wilbur — this lovely world, these golden days ...'

Charlotte stopped. A moment later a tear came to Wilbur's eye. 'Oh, Charlotte,' he said. 'To think that when I first met you I thought you were cruel and bloodthirsty!'

When he recovered from his emotion, he spoke again.

'Why did you do all this for me?' he asked. 'I don't deserve it. I've never done anything for you.'

'You have been my friend,' replied Charlotte. 'That in itself is a tremendous thing. I wove my webs for you because I liked you. After all, what's a life, anyway? We're born, we live a little while, we die. A spider's life can't help being something of a mess, with all this trapping and eating flies. By helping you, perhaps I was trying to lift up my life a trifle. Heaven knows anyone's life can stand a little of that.'

'Well,' said Wilbur. 'I'm no good at making speeches. I haven't got your gift for words. But you have saved me, Charlotte, and I would gladly give my life for you — I really would.'

'I'm sure you would. And I thank you for your generous sentiments.'

'Charlotte,' said Wilbur. 'We're all going home today. The Fair is almost over. Won't it be wonderful to be back home in the barn cellar again with the sheep and the geese? Aren't you anxious to get home?'

For a moment Charlotte said nothing. Then she spoke in a voice so low Wilbur could hardly hear the words.

'I will not be going back to the barn,' she said.

Wilbur leapt to his feet. 'Not gόing back?' he cried. 'Charlotte, what are you talking about?'

'I'm done for,' she replied. 'In a day or two I'll be dead. I haven't even strength enough to climb down into the crate. I doubt if I have enough silk in my spinnerets to lower me to the ground.'

Hearing this, Wilbur threw himself down in an agony of pain and sorrow. Great sobs racked his body. He heaved and grunted with desolation. 'Charlotte,' he moaned. 'Charlotte! My true friend!'

'Come now, let's not make a scene,' said the spider. 'Be quiet, Wilbur. Stop thrashing about!'

'But I can't *stand* it,' shouted Wilbur. 'I won't leave you here alone to die. If you're going to stay here I shall stay, too.'

'Don't be ridiculous,' said Charlotte. 'You can't stay here. Zuckerman and Lurvy and John Arable and the others will be back any minute now, and they'll shove you into that crate and away you'll go. Besides, it wouldn't make any sense for you to stay. There would be no one to feed you. The Fair Grounds will soon be empty and deserted.'

Wilbur was in a panic. he raced round and round the pen. Suddenly he had an idea—he thought of the egg sac and the five hundred and fourteen little spiders that would hatch in the spring. If Charlotte herself was unable to go home to the barn, at least he must take her children along.

Wilbur rushed to the front of his pen. He put his front feet up on the top board and gazed around. In the distance he saw the Arables and the Zuckermans approaching. He knew he would have to act quickly.

'Where's Templeton?' he demanded.

'He's in that corner, under the straw, asleep,' said Charlotte.

Wilbur rushed over, pushed his strong snout under the rat, and tossed him into the air.

'Templeton!' screamed Wilbur. 'Pay attention!'

The rat, surprised out of a sound sleep, looked first dazed then disgusted.

'What kind of monkeyshine is this?' he growled. 'Can't a rat catch a wink of sleep without being rudely popped into the air?'

'Listen to me!' cried Wilbur. 'Charlotte is very ill. She has only a short time to live. She cannot accompany us home, because of her condition. Therefore, it is absolutely necessary that I take her egg sac with me. I can't reach it, and I can't climb. You are the only one that can get it. There's not a second to be lost. The people are coming – they'll be here in no time. Please, please, *please*, Templeton, climb up and get the egg sac.'

The rat yawned. He straightened his whiskers. Then he looked up at the egg sac.

'So!' he said, in disgust. 'So it's old Templeton to the rescue again, is it? Templeton do this, Templeton do that, Templeton please run down to the dump and get me a magazine clipping, Templeton please lend me a piece of string so I can spin a web.'

'Oh, hurry!' said Wilbur. 'Hurry up, Templeton!'

But the rat was in no hurry. He began imitating Wilbur's voice.

'So it's "Hurry up, Temple", is it?' he said. 'Ho, ho. And what thanks do I ever get for these services, I would like to know? Never a kind word for old Templeton, only abuse and wisecracks and side remarks. Never a kind word for a rat.'

'Templeton,' said Wilbur in desperation, 'if you don't stop talking and get busy, all will be lost, and I will die of a broken heart. Please climb up!'

Templeton lay back in the straw. Lazily he placed his forepaws behind his head and crossed his knees, in an attitude of complete relaxation.

'Die of a broken heart,' he mimicked. 'How touching! My, my! I notice that it's always me you come to when in trouble. But I've never heard of anyone's heart breaking on *my* account. Oh, no. Who cares anything about old Templeton?'

'Get up!' screamed Wilbur. 'Stop acting like a spoiled child!'

Templeton grinned and lay still. 'Who made trip after trip to the dump?' he asked. 'Why, it was old Templeton! Who saved Charlotte's life by scaring that Arable boy away with a rotten goose egg? Bless my soul, I believe it was old Templeton. Who bit your tail and got you back on your feet this morning after you had fainted in front of the crowd? Old Templeton. Has it ever occurred to you that I'm sick of running errands and doing favours? What do you think I am, anyway, a rat-of-all-work?'

Wilbur was desperate. The people were coming. And the rat

was failing him. Suddenly he remembered Templeton's fondness for food.

'Templeton,' he said, 'I will make you a solemn promise. Get Charlotte's egg sac for me, and from now on I will let you eat first, when Lurvy slops me. I will let you have your choice of everything in the trough and I won't touch a thing until you're through.'

The rat sat up. 'You mean that?' he said.

'I promise. I cross my heart.'

'All right, it's a deal,' said the rat. He walked to the wall and started to climb. His stomach was still swollen from last night's gorge. Groaning and complaining, he pulled himself slowly to the ceiling. He crept along till he reached the egg sac. Charlotte moved aside for him. She was dying, but she still had strength enough to move a little. Then Templeton bared his long ugly teeth and began snipping the threads that fastened the sac to the ceiling. Wilbur watched from below.

'Use extreme care!' he said. 'I don't want a single one of those eggs harmed.'

'Thith thruff thticks in my mouth,' complained the rat. 'It'th worth than caramel candy.'

But Templeton worked away at the job, and managed to cut the sac adrift and carry it to the ground, where he dropped it in front of Wilbur. Wilbur heaved a great sigh of relief.

'Thank you, Templeton,' he said. 'I will never forget this as long as I live.'

'Neither will I,' said the rat, picking his teeth. 'I feel as though I'd eaten a spool of thread. Well, home we go!'

Templeton crept into the crate and buried himself in the straw. He got out of sight just in time. Lurvy and John Arable and Mr Zuckerman came along at that moment, followed by Mrs Arable and Mrs Zuckerman and Avery and Fern. Wilbur had already decided how he would carry the egg sac — there was only one way possible. He carefully took the little bundle in his mouth and held it there on top of his tongue. He remembered what Charlotte had told him — that the sac was waterproof and strong. It felt funny on his tongue and made him drool a bit. And of course he couldn't say anything. But as he was being shoved into the crate, he looked up at Charlotte and gave her a wink. She knew he was saying good-bye in the only way he could. And she knew her children were safe.

'Good-bye!' she whispered. Then she summoned all her strength and waved one of her front legs at him.

She never moved again. Next day, as the Ferris wheel was being taken apart and the race horses were being loaded into vans and the entertainers were packing up their belongings and driving away in their trailers, Charlotte died. The Fair Grounds were soon deserted. The sheds and buildings were empty and forlorn. The infield was littered with bottles and trash. Nobody, of the hundreds of people that has visited the Fair, knew that a grey spider had played the most important part of all. No one was with her when she died.

22.

A Warm Wind

And so Wilbur came home to his beloved manure pile in the barn cellar. His was a strange homecoming. Around his neck he wore a medal of honour; in his mouth he held a sac of spider's eggs. There is no place like home, Wilbur thought, as he placed Charlotte' s five hundred and fourteen unborn children carefully in a safe corner. The barn smelled good. His friends the sheep and the geese were glad to see him back.

The geese gave him a noisy welcome.

'Congratu–congratu–congratulations!' they cried. 'Nice work.'

Mr Zuckerman took the medal from Wilbur's neck and hung it on a nail over the pigpen, where visitors could examine it. Wilbur himself could look at it whenever he wanted to.

In the days that followed, he was very happy. He grew to a great size. He no longer worried about being killed, for he knew that Mr Zuckerman would keep him as long as he lived. Wilbur often thought of Charlotte. A few strands of her old web still hung in the doorway. Every day Wilbur would stand and look at the torn, empty web, and a lump would come to his throat. No one had ever had such a friend—so affectionate, so loyal, and so skilful.

The autumn days grew shorter, Lurvy brought the squashes and pumpkins in from the garden and piled them on the barn floor, where they wouldn' t get nipped on frosty nights. The maples and birches turned bright colours and the wind shook them and they dropped their leaves one by one to the ground. Under the wild apple trees in the pasture, the red little apples lay thick on the ground, and the sheep gnawed them and the geese gnawed them and foxes came in the night and sniffed them. One evening, just before Christmas, snow began falling. It covered house and barn and fields and woods. Wilbur had never seen snow before. When morning came he went out and ploughed the drifts in his yard, for the fun of it. Fern and Avery arrived, dragging a sledge. They coasted down the lane and out on to the frozen pond in the pasture.

'Coasting is the most fun there is,' said Avery.

'The most fun there is,' retorted Fern, 'is when the Ferris wheel stops and Henry and I are in the top car and Henry makes the car swing and we can see everything for miles and miles and miles.'

'Goodness, are you still thinking about that ol' Ferris wheel?' said Avery in disgust. 'The Fair was weeks and weeks ago.'

'I think about it all the time,' said Fern, picking snow from her ear.

After Christmas the thermometer dropped to ten below zero. Cold settled on the world. The pasture was bleak and frozen. The cows stayed in the barn all the time now, except on sunny mornings when they went out and stood in the barnyard in the lee of the straw pile. The sheep stayed near the barn too, for protection. When they were thirsty they ate snow. The geese hung around the barnyard the way boys hang around a drug store, and Mr Zuckerman fed them corn and turnips to keep them cheerful.

'Many, many, many thanks!' they always said, when they saw food coming.

Templeton moved indoors when winter came. His ratty home under the pig trough was too chilly, so he fixed himself a cosy nest in the barn behind the grain bins. He lined it with bits of dirty newspapers and rags, and whenever he found a trinket or a keepsake he carried it home and stored it there. He continued to visit Wilbur three times a day, exactly at mealtime, and Wilbur kept the promise he had made. Wilbur let the rat eat first. Then, when Templeton couldn't hold another mouthful, Wilbur would eat. As a result of overeating, Templeton grew bigger and fatter than any rat you ever saw. He was gigantic. He was as big as a young woodchuck.

The old sheep spoke to him about his size one day. 'You would live longer,' said the old sheep, 'if you ate less.'

'Who wants to live for ever?' sneered the rat. 'I am naturally a heavy eater and I get untold satisfaction from the pleasures of the feast.' He patted his stomach, grinned at the sheep, and crept upstairs to lie down.

All winter Wilbur watched over Charlotte's egg sac as though he were guarding his own children. He had scooped out a special place in the manure for the sac, next to the board fence. On very cold nights he lay so that his breath would warm it. For Wilbur, nothing in life was so important as this small round object — nothing else mattered. Patiently he awaited the end of winter and the coming of the little spiders. Life is always a rich and steady time when you are waiting for something to happen or to hatch. The winter ended at last.

'I heard the frogs today,' said the old sheep one evening. 'Listen! You can hear them now.'

Wilbur stood still and cocked his ears. From the pond, in shrill chorus, came the voices of hundreds of little frogs.

'Springtime,' said the old sheep, thoughtfully. 'Another spring.' As she walked away, Wilbur saw a new lamb following her. It was only a few hours old.

The snows melted and ran away. The streams and ditches bubbled and chattered with rushing water. A sparrow with a streaky breast arrived and sang. The light strengthened, the mornings came sooner. Almost every morning there was another new lamb in the sheepfold. The goose was sitting on nine eggs. The sky seemed wider and a warm wind blew. The last remaining strands of Charlotte' s old web floated away and vanished.

One fine sunny morning, after breakfast, Wilbur stood watching his precious sac. He wasn' t thinking of anything much. As he stood there, he noticed something move. He stepped closer and stared. A tiny spider crawled from the sac. It was no bigger than a grain of sand, no bigger than the head of a pin. Its body was grey with a black stripe underneath. Its legs were grey and tan. It looked just like Charlotte.

Wilbur trembled all over when he saw it. The little spider waved at him. Then Wilbur looked more closely. Two more little spiders crawled out and waved. They climbed round and round on the sac, exploring their new world. Then three more little spiders. Then eight. Then ten. Charlotte's children were here at last.

Wilbur's heart pounded. He began to squeal. Then he raced in circles, kicking manure into the air. Then he turned a back flip. Then he planted his front feet and came to a stop in front of Charlotte's children.

'Hello there!' he said.

The first spider said hello, but its voice was so small Wilbur couldn't hear it.

'I am an old friend of your mother's,' said Wilbur. 'I'm glad to see you. Are you all right? Is everything all right?'

The little spiders waved their forelegs at him. Wilbur could see by the way they acted that they were glad to see him.

'Is there anything I can get you? Is there anything you need?'

The young spiders just waved. For several days and several nights they crawled here and there, up and down, around and about, waving at Wilbur, trailing tiny draglines behind them, and exploring their home. There were dozens and dozens of them. Wilbur couldn't count them, but he knew that he had a great many new friends. They grew quite rapidly. Soon each was as big as a BB shot. They made tiny webs near the sac.

Then came a quiet morning when Mr Zuckerman opened a door on the north side. A warm draught of rising air blew softly through the barn cellar. The air smelt of the damp earth, of the spruce woods, of the sweet springtime. The baby spiders felt the warm updraught. One spider climbed to the top of the fence. Then it did something that came as a great surprise to Wilbur. The spider stood on its head, pointed its spinnerets in the air, and let loose a cloud of fine silk. The silk formed a balloon. As Wilbur watched, the spider let go of the fence and rose into the air.

'Good-bye!' it said, as it sailed through the doorway.

'Wait a minute!' screamed Wilbur. 'Where do you think you' re going?'

But the spider was already out of sight. Then another baby spider crawled to the top of the fence, stood on its head, made a balloon, and sailed away. Then another spider. Then another. The air was soon filled with tiny balloons, each balloon carrying a spider.

Wilbur was frantic. Charlotte' s babies were disappearing at a great rate.

'Come back, children!' he cried.

'Good-bye!' they called. 'Good-bye, good-bye!'

At last one little spider took time enough to stop and talk to Wilbur before making its balloon.

'We're leaving here on the warm updraught. This is our moment for setting forth. We are aeronauts and we are going out into the world to make webs for ourselves.'

'But *where*?' asked Wilbur.

'Wherever the wind takes us. High, low. Near, far. East, west. North, south. We take to the breeze, we go as we please.'

'Are *all* of you going?' asked Wilbur. 'You can't all go. I would be left alone, with no friends. Your mother wouldn't want that to happen, I'm sure.'

The air was now so full of balloonists that the barn cellar looked almost as though a mist had gathered. Balloons by the dozen were rising, circling, and drifting away through the door, sailing off on the gentle wind. Cries of 'Good-bye, good-bye, good-bye!' came weakly to Wilbur's ears. He couldn't bear to watch any more. In sorrow he sank to the ground and closed his eyes. This seemed like the end of the world, to be deserted by Charlotte's children. Wilbur cried himself to sleep.

When he woke it was late afternoon. He looked at the egg sac. It was empty. He looked into the air. The balloonists were gone. Then he walked drearily to the doorway, where Charlotte's web used to be. He was standing there, thinking of her, when he heard a small voice.

'Salutations!' it said. 'I'm up here.'

'So am I,' said another tiny voice.

'So am I,' said a third voice. 'Three of us are staying. We like this place, and we like *you*.'

Wilbur looked up. At the top of the doorway three small webs were being constructed. On each web, working busily was one of

Charlotte's daughters.

'Can I take this to mean,' asked Wilbur, 'that you have definitely decided to live here in the barn cellar, and that I am going to have *three* friends?'

'You can indeed,' said the spiders.

'What are your names, please?' asked Wilbur, trembling with joy.

'I'll tell you my name,' replied the first little spider, 'if you'll tell me why you are trembling.'

'I'm trembling with joy,' said Wilbur.

'Then my name is Joy,' said the first spider.

'What was my mother's middle initial?' asked the second spider.

'A,' said Wilbur.

'Then my name is Aranea,' said the spider.

'How about me?' asked the third spider. 'Will you just pick out a nice sensible name for me — something not too long, not too fancy, and not too dumb?'

Wilbur thought hard.

'Nellie?' he suggested.

'Fine, I like that very much,' said the third spider. 'You may call me Nellie.' She daintily fastened her orb–line to the next spoke of the web.

Wilbur's heart brimmed with happiness. He felt that he should make a short speech on this very important occasion.

'Joy! Aranea! Nellie!' he began. 'Welcome to the barn cellar. You have chosen a hallowed doorway from which to string your webs. I think it is only fair to tell you that I was devoted to your mother. I owe my very life to her. She was brilliant, beautiful, and loyal to the end. I shall always treasure her memory. To you, her daughters, I pledge my friendship, for ever and ever.'

'I pledge mine,' said Joy.

'I do, too,' said Aranea.

'And so do I,' said Nellie, who had just managed to catch a small gnat.

It was a happy day for Wilbur. And many more happy, tranquil days followed.

As time went on, and the months and years came and went, he was never without friends. Fern did not come regularly to the barn any more. She was growing up, and was careful to avoid childish things, like sitting on a milk stool near a pigpen. But Charlotte' s children and grandchildren and great-grandchildren, year after year, lived in the doorway. Each spring there were new little spiders hatching out to take the place of the old. Most of them sailed away, on their balloons. But always two or three stayed and set up housekeeping in the doorway.

Mr Zuckerman took fine care of Wilbur all the rest of his days, and the pig was often visited by friends and admirers, for nobody ever forgot the year of his triumph and the miracle of the web. Life in the barn was very good — night and day, winter and summer, spring and autumn, dull days and bright days. It was the best place to be, thought Wilbur, this warm delicious cellar, with the garrulous geese, the changing seasons, the heat of the sun, the passage of swallows, the nearness of rats, the sameness of sheep, the love of spiders, the smell of manure, and the glory of everything.

Wilbur never forgot Charlotte. Although he loved her children and grandchildren dearly, none of the new spiders ever quite took her place in his heart. She was in a class by herself. It is not often that someone comes along who is a true friend and a good writer. Charlotte was both.

〔美〕E.B.怀特 著 任溶溶 译

夏洛的网

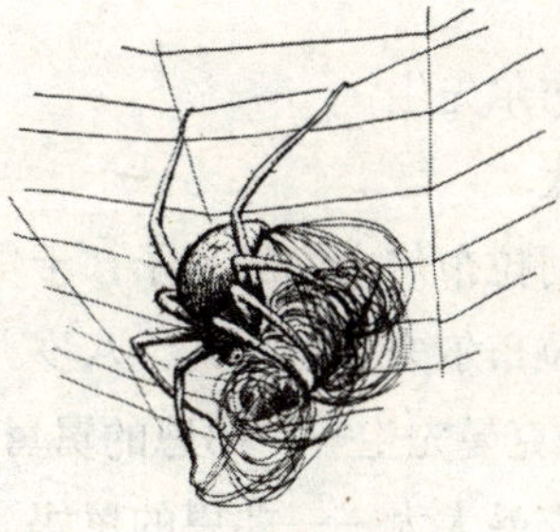

上海译文出版社

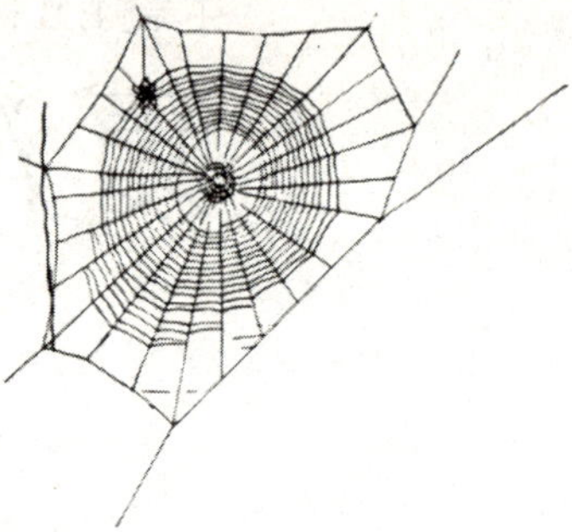

“人物”表

约翰·阿拉布尔先生

阿拉布尔太太

艾弗里——阿拉布尔夫妇的儿子，十岁

弗恩——阿拉布尔夫妇的女儿，八岁

霍默·L·朱克曼先生——弗恩的舅舅

伊迪丝·朱克曼太太——弗恩的舅妈

勒维——朱克曼夫妇的雇工

多里安医生

威尔伯——小猪

夏洛·阿·卡瓦蒂卡——蜘蛛

坦普尔顿——老鼠

目　录

1．早饭前 / 161
2．小猪威尔伯 / 166
3．逃走 / 169
4．孤独 / 177
5．夏洛 / 183
6．夏日 / 191
7．坏消息 / 196
8．家里的谈话 / 199
9．威尔伯说大话 / 202
10．臭弹爆炸 / 211
11．奇迹 / 219
12．会议 / 226
13．进展顺利 / 231
14．多里安医生 / 241
15．蟋蟀 / 247
16．上集市去 / 251
17．叔叔 / 260
18．凉爽的晚上 / 266
19．卵袋 / 271
20．胜利时刻 / 279
21．最后一天 / 285
22．温暖的风 / 292

译后记 / 3 0 3

1.

早饭前

“爸爸拿着那把斧子去哪儿？”摆桌子吃早饭的时候，弗恩问她妈妈。

“去猪圈，”阿拉布尔太太回答说，“昨天夜里下小猪了。”

“我不明白，他干吗要拿着把斧子去，”只有八岁的弗恩又说。

“这个嘛，”她妈妈说，“有一只小猪是落脚猪。它太小太弱，不会有出息。因此你爸爸拿定主意不要它。”

“不要它？”弗恩一声尖叫，“你是说要杀掉它？只为了它比别的猪小？”

阿拉布尔太太在桌子上放下奶油缸。“别嚷嚷，弗恩！”她说，“你爸爸是对的。那小猪反正活不了。”

弗恩推开挡道的一把椅子，跑出去了。青草湿湿的，泥土散发着一股春天的气息。等到追上爸爸，弗恩的帆布鞋都湿了。

“请不要杀它！”她眼泪汪汪地说，“这不公平。”

阿拉布尔先生停下了脚步。

“弗恩，”他温和地说，“你得学会控制自己。”

“控制自己？”弗恩叫道，“这是生死攸关的事，你还说什么控制自己。”泪珠滚滚滑落她的面颊，她一把抓住斧子，打算把它从爸爸手里抢下来。

“弗恩，”阿拉布尔先生说，“养小猪的事我比你懂。落脚猪麻烦大着呢。现在让开吧！”

“可是这不公平，”弗恩叫道，“小猪生下来小，它自己也没办法，对不对？要是我生下来的时候很小很小，你也把我给杀了吗？”

阿拉布尔先生微笑了。“当然不会，”他说着，疼爱地低头看着女儿，“不过这是两码事。女孩小是一回事，落脚猪小又是一回事。”

“我看不出有什么两样，”弗恩回答说，仍旧抓住斧头不放，“我听到过那么多不公平的事，这件事是最最不公平的。”

约翰·阿拉布尔先生脸上掠过一种古怪的神情。他自己好像也要哭了。

“好吧好吧，”他说，“你先回去，我回家的时候把这落脚猪带回来，让你用奶瓶喂它奶，像喂小宝宝似的。这下子你就会看到，对付一只小猪有多么麻烦了。”

半小时后，阿拉布尔先生回家来了，胳肢窝里真夹着一个纸箱。这时候弗恩正在楼上换她的帆布鞋。厨房的桌子上，早饭已经摆好，房间里透着咖啡、熏肉的香味，湿灰泥的气味，还有从炉子里飘出来的柴火烟味。

“把它放到她的椅子上去！”阿拉布尔太太说。阿拉布尔先生就把

纸箱放在弗恩的位子上，然后走到水池旁边洗了手，还用滚筒架上的擦手毛巾擦擦干。

弗恩慢慢地一步一步下楼。她的眼睛哭红了。当她走近她那把椅子的时候，那纸箱摇摇晃晃的，里面发出抓扒的声音。弗恩看看她爸爸。

接着她掀起纸箱盖。从里面抬头看着她的，正是刚生下来的那只小猪。是只小白猪。晨光透过它的耳朵，把它们映成了粉红色。

“它是你的了，”阿拉布尔先生说，“你让它免于生下来就死。愿老天爷原谅我做了这傻事。”

弗恩盯着小猪看，眼睛怎么也离不开它。“噢，”她很轻很轻地说，“噢，瞧它！它棒极了。”

她小心地盖上纸箱。她先亲亲爸爸，再亲亲妈妈。然后她又打开箱盖，把小猪抱出来，贴在脸蛋上。这时候她哥哥艾弗里走进房间。艾弗里十岁。他全副武装——一只手握住一支气枪，一只手握住一把木头短刀。

“那是什么玩意儿？”他问道，“弗恩得到什么了？”

“她来了位客人吃早饭，”阿拉布尔太太说，“你去洗洗手洗洗脸吧，艾弗里！”

“让我看看它，”艾弗里放下枪说，“这么可怜的小东西也能叫做猪？它真是猪呱呱叫的样板——还没有一只白老鼠大。”

“快去洗洗，来吃早饭，艾弗里！”他妈妈说，“还有半个钟头校车就到了。”

“我也可以有只猪吗，爸爸？”艾弗里问道。

“不，我只把猪送给早起的人，”阿拉布尔先生说，“弗恩天一亮就起来打抱不平，要扫尽天下不平事。结果呢，她现在得到了一只小猪。没错，它是很小，只有一丁点大，不过到底还是猪。这正好证明，早起的人会有什么好处。好了，我们吃早饭吧！”

可宝贝小猪不先喝上牛奶，弗恩是吃不下去的。阿拉布尔太太找来一个婴儿奶瓶和一个橡皮奶嘴。她把热牛奶灌进奶瓶，套上奶嘴，递给弗恩说：“给它吃它的早饭吧！”

紧接着，弗恩坐在厨房角落的地板上，把她的小宝宝放在膝间，教小猪吸奶瓶。小猪虽然小，胃口却很好，很快就学会了。

校车在大路上按喇叭了。

“快跑！”阿拉布尔太太抱起弗恩怀里的小猪，在她手里塞了个炸面圈，吩咐说。艾弗里抓起他的枪，又拿了一个炸面圈。

两个孩子奔到外面大路上，上了车。弗恩不理车上的其他同学。她只是坐在那里看着车窗外，一个劲儿地想，这是一个多么快乐的世界啊，她一个人拥有一只小猪，又是多么福气啊。等校车来到学校时，弗恩已经给她的宝贝猪取好了名字，一个她想得出来的最漂亮的名字。

“它的名字叫威尔伯，”她悄悄地对自己说了一声。

她正在想着她的小猪，这时老师问道：“弗恩，宾夕法尼亚州的首府叫什么名字？”

“威尔伯①，”弗恩像做梦似的说。同学们格格笑起来。弗恩脸都红了。

① 美国宾夕法尼亚州的首府应该是哈里斯堡。

2.

小猪威尔伯

弗恩爱威尔伯胜过一切。她爱抚摩它，喂它，把它放在床上。每天早晨一起来，她就去热牛奶，给它围上围涎，拿着奶瓶喂它。每天下午，校车在家门口一停下来，她马上跳下车，登登登跑到厨房，又给它弄牛奶。吃晚饭的时候再喂一次，睡觉前又喂一次。弗恩上学的时候，就由阿拉布尔太太每天中午喂它。威尔伯爱喝牛奶，再没有什么比看到弗恩给它热牛奶更让它开心的了。它会站来起，抬头用深情的眼睛看着她。

在威尔伯生下来的头几天，它给安置在厨房炉子旁边的箱子里。后来阿拉布尔太太说话了，它就给搬到板棚里，换了一个大一点的箱子。长到两个星期时，它又给转移到户外。这是苹果开花的时节，天气越来越暖和。阿拉布尔先生特地在一棵苹果树下圈了一小块地给威尔伯做猪栏，为它备了一个大木箱，里面堆满麦草，木箱开了一个门，这样它就能随意进进出出了。

"夜里它不会冷吗？"弗恩问道。

"不会，"她爸爸说，"你看着吧，看它会怎么办？"

弗恩拿来一瓶牛奶，在苹果树下的猪栏里坐下来。威尔伯跑到她面前，她端着奶瓶让它吸。喝完最后一滴牛奶，它呼噜呼噜着，瞌睡蒙眬地走进木箱。弗恩低下头朝门里看。威尔伯正用它的鼻子拱麦草。转眼间，它就在麦草里拱出了一条地道。它钻进地道，完全被麦草盖住，不见了。弗恩看得入了神。知道她这小宝宝盖上麦草睡觉不会冷，她放心了。

每天早晨吃过早饭，威尔伯就和弗恩一起走到大路上，陪她等校车。她朝它挥手告别，它就站在那里一直等到校车拐弯看不见为止。弗恩在学校的时候，威尔伯给关在它的小猪栏里。她下午一回家，就把它放出来，它跟着她到处溜达。她进屋它也进屋。要是她上楼，威尔伯就等在楼梯脚边，直到她再下楼来。碰到她用玩具婴儿车推她的洋娃娃去散步，威尔伯会在后面跟着。有时候，在散步的过程中，威尔伯走累了，弗恩干脆把它抱起来，放到婴儿车上，躺在洋娃娃的身边。威尔伯最喜欢这样。要是实在太累，它会闭上眼睛，在洋娃娃的毯子底下睡觉。它闭上眼睛时的样子真好看，因为它的眼睫毛很长很长。洋娃娃也会闭上眼睛，这时弗恩就把车子推得很慢很轻，以免吵醒她的两个小宝宝。

一个暖和的下午，弗恩和艾弗里穿上泳衣到下面的小河去游泳。威尔伯紧跟着弗恩。她涉水，威尔伯也跟着她涉水。可是它觉得水很凉——凉得它受不了。因此，当两个孩子游泳、玩耍、用水你泼我我泼你时，威尔伯就待在河边的烂泥里自得其乐，烂泥暖和，湿嗒嗒的，黏黏糊糊，舒服极了。

天天这样，白天快快活活，夜里安安静静。

威尔伯是农民说的那种春猪，意思不过是指它出生在春天。它长到五个星期大的时候，阿拉布尔先生说它已经够大，可以卖掉了。弗恩听了忍不住大哭起来，可她爸爸对这件事铁了心。威尔伯胃口大了，除了喝牛奶还开始吃剩菜。阿拉布尔先生不愿意再养它。威尔伯的十个兄弟姐妹都已经卖了。

“它得走，弗恩，”他说，“把猪宝宝养大的乐趣你已经享受过了，如今威尔伯不再是猪宝宝，它得卖出去了。”

“给朱克曼家打个电话吧，”阿拉布尔太太劝弗恩说，“你的霍默舅舅有时候会弄只猪养养。要是威尔伯卖到他家里去，你只要高兴就可以常常走大路去看它。”

“我该问他要多少钱呢？”弗恩问道。

“这个嘛，”她爸爸说，“它是只落脚猪。你对你霍默舅舅说，你有只小猪要卖，只卖六块钱，看看他怎么说。”

这事儿很快就办妥了。弗恩打电话给她的伊迪丝舅妈，伊迪丝舅妈去叫霍默舅舅，霍默舅舅从谷仓回来接弗恩的电话。他听说只要六块钱，便说这猪他买下了。第二天，威尔伯就从它苹果树下的家给搬到朱克曼家谷仓底的肥料堆里。

3.

逃走

谷仓很大。它很旧了。里面有干草的气味，有肥料的气味。里面有干活累了的马的汗味，有吃苦耐劳的母牛的极好闻的气息。谷仓让人闻上去感到天下太平，什么坏事都不会再发生。它充满了谷物、马具套、车轴油、橡胶靴和新绳索的气味。碰上猫叼着给它的鱼头到这儿来享受，谷仓里还会多股鱼腥气。不过最强烈的是干草气味，因为谷仓上面的阁楼里一直堆着干草。总是有干草给扔下来喂牛、喂马、喂羊。

冬天谷仓很暖和，牲口大部分时间在室内；夏天所有的大门敞开透风，它又很凉爽。谷仓里面有马栏，有牛栏，谷仓底下有羊圈，有威尔伯待的猪圈。谷仓里有凡是谷仓都有的各种东西：梯子、磨子、叉子、扳手、镰刀、割草机、雪铲、斧头柄、牛奶桶、水桶、空麻袋、生锈的老鼠夹。它是燕子喜欢筑巢的那种谷仓。它是孩子们喜欢在里面玩耍的那种谷仓。这谷仓连同里面所有的东西，都是弗恩的舅舅霍默·朱克曼先生的。

威尔伯的新家在谷仓底层，就在牛栏下面。朱克曼先生知道，肥料堆是养小猪的好地方。猪需要温暖，向阳的谷仓底层又温暖又舒适。

弗恩几乎天天来看威尔伯。她找来一个丢弃不用的挤奶凳，放在挨着威尔伯那猪圈的羊圈里。漫长的下午，她静静地坐在那里，想着心事，听着、看着威尔伯。那些羊很快就跟她熟了，信任她。和羊待在一起的那些鹅也一样。所有的牲口都信任她，她是那么安静友好。朱克曼先生不让她把威尔伯带到外面去，也不让她进猪圈。不过他对弗恩说，只要她高兴，她可以坐在凳子上看威尔伯，爱看多久就看多久。

只要能和小猪待在一起，她就够高兴了。只要知道弗恩就坐在它的猪圈外面，威尔伯也就够快活了。只是它一点乐趣也没有——不能散步，不能坐婴儿车，不能游泳。

六月里，威尔伯已经快两个月大了。一天下午，它走到谷仓外的小院子里。这时候天天来看它的弗恩还没到。威尔伯站在阳光里，感到寂寞无聊。

“在这里什么事也不能做，”它想。它慢慢地走到它的食槽边，用鼻子闻闻，看有没有中午时吃漏的东西。它找到一小块土豆皮，把它吃了。它觉得背痒，于是靠着围栏，在栏板上磨蹭它的背。磨蹭够了，它又回到屋里，爬到肥料堆上，坐下来。它不想睡，不想刨地，它站厌了，也躺厌了。“我还没活到两个月，可已经活腻了，”它说。它又走到外面的院子里。

“来到外面，”它说，“除了进去再没有地方可去。回到里面，除了出来也再没有地方可去。”

“你这话就错了，我的朋友，我的朋友，我的朋友，”一个声音说。

威尔伯朝栏板外面望去，看到一只母鹅站在那里。

“你用不着待在那脏兮兮小兮兮脏兮兮小兮兮脏兮兮小兮兮的猪栏里，”那母鹅飞快地说，“有一块栏板松了。顶顶它，顶顶——顶顶——顶顶它，照我说的做，出来吧！”

“什么？”威尔伯说，“请你说得慢些！”

“我豁出去——豁出去——豁出去再说一遍，”那母鹅说，“我劝你出来。外面棒极了。”

“你刚才说有一块板松了吗？”

“我说了，我说了，我说了。”那鹅说。

威尔伯走到栏板旁边，看到母鹅说得没错——是有一块木板松了。它低下头，闭上眼睛去顶。木板给顶开了。转眼工夫，它已经钻出了围栏，站在猪栏外面高高的草丛里。那只母鹅咯咯地笑起来。

“自由自在的感觉怎么样？”它问道。

“我喜欢，”威尔伯说，“我是说，我想我喜欢。”真的，到了围栏外面，没有东西把它和浩大的世界隔开，它觉得怪怪的，十分特别。

“依你看，我最好上哪儿去呢？”

“你爱上哪儿就上哪儿，爱上哪儿就上哪儿，”母鹅说，“穿过果园，拱草皮！穿过花园，拱出萝卜！拱出所有的东西！吃草！找玉米！找燕麦！到处跑！蹦蹦跳跳！穿过果园，到林子里去游荡！你年纪小，会觉得世界真奇妙。”

“我看得出它奇妙，”威尔伯回答说。它蹦起来，跳得半天高，打了个转，跑了几步，停下来朝四周看，闻闻下午的各种气味，然后动身穿过果园。它在一棵苹果树的树阴下停住，开始用有力的鼻子拱地，又拱又掘。它觉得非常快活。还没有人看到它时，它已经拱了一大片地。是朱克曼太太第一个看到它。她从厨房窗子里看到了它，马上大声喊人。

“霍——默！”她叫道，“小猪出去了！勒维！小猪出去了！霍默！勒维！小猪出去了。它在那棵苹果树底下。”

“现在麻烦开始了，”威尔伯想，“现在我闯祸了。”

那只母鹅听到了喧闹声，也嚷嚷起来。“跑——跑——跑，跑下山，到林子——林子——林子里去！”它对威尔伯大叫，“到了林子里，他们永远——永远——永远捉不到你。”

那只小猎狗听到了喧闹声，从谷仓里奔出来参加追捕。朱克曼先生听到了叫声，从他正在修理工具的机器棚出来。雇工勒维听到了叫声，从他正在拔野草的芦笋地跑来。大家朝威尔伯追去，威尔伯不知道怎么办才好。林子看来离得很远，再说它也从未进过林子，吃不准是不是喜欢它。

“绕到它后面，勒维，”朱克曼先生说，“把它朝谷仓赶！悠着点——别推它拖它！我去拿一桶泔脚来。”

威尔伯逃走的消息，很快在那群牲口当中传开了。不论什么时候，只要有牲口逃出朱克曼的农场，其他牲口就都大感兴趣。那只母鹅对离它最近的那头牛大叫，说威尔伯已经自由了，很快所有的牛都知道了。接下来有一头牛告诉一只羊，很快所有的羊也都知道了。小羊羔又从它们的妈妈那里知道。谷仓马栏里的马听到母鹅嚷嚷大叫时竖起了耳朵，也马上知道出了什么事。“威尔伯走掉了。”它们说。所有的牲口全都晃头晃脑，很高兴知道它们的一个朋友自由了，不再被关起来，或者被捆得紧紧的。

威尔伯不知道怎么办才好，也不知道该朝哪里跑。看着个个都像在追它。“如果这就是所谓的自由，”它心里说，“我想，我情愿被关在自己的猪栏里。”

那条小猎狗从一边悄悄地靠近威尔伯。雇工勒维从另一边悄悄地靠近威尔伯。朱克曼太太站在那里做好准备，万一威尔伯朝花园跑就拦住它。朱克曼先生提着一桶东西朝威尔伯走过来。“太可怕了，”威尔伯心里说，“弗恩为什么还不来啊？”它开始哭了。

那只母鹅充当指挥，开始发号施令。

“不要光站在那里，威尔伯！躲开啊，躲开啊！”那鹅叫着，“绕开，向我这边跑来，溜进溜出，溜进溜出，溜进溜出！向林子跑！转过身跑！”

那条小猎狗朝威尔伯的后腿扑上去，威尔伯一跳，跑掉了。勒维伸手来抓。朱克曼太太对勒维尖叫。那只母鹅为威尔伯当啦啦队助威。威尔伯在勒维的两腿间溜了过去。勒维没抓到威尔伯，反而抓住了那条小猎狗。“干得好，干得好，干得好！”母鹅欢呼，“再来一次，再来一次，再来一次！”

“朝山下跑！”那些牛劝威尔伯。

“朝我这边跑！”公鹅大叫。

“朝山上跑！”那些羊嚷嚷。

“转过身跑！”母鹅嘎嘎喊。

“跳，跳！”那只公鸡叫道。

“小心勒维！”那些牛喊道。

"小心朱克曼！"公鹅喊道。

"提防那狗！"那些羊嚷。

"听我说，听我说，听我说！"母鹅尖叫。

你叫我嚷，可怜的威尔伯被这些喧闹声弄得昏头昏脑，吓坏了。它不愿意成为这场大乱的中心人物。它很想听从它那些朋友给它发出的指示，可它不能同时上山又下山，它不能在蹦蹦跳跳时又转来转去，它哭得那么厉害，简直看不清正在它眼前发生的事。再说威尔伯只是一只小乳猪——实际上跟个婴儿差不多。它只巴望弗恩在这里，把它抱在怀里安慰它。当它抬头看到朱克曼先生站在离它很近的地方，提着一桶热的泔脚，它觉得放了心。它抬起鼻子闻。气味真香——热牛奶、土豆皮、麦麸、凯洛牌爆米花，还有朱克曼家早饭吃剩的膨松饼。

"来吧，小猪！"朱克曼先生拍着桶子说，"小猪，来吧！"

威尔伯朝桶子上前一步。

"不不不！"母鹅说，"这是桶子老把戏了。威尔伯。别上当，别上当，别上当！他在引你回到牢——牢——牢笼里去。他在引诱你的肚子。"

威尔伯不管。食物的气味太吊人胃口了。它朝桶子又走了一步。

"小猪，小猪！"朱克曼先生好声好气地说，开始慢慢地朝谷仓院子走，一副没事人似的样子朝四下里看，好像根本不知道后面跟着一只小白猪。

"你要后悔——后悔——后悔的。"母鹅叫道。

威尔伯不管。它继续朝那桶泔脚走去。

“你会失去你的自由，”母鹅嘎嘎叫，“一小时的自由抵得上一桶泔脚。”

威尔伯不管。

等朱克曼先生来到猪栏那里，他爬过围栏，把泔脚倒进食槽。接着他拉掉围栏上那块松了的木板，露出一个大洞让威尔伯钻进去。

“再想想，再想想，再想想！”母鹅叫道。

威尔伯不听它的。它迈步穿过围栏，走进它的猪栏。它走到食槽旁边，希哩哗啦地吃了半天泔脚，贪馋地吸牛奶嚼膨松饼。重新回到家真好。

趁威尔伯在大吃大喝，勒维拿来槌子和钉子，把木板重新钉好。接着他和朱克曼先生用根棍子挠威尔伯的背。

“这只小猪真不赖。”勒维说。

“没错，它会长成头好猪。”朱克曼先生说。

威尔伯听到了这两句夸它的话。它感觉到了肚子里的热牛奶。它感觉到棍子舒服地在挠它痒痒的背。它感觉到安宁、快乐和睡意。这真是一个累人的下午。才不过四点钟左右，可威尔伯已经要睡了。

“我独自一个去闯世界实在还太小。”它躺下来时在心里这样说。

4.

孤独

第二天下雨，天色阴沉沉的。雨水落在谷仓顶上，不停地从屋檐上滴落下来；雨水落到谷仓院子里，弯弯曲曲地一道一道流进长着蓟草和藜草的小路；雨水噼噼啪啪地打在朱克曼太太的厨房窗上，咕咚咕咚地涌出水管；雨水落在正在草地上吃草的羊的背上。羊在雨中站累了，就沿着小路慢慢地走回羊圈。

雨水打乱了威尔伯的计划。威尔伯原打算今天出去，在它那猪栏里挖个新洞。它还有别的计划。它今天的打算大致上是这样的：

六点半吃早饭。脱脂牛奶、面包皮、麦麸、炸面圈碎块、上面滴着槭糖浆的麦饼、土豆皮、吃剩的葡萄干蛋奶布丁、脆麦片条屑屑。

这顿早饭预计七点吃完。

从七点到八点，威尔伯打算跟坦普尔顿聊聊天。坦普尔顿是住在食槽底下的那只老鼠。跟坦普尔顿聊天算不得世界上最有趣的事，不过聊胜于无。

从八点到九点，威尔伯打算在外面太阳底下打个盹。

从九点到十一点，它打算挖个洞，或者挖条沟，这样做也许能找到点埋在土里的好吃东西。

从十一点到十二点，它打算一动不动地站着看木板上的苍蝇，看红花草丛中的蜜蜂，看天上的燕子。

十二点吃中饭。麦麸、热水、苹果皮、肉汁、胡萝卜皮、肉屑、不新鲜的玉米片粥、干酪包装纸。中饭吃完大约一点。

从一点到两点，威尔伯打算睡觉。

从两点到三点，它打算抵着栏板挠身上的痒痒。

从三点到四点，它打算站着一动不动，想想活着是什么滋味，同时等弗恩来。

四点钟，晚饭大概送来了。脱脂牛奶、干饲料、勒维饭盒里吃剩下的三明治、洋李皮、这样一点那样一点、煎土豆、几滴果酱、又是这样一点那样一点、一块烤苹果、一点水果蛋糕。

威尔伯想着这些计划，想着想着睡着了。它六点醒来，看到在下雨，它简直受不了。

“我什么事情都美美地计划好了，偏偏下雨。”它说。

它在圈里扫兴地站了好一会儿。接着它走到门口，望出去。雨点打在它脸上。它的猪栏又冷又湿嗒嗒。它的食槽里面积了一英寸的水。坦普尔顿连个影子也见不着。

“你在外面吗，坦普尔顿？”威尔伯叫道。没有回答。威尔伯一下子感到孤独了，一个朋友也没有。

“天天一个样，”它抱怨说，“我太小，在谷仓这儿我没有真正的朋友，雨要下一整个上午一整个下午，天气这么坏，弗恩不会来了。噢，天啊！”威尔伯又哭了，两天当中这是第二回了。

六点半，威尔伯听到桶子砰砰响。勒维正站在外面顶着雨搅拌它的早饭。

“来吧，小猪！”勒维叫它。

威尔伯一动不动。勒维倒下泔脚，刮干净桶子，走了。他注意到这小猪有点不对头。

威尔伯不要食物，它要爱。它要一个朋友——一个肯和它一起玩的朋友。它对静静地坐在羊栏角落的母鹅讲话。

“你肯过来和我一起玩吗？”它问道。

“对不起——对不起——对不起，”母鹅说，“我在孵——孵——孵我的蛋。一共八个蛋。我得让它们热乎乎——热乎乎——热乎乎的。我得蹲在这里不动，我是个负责任——负责任——负责任的鹅妈妈。有蛋要孵我连玩也不玩。我在等着小鹅出世。”

“当然，我不会以为你在等着啄木鸟出世。”威尔伯挖苦说。

威尔伯接下来试试看问一只小羊羔。

“你能跟我玩吗？”它问道。

“当然不能，”那小羊羔说，“第一，我没法到你的圈里去，我还没大到能跳过围栏。第二，我对猪没兴趣。对我来说，猪的价值比零还要少。”

“比零还要少，你这话是什么意思？”威尔伯应道，“我不认为有什么东西会比零还要少。零就是零，什么也没有，这已经到了极限，少到了极限，怎么能有东西比零还要少呢？如果有什么东西比零还要少，那么这零就不能是零，一定要有些东西——哪怕只是一丁点东西。如果零就是零，那就没有什么东西比它还要少。”

“噢，别说了！”小羊羔说，“你自个儿去玩吧！反正我不跟猪玩。”

威尔伯很难过，只好躺下来，听雨声。很快它看到那只老鼠从一块斜板上爬下来，它把它当楼梯使。

“你肯跟我一起玩吗？坦普尔顿？”威尔伯问它。

"玩？"坦普尔顿捻捻它的小胡子，"玩？我简直不知道玩这个字是什么意思。"

"玩嘛，"威尔伯说，"它的意思是游戏、耍、又跑又跳、取乐儿。"

"这种事我从来能不干就不干，"老鼠尖刻地回答说，"我情愿把时间花在吃啊，啃啊，窥探啊，躲藏啊这些上头。我是个大食鬼而不是个寻欢作乐者。这会儿我正要上你的食槽去吃你的早饭，既然你自己不想吃。"坦普尔顿这老鼠说着偷偷地顺着墙爬，钻进了它在门和猪栏的食槽之间挖的地道。坦普尔顿是只诡计多端的机灵老鼠，它办法多多。这条地道就是它的技巧和狡猾的一个例子，让它不用上地面就能从谷仓到达它在食槽底下的藏身处。它的地道和通路遍布朱克曼先生的整个农场，能够从一个地方到另一个地方而不被人看见。白天它通常睡觉，天黑了才外出活动。

威尔伯看着它钻进地道不见了，转眼就见它的尖鼻子从食槽底下伸出来。坦普尔顿小心翼翼地爬过食槽的边进了食槽。在这可怕的下雨天，眼睁睁地看着自己的早饭被别人吃掉，这简直叫威尔伯无法容忍。就算它知道，瓢泼大雨中，坦普尔顿在那儿浑身都湿透了，也不能让它心里好过些。没有朋友，情绪低落，饿着肚子，它不由得扑倒在肥料上抽抽搭搭哭起来。

那天下午后半晌，勒维去对朱克曼先生说："我觉得你那只小猪有点不对头。吃的东西它连碰也不碰。"

"给它两匙羹硫和一点蜂蜜吧。"朱克曼先生说。

当勒维抓住威尔伯，把药硬灌进它的喉咙时，威尔伯简直不能相信会碰到这种事。这真正是它一生中最糟糕的一天。这种可怕的孤独，它真不知道是不是还能再忍耐下去。

黑暗笼罩了一切。很快就只有影子和羊嚼草的声音了，偶尔还有头顶上牛链子的格格声。因此，当黑暗中传来一个威尔伯从没听到过的细小声音时，它有多么吃惊，你们也就可想而知了。这声音听上去很细，可是很好听。“你要一个朋友吗，威尔伯？”那声音说，“我可以做你的朋友。我观察你一整天了，我喜欢你。”

“可我看不见你，”威尔伯跳起来说，“你在哪里？你是谁？”

“我就在上面这儿，”那声音说，“睡觉吧。明天早晨你就看见我了。”

5.

夏洛

这一夜好像特别长。威尔伯肚子空空的，可是心满满的，都是心事。一个人肚子空空，心事重重，总是睡不好觉的。

这天夜里威尔伯醒来十几次，看着黑暗，听着响声，想要琢磨出这是什么时间了。一间谷仓是永远不可能十分安静的。连半夜里也总是有动静。

第一次醒来时，它听到坦普尔顿在粮仓里啃洞。坦普尔顿的牙齿很响地啃着木头，发出很大的叽嘎声。“那发疯的老鼠！”威尔伯在心里说，“为什么它一定要整夜醒着，叽嘎叽嘎磨它的牙齿，破坏人的财产呢？为什么它不能像所有正正经经的动物那样睡觉呢？”

威尔伯第二次醒来，听见母鹅在窝里转来转去，自个儿在咯咯笑。

“这是什么时候了？”威尔伯悄悄地问它。

“大概——大概——大概是十一点半吧，”母鹅说，“你为什么不睡啊，威尔伯？”

“我心里想的东西太多了，”威尔伯说。

“唉，”母鹅说，“我倒不为这个烦。我心里什么东西也没有，可我屁股底下东西太多了。你试过蹲在八个蛋上面睡觉吗？”

“没有，”威尔伯回答，“我想那是很不舒服的。一个鹅蛋孵出小鹅来要多少时间呢？”

“大家说，大概——大概——大概三十天，”母鹅答道，“不过我也玩点小把戏。下午天气暖和，我拉点麦草把蛋盖上，自己到外面去溜达一会儿。”

威尔伯打了几个哈欠，回头继续睡它的觉。在梦里，它又听到那声音说：“我要做你的朋友。睡觉吧——明天早晨你就看到我了。”

离天亮大约半个钟头，威尔伯醒来竖起耳朵听。谷仓还是黑黑的。羊躺着一动不动。连母鹅也没有声音。头顶上那层也没有一点儿动静：牛在休息，马在打盹。坦普尔顿已经不啃洞，有事上什么地方去了。惟一的声音是屋顶上轻轻的叽嘎声，风标在转来转去。威尔伯喜欢谷仓这个样子——安安静静，等着天亮。

“天就要亮了。”它心里说。

微光透进一扇小窗子。星星一颗接一颗消失。威尔伯已经能看到离它几英尺远的母鹅。它蹲在那里，头塞在翅膀底下。接着威尔伯又认出羊和小羊羔。天空亮起来了。

“噢，美丽的白天，它终于来了！今天我将找到我的朋友。”

威尔伯到处看。它彻底搜索它的猪圈。它察看了窗台，抬头看天花板。可它没看到新的东西。最后它决定只好开口了。它不想用它的声音打破黎明时分这可爱的寂静，可它想不出别的办法来判断它那位神秘朋友在什么地方，哪儿也看不见它。于是威尔伯清清它的嗓子。

“请注意！”它用坚定的口气大声说，“昨天夜里临睡时对我说话的那位先生或者女士，能够好心地给我点什么指示或者信号，让我知道他或者她是谁吗？”

威尔伯停下来倾听。其他所有牲口都抬起头来看它。威尔伯脸都红了。可它拿定了主意，一定要和它这位不认识的朋友取得联系。

“请注意！”它又说，“我把我的话再说一遍。昨天夜里临睡时对我说话的那位，能够好心开开口吗？如果你是我的朋友，请告诉我你在什么地方！”

那些羊厌恶地你看看我我看看你。

“别乱叫了，威尔伯！”最老的那只羊说，“如果你在这里真有个新朋友，你这样叫恐怕只会打搅他休息，大清早人家还在睡觉，你却把他吵醒，这最容易伤害感情，破坏友谊了。你怎么能肯定，你那位朋友是早起的呢？”

“我请大家原谅，”威尔伯低声说，“我无意让大家不高兴。”

它乖乖地在肥料堆上躺下来，面对着门。它不知道，其实它那位朋友就在附近。老羊说得对——这位朋友还在睡觉。

很快勒维就拿来泔脚给它当早饭吃。威尔伯冲出去，急急忙忙地吃了个精光，舔着食槽。羊群顺着小路走了，公鹅一摇一摆地跟在它们后面，啄着青草吃。接下来，正当威尔伯躺下要打它的早盹时，它又听见了头天夜里叫过它的细小声音。

"敬礼！"那声音说。

威尔伯一下子跳起来。"敬——什么？"它叫道。

"敬礼！"那声音再说一遍。

"这话是什么意思，你在哪里？"威尔伯尖声大叫，"谢谢你，谢谢你告诉我，你在什么地方。什么是敬礼？"

"敬礼是句问候话，"那声音说，"我说'敬礼'，这只是我喜欢用这种方式来表示'你好'或者'你早'。说实在的，这种方式有点傻，我也奇怪我怎么会说惯了。至于我在什么地方，那很简单。你只要抬头朝门犄角这儿看看！我就在这上面。看，我在挥腿呢！"

威尔伯终于看到了那么好心好意地对它说话的东西。门口上端张着一个大蜘蛛网，从网顶头朝下吊着的是只灰色大蜘蛛。它有一颗橡皮糖大小，八条腿，它正在向威尔伯挥动其中一条腿，友好地打着招呼呢。"现在看见我啦？"它问道。

"噢，看见了，还用说，"威尔伯说，"看见了，一点不错，看见了！你好！你早！敬礼！很高兴看到你。请问你叫什么名字？我可以请问你的名字吗？"

"我的名字嘛，"那蜘蛛说，"叫夏洛。"

"夏洛什么？"威尔伯急着问。

"夏洛·阿·卡瓦蒂卡。不过叫我夏洛就行了。"

"我觉得你很美。"威尔伯说。

"这个嘛，我是美，"夏洛回答说，"这是没说的。几乎所有的蜘蛛

都十分美。我还不及有一些蜘蛛耀眼，不过我会做到的。我真希望我看你能跟你看我那样清清楚楚，威尔伯。”

“你为什么不能呢？”小猪问道，“我就在这里。”

“没错，不过我近视眼，”夏洛回答说，“我一向近视得厉害。在某些方面这也很好，可在某些方面就不那么好。看我捆住这只苍蝇吧。”

一只苍蝇本来在威尔伯的食槽上爬，这会儿飞起来，撞到夏洛那个网的底下部分，给黏性的蜘蛛丝缠住了。苍蝇拼命扑打翅膀，想要挣脱逃走。

“首先，”夏洛说，“我向它潜下去。”它头朝前向苍蝇扑下去。它下来时，一根细丝从它后面吐出来。

“接下来，我把它捆住，”它抓住苍蝇，吐出几根丝捆住它，把它翻过来翻过去，捆得它动也不能动。威尔伯惊恐地看着。它简直不能相信它所看到的事，虽然它讨厌苍蝇，可却为这一只感到难过。

“好了！”夏洛说，“现在我让它失去知觉，好叫它舒服些。”它咬了苍蝇一口。“它现在什么感觉也没有了，”它说，“它可以当我的美味早餐了。”

“你是说，你吃苍蝇？”威尔伯倒抽一口冷气。

“当然。苍蝇、甲虫、蚱蜢、精选的昆虫、飞蛾、蝴蝶、美味蟑螂、蚊蚋、摇蚊、大蚊、蜈蚣、蚊子、蟋蟀——一切太不小心给我的网捉住了的东西。我得活啊，对吗？”

“当然，当然，”威尔伯说，“它们味道好吗？”

"太美了。自然，我不是真的吃掉它们。我是喝它们——喝它们的血。我嗜血。"夏洛说，它悦耳的细小声音更细了，更悦耳了。

"别这么说！"威尔伯呻吟道，"请别说这样的话！"

"为什么不说？这是真的，我得说实话。我对吃苍蝇和甲虫并不真正感到快活，可我天生就这样。蜘蛛总得想办法活下去啊，碰巧我是一个结网捉虫的。我正是生来就结网捉苍蝇和其他昆虫。在我之前，我妈妈结网捉虫。在它之前，它妈妈结网捉虫。我们一家都结网捉虫。再回过去几千几万年，我们蜘蛛一直埋伏着捉苍蝇和甲虫。"

"这真是一种悲惨的遗传，"威尔伯难过地说。它之所以这么难过，是因为它这位新朋友那么嗜血。

"不错，是这样，"夏洛同意说，"可我没办法。我不知道开天辟地以来，第一只蜘蛛是怎么想出结网这个异想天开的主意的，可它做到了，它也真叫聪明。从此以后，我们所有的蜘蛛都得玩同样的把戏。总的说来，这不是个坏点子。"

"这很残忍。"威尔伯回答说，它不打算被说服而放弃自己的立场。

"这个嘛，你没有发言权，"夏洛说，"你是有人用桶子送东西给你吃。可没有人给我东西吃。我得自己谋生。我靠自己的本事过活。我得机智灵活，要不然就挨饿。我得自己想办法，能捉什么捉什么，来什么捉什么。我的朋友，碰巧来的都是苍蝇、昆虫和甲虫。再说，"夏洛抖着它的一条腿说，"你知道吗，如果我不捉甲虫，不吃掉它们，甲虫就会增加，成倍成倍地增加，多得会破坏地球，把所有的东西一扫而光？”

“真的？”威尔伯说，“我不希望出这样的事。这么说，你的网也许还是个好东西。”

母鹅听到了它们这番对话，在那里咯咯暗笑。“生活里有许多事威尔伯还不懂，”它想，“它的确是只非常天真的小猪。它甚至不知道到了圣诞节有什么事要临头；它一点不知道，朱克曼先生和勒维正在阴谋杀掉它。”母鹅挺起点身子，把底下那些蛋拨开一点，好叫它们充分得到它暖和的身体和蓬松的羽毛的温暖。

夏洛静静地站在苍蝇上面，准备去吃它。威尔伯躺下来闭上眼睛。由于一夜没有睡好，又和陌生人第一次相识太兴奋了，它觉得十分疲倦。微风给它送来红花草的香气——它的围栏外面芬芳天地的香气。“好了，”它心里说，“我终于有一个新朋友了，错不了。可这友谊多么冒风险啊！夏洛凶狠、残忍、狡诈、嗜血——样样都不是我喜欢的。我怎么能学会喜欢它呢？哪怕它好看，当然，又聪明？”

找到一个新朋友，在喜悦之外，常常会同时有一些疑惑和恐惧，可威尔伯却只感受到了疑惑和恐惧。不过到时候它就会发现，它这是错看了夏洛。在夏洛凶猛残忍的外表下，有一颗善良的心，到头来，它会显示出自己是个多么忠实的朋友。

6.

夏日

在农场里，初夏的日子是一年当中最快活最美好的日子。丁香开花，让空气芳香扑鼻。接下来丁香花谢了，苹果树又紧接着开花，蜜蜂围着苹果树飞来飞去。天气越来越暖和。学校放假了，孩子们有工夫玩了，可以到小河边去钓鲑鱼。艾弗里常常在他那衣袋里带条鲑鱼回家，它硬邦邦的，热热的，马上就好煎来在中饭时吃。

现在学校放假，弗恩几乎天天上谷仓去，静静地坐在她那张凳子上。牲口把她当作自己人。那些羊安静地躺在她的脚旁。

七月初，那些耕马给拴到割草机上，朱克曼先生坐到割草机的座位上面，把割草机拉到地里去。整个上午可以听到割草机绕过来绕过去的嘎嘎声，这时高高的草在割草机横档后面倒下来，排成绿色的长排。到第二天，如果没有雷阵雨，所有的人手都来帮忙耙啊，叉啊，装车啊，这些干草就被高高的干草车运到谷仓去，弗恩和艾弗里高高地坐在干草顶上。接下来，这些香喷喷热烘烘的干草给吊到那大阁楼上，直到整个谷仓像是一张猫尾草和红花草的大草床。跳进去真痛快，躲在草里连人都找不到。有时候艾弗里会在草里找到一条小草蛇，把它塞进衣袋，衣袋里杂七杂八的东西又多了一样。

初夏的日子对于小鸟来说是个喜庆时节。田野上，房子周围，谷仓里，林子里，沼地里——到处是小鸟在谈情说爱，在唱歌，到处是鸟窝，是鸟蛋。在林边，白喉带鹀(一定是老远从波士顿飞来的)大叫："噢，皮博迪，皮博迪，皮博迪！"在一根苹果树枝上，那东菲比霸鹟摇头摆尾说："菲比，菲——比！"知道生命有多短促和可爱的歌雀说："甜滋滋、甜滋滋、甜滋滋的插曲；甜滋滋、甜滋滋、甜滋滋的插曲！"你一走进谷仓，燕子就会从它们的窝里飞下来责备你说："放肆，放肆！"

在初夏的日子里有许多东西可以给孩子吃、喝、吸、嚼。蒲公英秆充满乳液，红花草球充满蜜汁，电冰箱里当然装满冰凉的饮料。不管朝哪里看都是勃勃生机；甚至把野草梗上的小绒球拨开，里面也会有一条青虫。土豆藤上的叶片背后有马铃薯甲虫发亮的橙色虫卵。

在初夏的一天，那些鹅蛋终于孵出小鹅来了。在仓底这儿，这可是一件大事。小鹅孵出来时，弗恩正坐在她的凳子上。

除了母鹅自己，夏洛是第一个知道小鹅终于出世的。母鹅早一天就知道它们要诞生——它能听到它们在蛋里很微弱的叫声。它知道它们在蛋壳里姿势极其别扭，急着要把蛋壳啄破出来。因此它很镇静，说话比平时少。

当第一只小鹅刚从母鹅羽毛间伸出它深绿色的小脑袋朝四周张望时，就被夏洛看到了，它马上向大家宣布。

"我想，"它说，"我们仓底这儿的每一位都会很高兴地知道，我们的母鹅老朋友经过四个礼拜持续的努力和耐心照料，现在有些宝贝要给我们看看了。小鹅诞生啦。请允许我表示衷心的祝贺！"

"谢谢你，谢谢你，谢谢你！"母鹅不怕难为情地点头鞠躬说。

"谢谢你，谢谢你，谢谢你！"公鹅说。

"祝贺你！"威尔伯大叫，"有多少只小鹅啊？我只看到一只。"

"一共七只。"母鹅说。

"好极了！"夏洛说，"七是个幸运数字。"

"这跟幸运没有关系，"母鹅说，"这是精心照料和辛苦工作的结果。"

这时候，坦普尔顿从威尔伯的食槽底下露出鼻子。它看看弗恩，然后紧靠着墙边，小心翼翼地向母鹅爬去。大家盯住它看，因为它不受大家欢迎，不被大家信任。

"我说，"它用它那尖嗓子说起来，"你说你有七只小鹅。可原来有八个鹅蛋啊。还有一个蛋出什么事啦？它为什么没有孵出小鹅来啊？"

"我猜想这是个孵不出小鹅的蛋。"母鹅说。

"你打算把它怎么样呢？"坦普尔顿说下去，它那双圆滚滚的小眼睛盯住母鹅看。

"就给你吧，"母鹅回答说，"把它滚走，加到你那些该死的收藏品里去吧。"（坦普尔顿有这样一个嗜好，爱把农场周围不寻常的东西收来，藏在它的家里。它积攒各种东西。）

“当然，当然，当然，”公鹅说，“这个蛋你可以拿走，不过有一件事我告诉你，坦普尔顿，万一让我看到你在我这些小鹅身边探头探脑，伸出——伸出——伸出你的丑鼻子，我会给你老鼠从没挨过的最狠的打击。”公鹅张开它强壮的翅膀，扑打空气，表现它多么有力气。它又强壮又勇敢，不过事实是，母鹅公鹅都很担心这个坦普尔顿。这是完全有道理的。这老鼠不讲道德，没有良心，无所顾忌，不想别人，毫不正派，没有啮齿动物的善良天性，没有内疚，没有高尚的感情，没有交情，什么也没有。如果它咬死了小鹅能逃脱罪责，它是会咬死小鹅的——母鹅心中有数。个个心中都有数。

母鹅用它宽宽的硬嘴把那个孵不出小鹅的蛋从窝里拨出来，大家大倒胃口地看着老鼠把它滚走。连几乎什么都吃的威尔伯也吓坏了。它咕噜说："想一想吧，连一个毫无用处的老坏蛋也要！"

"老鼠到底是老鼠，"夏洛说。它发出轻轻的银铃般的笑声。"不过我的朋友们，万一那老掉牙的蛋破了，谷仓可就受不了啦。"

"什么意思？"威尔伯问道。

"我是说，由于它的气味，在这里谁也没法待下去。一个坏蛋等于一个地地道道的臭蛋。"

"我不会让它打破的，"坦普尔顿叫道，"我知道我在干什么。这样的东西我一直在摆弄。"

它把那鹅蛋推在前面，钻进它的地道不见了。它推啊推，直到成功地把它滚进食槽底下的老鼠洞里。

那天下午，等到风停了，谷仓院子静悄悄暖洋洋的，灰母鹅带着七只小鹅离开它的窝，来到外面的大世界。朱克曼先生来给威尔伯送饭时，看到了。

"哎呀，好啊，"他满面笑容地说，"让我数数看……一，二，三，四，五，六，七。一共七只鹅宝宝。那不是好极了嘛！"

7.

坏消息

威尔伯一天比一天喜欢夏洛。它和昆虫作战似乎是有道理的，是有用的。农场没有谁会说苍蝇的好话。苍蝇一辈子都在骚扰别人。牛恨它们。马讨厌它们。羊憎恶它们。朱克曼先生和太太一直抱怨它们，还装上了纱窗。

威尔伯佩服夏洛的做法，特别欣赏它在吃它们之前先让它们睡着。

“你这样做实在有头脑，夏洛。”它说。

“是的，”夏洛用它唱歌似的甜美的声音说，“我一直先麻醉它们，让它们不感到痛苦。这是我能帮的一点小小的忙。”

日子一天天过去，威尔伯越长越大。它一天大吃三顿。它舒舒服服地侧身躺上很长时间，半睡半醒，做着美梦。它身体很棒，胖了许多。一天下午，当弗恩正坐在她的凳子上时，最老的那只羊走进谷仓，停下来看威尔伯。

“你好，”它说，“我觉得你发福了。”

“是的，我想是的，”威尔伯回答说，“在我这个岁数，不断长胖是件好事。”

“反正我不羡慕你，”那老羊说，“你知道他们为什么让你长胖吗？”

“不知道，”威尔伯说。

“唉，我不想当小广播，”老羊说，“不过他们让你长胖只为了要杀你，就是这么回事。”

“他们要做什么？”威尔伯尖叫起来。弗恩在她的凳子上呆住了。

“杀你，把你变成熏肉火腿，”老羊说下去，“一到天气变得实在太冷时，几乎所有的猪年纪轻轻地就都被农民杀了。在这里，圣诞节杀你们是一种固定的阴谋活动。人人参与——勒维，朱克曼，甚至约翰·阿拉布尔。”

“阿拉布尔先生？”威尔伯哭起来，“弗恩的爸爸？”

“当然，杀猪人人帮忙。我是只老羊，一年又一年，这同样的事情看多了，都是老一套。那个阿拉布尔拿着他那支点二二口径步枪到这里，一枪……”

“别说了！”威尔伯尖叫，“我不要死！救救我，你们哪一位！救救我！”弗恩正要跳起来，听见了一个声音。

“安静点，威尔伯！”一直在听这番可怕谈话的夏洛说。

“我没法安静，”威尔伯跑过来跑过去，尖叫着说，“我不要给一枪射死。我不要死。老羊说的是真的吗，夏洛？天冷了他们要杀我，这是真的吗？”

“这个嘛，”蜘蛛弹拨着它的网，动着脑筋，“老羊在这谷仓里很久

了。它看到许多春猪来了又走了。如果它说他们打算杀你，我断定这是真的。这也是我听到过的最肮脏的勾当。有什么事人想不出来啊！”

威尔伯哇哇大哭。“我不要死，”它呻吟说，“我要活，我要活在这舒服的肥料堆上，和我所有的朋友在一起。我要呼吸美丽的空气，躺在美丽的太阳底下。”

“你发出的吵闹声实在够美丽。”老羊厉声对它说。

“我不要死！”威尔伯扑倒在地上尖叫。

“你不会死。”夏洛马上说。

“什么？真的吗？”威尔伯叫道，“谁来救我呢？”

“我救你。”夏洛说。

“怎么救？”威尔伯问道。

“这得走着瞧。不过我要救你的，你给我马上安静下来。你太孩子气了。你马上停止，别哭了！这种歇斯底里我受不了。”

8.

家里的谈话

星期日早晨，阿拉布尔先生和太太跟弗恩一起坐在厨房里吃早饭。艾弗里已经吃好，正在楼上找他的弹弓。

“你们知道吗，霍默舅舅的小鹅已经孵出来了？”弗恩问道。

“多少只？”阿拉布尔先生问道。

“七只，”弗恩回答，“蛋有八个，可其中一个没孵出小鹅来，母鹅对坦普尔顿说，这蛋它不要了，坦普尔顿可以把它拿走。”

“你说母鹅什么？”阿拉布尔太太用奇怪又担心的目光看着女儿，问道。

“它对坦普尔顿说，这蛋它不要了，”弗恩再说一遍。

“这坦普尔顿是谁？”阿拉布尔太太又问。

“是只老鼠，”弗恩回答说，“我们没有一个喜欢它。”

“你说的‘我们’是谁？”阿拉布尔太太问道。

“哦，在仓底的大伙儿啊。威尔伯，大羊小羊，母鹅公鹅小鹅，夏洛，还有我。”

“夏洛？”阿拉布尔太太说，“夏洛是谁？”

"是威尔伯最好的朋友。它聪明极了。"

"是什么样子的？"阿拉布尔太太问道。

"这——个嘛，"弗恩一边想一边回答，"它有八条腿。我想所有的蜘蛛都有八条腿。"

"夏洛是只蜘蛛？"弗恩的妈妈问道。

弗恩点点头。"一只灰色的大蜘蛛。它在威尔伯的门口顶上织了张网。它捉苍蝇吸它们的血。威尔伯对它佩服极了。"

"威尔伯真这样？"阿拉布尔太太含含糊糊地说。她看着弗恩的脸，十分担心的样子。

"噢，是的，威尔伯佩服夏洛，"弗恩说，"你知道那些小鹅孵出来那会儿，夏洛说了什么吗？"

"我一点也想不出来，"阿拉布尔太太说，"告诉我吧。"

"嗯，当第一只小鹅从母鹅底下伸出它那小脑袋的时候，我正坐在角落的那张凳子上，夏洛蹲在它的网上。它发表了一篇演讲。它说：'我想我们仓底这儿的每一位都会很高兴地知道，我们的母鹅老朋友经过四个星期不懈的努力和耐心照料，它现在有些宝贝要给我们看看了。'你不觉得，它说出这样的话来很棒吗？"

"是的，我觉得是很棒，"阿拉布尔太太说，"不过现在，弗恩，该上主日学校①去了。叫艾弗里快准备好。你可以下午再告诉我霍默舅

① 主日学校是星期日对儿童进行宗教教育的学校，大多附设在教堂里。

舅那谷仓里的事。你在那里是不是花了许多时间啊？你几乎天天下午都到那里去，对不对？”

“我喜欢那里，”弗恩回答说。她擦过嘴就上楼去了。她离开厨房以后，阿拉布尔太太小声对她的丈夫说话。

“我为弗恩担心，”她说，“你听到她嘟噜嘟噜谈那些动物了吗？说得好像它们会讲话似的。”

阿拉布尔先生格格笑。“也许它们真会说话，”他说，“我有时候也怀疑它们是不是会说话。反正不用为弗恩担心——一切只是出于她活灵活现的想象。小娃娃以为他们听到了各种东西。”

“我还是真为她担心，”阿拉布尔太太回答说，“下一回我看到多里安医生，我想问问他弗恩这事。他几乎和我们一样爱弗恩，我要让他知道，她对于那只小猪和所有事情的举动有多么古怪。我认为这不正常。你很清楚，动物不会说话的。”

阿拉布尔先生咧开嘴笑。“也许我们的耳朵没有弗恩的尖。”他说。

9.

威尔伯说大话

蜘蛛网比它看上去的样子结实。它虽然由纤细的丝织成，可是不容易坏。不过每天有那么多昆虫在它里面乱踢，等到它满是窟窿时，蜘蛛只好重新再织。夏洛喜欢在下午后半晌结网，弗恩喜欢在旁边看。有一天下午，她听到一番再有趣不过的谈话，也亲眼看到了一件怪事。

“你有毛茸茸的腿啊，夏洛，”当蜘蛛忙着结网的时候，威尔伯对它说。

“我的腿毛茸茸是有道理的，”夏洛回答说，“而且我的每条腿有七个节——基节、转节、腿节、吸跗节、胫节、跖节、跗节。”

威尔伯一下子坐直了身子。“你在开玩笑，”它说。

“不，我一点不开玩笑。”

“请把这些名称再说一遍好吗？刚才那一遍我没听清楚。”

“基节、转节、腿节、吸跗节、胫节、跖节、跗节。”

“天啊！”威尔伯低头看着自己的胖腿。“我想我的腿没有七节。”

“这个嘛，”夏洛说，“你和我过的生活不同。你用不着结网。结网是真正的腿上功夫。”

“我要想结网也能结，”威尔伯说大话，“我只是不结罢了。”

“那就让我们看看你结网吧，”夏洛说。弗恩轻轻地格格笑，眼睛都睁大了，对小猪充满了爱意。

“好吧，”威尔伯回答说，“你给我指点一下，我来结一个。结网一定很好玩。我怎么开头呢？”

“深深吸口气！”夏洛微笑着说。威尔伯深深吸了口气。“现在你能爬多高就爬多高，像这样。”夏洛飞快地爬上门顶。威尔伯爬到肥料堆的顶上。

“很好！”夏洛说，“现在用你的吐丝器吐丝，然后跳到空中，一路下来时吐出丝来拉着你。”

威尔伯犹豫了一下，接着悬空往下跳。它赶快往身后瞧，看后面是不是有根绳子拉住它不让它掉下去，可是它身后似乎一无所有，紧接着就扑通一声落到地上了。“哎哟！”它哼哼叫了一声。

夏洛哈哈大笑，笑得它的网晃来晃去。

“我做错什么了？”小猪从摔跤中缓过气来，问道。

“什么也没做错，”夏洛说，“这个尝试做得很好。”

“我想再试一次，”威尔伯开心地说，“我认为我要的是根绳子把我拉住。”

小猪走到外面它的猪栏去。“喂，坦普尔顿，你在那里吗？”它叫道。老鼠从食槽底下伸出它的脑袋。

“有没有一小段绳子借给我用用？”威尔伯问道，“我要用它来结网。”

“当然有，”坦普尔顿回答说，它就爱收藏绳子。“一点没问题。你要什么给你什么。”它爬进老鼠洞，把鹅蛋推开，叼着一条肮脏的白色旧绳子上来。威尔伯仔细看看绳子。

“正合适，”它说，“你把一头拴到我的尾巴上好吗，坦普尔顿？”

威尔伯蹲低身子，让它那条细细的弯尾巴对着老鼠。坦普尔顿抓住绳子，绕在小猪尾巴尖上，打了两个简单的半结。夏洛乐滋滋地看着。它和弗恩一样实在太喜欢威尔伯，它的臭猪圈和发臭的食物引来夏洛需要的苍蝇。看到威尔伯不是一个临阵脱逃的胆小鬼，愿意再试一次结网，它为它感到骄傲。

老鼠、蜘蛛和小姑娘就这样看着威尔伯再次爬上肥料堆顶上，精力充沛，充满信心。

“大家看好了！”威尔伯大叫一声，用尽全身力气，头向前腾空跳下去。绳子拖在它身后。可是它忘了把绳子另一头拴在什么东西上面，绳子一点不起作用，威尔伯扑通一声落在地上，跌疼了。眼泪从它眼睛里涌出来。坦普尔顿龇着大牙笑。夏洛只是静静地坐着。过了一会儿它开口了。

“你不会结网，威尔伯，我劝你就打消这个念头吧。要结网你少了两样东西。”

“什么东西？”威尔伯难过地问。

“你少了一个吐丝器，你也少了这门技术。不过高兴起来吧，你用不上网。朱克曼先生一天供你三顿大餐。你干吗要费心捉东西吃呢？”

威尔伯叹气。“你真是比我聪明伶俐得多，夏洛。我想我只是要出风头。我这是活该。”

坦普尔顿解下它的绳子，拿回家去了。夏洛回过头去结它的网。

“你用不着太难过，威尔伯，”它说，“没有多少动物会结网的。连人类也织不过蜘蛛，虽然他们自以为织得很好，想尽了办法。你听说过昆斯伯罗大桥①吗？”

威尔伯摇摇头。“是张网吗？”

“有点像，”夏洛说，“不过你知道，人类用了多长时间才把它造出

① 昆斯伯罗大桥（Queensborough），在纽约皇后区，是曼哈顿中城跨东河连接皇后区的干桥。

来吗？整整八个年头。天啊，等那么长，我都要饿死了。我一个晚上就结成一张网。”

“在昆斯伯罗大桥上，人类捉什么呢——甲虫吗？”威尔伯问道。

“不是，”夏洛说，“他们不捉任何东西。他们只是在桥上走过来走过去，老以为另一边有更好的东西。如果他们在这桥顶上倒过头来静静地等着，也许真有好东西会来。可是不——人类每分钟都向前冲啊，冲啊，冲啊。我很高兴我是一只坐网的蜘蛛。”

“坐网是什么意思？”威尔伯问道。

“意思是我大部分时间一动不动地坐在网上，不到处走。好东西我一看就知道，我的网是样好东西。我固定不动，等着东西送上门来。趁机可以好好想想。”

“这么说来，我想本猪是坐窝的，”小猪说，“不管我愿意不愿意，我都得待在这里。你知道今天晚上我实在想上哪里去吗？”

“上哪里去？”

“上一片森林去找山毛榉果子、块菌、甘美的树根，用我了不起的有力的鼻子拱开树叶，在地里又嗅又找，闻啊，闻啊，闻啊，闻啊……”

“你自己的气味就够闻的，”一只刚进来的小羊羔说，“我老远就闻到你了。你是这里最臭的东西。”

威尔伯侧着头。它的眼睛湿润了。夏洛看到它那么难过，狠狠地训那小羊羔。

“别烦威尔伯，”它说，“考虑到它的环境，它完全有理由有气味。

你自己也不是一捆香豌豆。而且你打断了一场非常愉快的谈话。我们刚才给它那么粗暴无礼地打断的时候，威尔伯，我们正谈到哪里啊？”

“噢，我不记得了，”威尔伯说，“没关系。我们歇一会儿，不要再谈了，夏洛。我很困了。你继续结你的网吧，我躺下来看你结网。这是一个美丽的傍晚。”威尔伯躺下来伸懒腰，长长叹了口气。

暮色笼罩了朱克曼的农场，带来了一种和平的感觉。弗恩知道晚饭时间要到了，可是她舍不得离开。燕子无声地扑动翅膀，在门口飞进飞出，给它们的小鸟带来食物。大路对面，一只小鸟在唱：唧唧喳，唧唧喳！勒维在苹果树下面坐下来，点燃他的烟斗；牲口吸着它们熟悉的强烈的烟草味。威尔伯听到树蛙咕咕叫，还有偶尔的厨房关门声。所有这些声音让它感到舒适和快活，因为它爱生活，爱成为夏夜世界的一份子。可它正躺在那里时，忽然想起老羊告诉它的话。关于死的想法来到它的脑子里，它吓得发起抖来。

“夏洛？”它轻轻地说。

“什么事啊，威尔伯？”

“我不要死。”

“你当然不要。”夏洛安慰它说。

“我就是爱谷仓这里，”威尔伯说，“我爱这里所有的东西。”

“你当然爱，”夏洛说，“我们全都爱。”

那母鹅来了，后面跟着它的七只小鹅。它们伸长自己的小脖子，一直不停地嘘嘘嘘吹着悦耳的声音，像是一小队风笛手。威尔伯满心爱意地谛听这嘘嘘声。

“夏洛？”它又说。

“什么事？”蜘蛛问它。

“你答应过不让他们来杀我，你这话是当真吗？”

“我这辈子说的话，没有比这话更当真的了，我不会让你死，威尔伯。”

“可你怎样救我呢？”威尔伯问道，对这一点，它的好奇心非常之大。

“这个嘛，”夏洛含糊地说，“我也说不准。不过我在盘算。”

“那太好了，”威尔伯说，“盘算得怎样啦，夏洛？盘算得差不多了吗？盘算得顺利吗？”威尔伯又哆嗦了，不过夏洛很冷静，很镇定。

“噢，很顺利，”它轻松地说，“这个计划还在初级阶段，没有完全定下来，不过我在盘算。”

“你是在什么时候做你的计划的？”威尔伯求着问它。

“在我头朝下吊在我那网顶的时候。我就是在这种时候想我的事情的，因为这时候全部血都流到我的脑袋里。”

“要是我能有什么办法帮帮你，我就太高兴了。”

“噢，我要独自把办法想出来，”夏洛说，“我独自想能够想得更加好。”

“那好吧，”威尔伯说，“不过要是有什么事我能帮上忙，不管事情多么小，请一定告诉我。”

“好的，”夏洛回答说，“你必须尽力打起精神来。我要你睡得足足的，不要担心。永远不要紧张，永远不要担心！把你的食物嚼嚼烂，把它们吃吃光，只除了必须给坦普尔顿留下够它吃的那一点。胖起来，过得好——这就是你能给我帮的忙了。保持健康，不要失去勇气。你认为你明白了吗？”

“是的，我明白了。”威尔伯说。

“那就去睡你的觉吧，”夏洛说，“睡觉顶重要。”

威尔伯于是快步走到它的猪圈最黑暗的角落，倒头躺下来。它闭上眼睛，可转眼间它又开口了。

“夏洛？”它说。

“什么事，威尔伯？”

“我可不可以到外面食槽去，看看我是不是还留下一点晚饭？我想我还留下了一点儿土豆泥。”

“很好，”夏洛说，“不过我要你马上回来睡觉。”

威尔伯赶紧起来，跑着上外面它的猪栏去。

“慢点跑，慢点跑！”夏洛说，“永远不要急急忙忙，永远不要担心！”

威尔伯停了下来，然后慢慢走到它的食槽那里。它找到一点土豆，小心地嚼烂，吞下去，又走回来睡觉。它闭上眼睛，沉默了一会儿。

“夏洛？”它又悄悄地说。

“什么事？”

“我可以喝一口牛奶吗？我想我的食槽里还留下几滴牛奶。”

“不，食槽是干的，我要你睡觉。别说话了！闭上你的眼睛，好好睡觉吧！”

威尔伯闭上眼睛。弗恩从她的凳子上站起来，动身回家，她的心里充满了她刚才看到和听到的东西。

“晚安，夏洛！”威尔伯说。

“晚安，威尔伯！”

沉默了一会儿。

“晚安，夏洛！”

“晚安，威尔伯！”

“晚安！”

“晚安！”

10.

臭弹爆炸

一天又一天，蜘蛛头朝下，等着一个好主意来到它的脑瓜子里。一个小时又一个小时，它坐在那里一动不动，冥思苦想。答应过威尔伯救它的命以后，蜘蛛决定说到做到，决不食言。

夏洛天生耐心好。它从经验当中知道，只要等得够久，苍蝇自然会飞到它的网上来；它断定，威尔伯的问题也一样，只要等得够久，好主意一定会来到它的脑瓜子里。

最后，在接近七月中旬的一个早晨，这主意真来了。“哎呀，多么简单啊！”它对自己说，“要救威尔伯的命，办法就是给朱克曼玩个把戏。我既然能戏弄一只甲虫，”夏洛想，“我就一定能戏弄一个人。人没有甲虫机灵。”

就在这节骨眼上，威尔伯走进它的猪栏。

“你在想什么啊，夏洛？”它问道。

“我正在想，”蜘蛛说，“人是阿木林。”

“‘阿木林’是什么意思？”

“就是傻瓜，容易上当受骗。”夏洛说。

“那真是太谢天谢地了，”威尔伯回答一声，随即在它的围栏阴影里躺下来，呼呼睡着了。可蜘蛛醒着，充满深情地看着它，做它的计划。夏天已经过去一半。它知道时间紧迫了。

那天早晨，正当威尔伯睡着的时候，艾弗里走进朱克曼家的前院，后面跟着弗恩。艾弗里手里拿着一只活青蛙。弗恩头发上戴着一个雏菊花环。两个孩子跑到厨房去。

“来得正好，吃一块果酱馅饼。”朱克曼太太说。

“你看看我的青蛙。”艾弗里说着，把青蛙放在水池边的滴水板上，伸出手来拿馅饼。

“把那东西拿到外面去！”朱克曼太太连忙说。

“它太热了，”弗恩说，“它差不多要热死了，我说那青蛙。”

“它没死，”艾弗里说，“它让我搔它的眉心。”青蛙猛跳起来，落到朱克曼太太那洗碟盆的肥皂水里。

“你把你的馅饼弄到身上了，”弗恩说，“我可以到鸡棚去找蛋吗，伊迪丝舅妈？”

“出去吧出去吧，你们两个！别去惊动那些鸡！”

“什么东西都弄上馅饼了，”弗恩大叫，“他把他前面弄得都是馅饼了。”

“来吧，青蛙！”艾弗里叫道。他把他的青蛙捞出来。青蛙踢着腿，把肥皂水溅到馅饼上面。

"又是一场灾难！"弗恩呻吟说。

"我们去荡秋千吧！"艾弗里说。

两个孩子跑到谷仓去。

朱克曼先生有全县最好的秋千。它是用一根又粗又长的绳索拴在北边门口的横梁上做成的。绳索下面一端的头上打了个大结，人可以骑坐在上面。荡这秋千不用人推，你只要爬梯子上堆干草的阁楼就行。抓住绳索，站在阁楼边朝下看，真会让人吓得头晕。然后你两腿夹住绳结坐在上面，鼓起全部勇气，深深吸口气，往下一跳。你仿佛一下子要掉落到下面离得很远的谷仓地板上去，可绳索猛地把你拽住，你用一分钟一英里的速度飞出谷仓门，风在你的眼睛、耳朵和头发间呼啸。这时候你飞上天空，看到天上的云彩，绳索会旋转，你也跟着绳索一起旋转。接着你从半空落下来，落啊落啊，然后又飞回谷仓里面，几乎飞上干草阁楼，然后又飞出去（这一回没飞那么远），然后又飞进来（这一回没飞那么高），然后又飞出去，然后又飞进来，然后又飞出去，然后又飞进来；直到最后你跳下来，落到地上，让别人来玩。

附近几英里范围内那些做妈妈的对朱克曼家这个秋千都提心吊胆。她们生怕孩子会从秋千上摔下来。可是没有一个孩子摔下来过。孩子们挂在东西上面抓住它们时，几乎总比他们父母想的要牢靠得多。

艾弗里把青蛙放进衣袋，爬上干草阁楼。"上一回我荡秋千时，几乎撞上了谷仓的一只燕子。"他叫道。

"把那只青蛙拿出来！"弗恩吩咐他。

艾弗里骑在绳索上，猛地往下一跳。他连同青蛙和身上所有的东西飞出了门，飞上了天。接着他又飞进谷仓。

“你的舌头发紫了！”弗恩大叫。

“你的也是！”艾弗里叫道，连同青蛙又飞出去。

“我衣服里有干草！弄得人痒痒的！”弗恩叫道。

“抓抓它吧！”艾弗里大叫，又飞回来。

“轮到我了，”弗恩说，“跳下来！”

“弗恩身上痒兮兮！”艾弗里唱道。

他跳下来，把秋千扔上阁楼给他妹妹。弗恩闭紧眼睛，往下一跳。她感觉到落下去时头都晕了，感觉到秋千把她带着飞走。等她睁开眼睛看到蓝天时，都几乎又飞进门里了。

他们轮着玩了一个钟头。

两个孩子荡够秋千后，一路朝牧场走去，采野悬钩子吃。他们的舌头从紫色变成红色。弗恩咬到一个悬钩子，里面有一只怪味道的甲虫，大倒胃口。艾弗里找到一个空糖果盒，把青蛙放进去。青蛙荡了一个上午秋千，似乎累了。两个孩子又慢慢地向谷仓走回来。他们也累了，走不动了。

“让我们在树上造房子吧，”艾弗里建议说，“我要和我的青蛙住到树上去。”

“我去看威尔伯。”弗恩说。

他们爬过围栏来到小路上，懒洋洋地朝猪圈走过来。威尔伯听见他们走来，站起身子。

艾弗里注意到蜘蛛网，走近一点，他看到了夏洛。

“嘿，看那大蜘蛛！”他说，“大极了。”

“别碰它！”弗恩吩咐说，“你已经有青蛙了——还不够吗？”

“这是只呱呱叫的蜘蛛，我要捉到它。”艾弗里说。他打开糖果盒盖。接着他折了一根树枝。“我要把那老蜘蛛敲到盒子里。”他说。

威尔伯一见这情景，心都停止跳动了。万一这小家伙捉住夏洛，夏洛就完了。

“你快住手，艾弗里！”弗恩大叫。

艾弗里单腿站在猪栏的围栏上。他正要举起树枝去打夏洛，一下子没站稳，摇摇晃晃，翻身倒了下来，落在威尔伯的食槽上。食槽一侧，扑通一声翻倒了。那个鹅蛋正好在底下，闷声爆开，一下子臭气熏天。

弗恩哇哇尖叫。艾弗里跳起来。空气里全是那个坏蛋的臭气。正在洞里休息的坦普尔顿跑进了谷仓。

“我的天！”艾弗里尖叫，“我的天！多么臭啊。我们离开这儿吧！”

弗恩哭了起来。她捂住鼻子朝房子跑。艾弗里在她后面跟着，也捂着鼻子。夏洛看到他走了，这才放了心。真是死里逃生啊。

这个上午后半晌，牲口从牧场回来了——大羊小羊、公鹅母鹅和七只小鹅。它们闻到那可怕的臭气都怨声载道，威尔伯得把这件事讲

一遍又一遍，艾弗里这小家伙怎样打算捉夏洛，幸亏这蛋破了，臭气及时把他熏走。“正是这个坏蛋救了夏洛的命。”威尔伯说。

母鹅由于在这重大事件中也有一份功劳，十分得意。“我很高兴这蛋没有孵出小鹅来。”它叽里咕噜说。

坦普尔顿失去它这心爱的蛋，自然十分伤心。不过它也禁不住夸口。“积攒东西也有好报，”它用傲慢的口气说，“老鼠就知道不定有什么东西在某个时候会派上用场，因此我从来不扔东西。”

“很好，”一只小羊说，“这整件事情让夏洛总算太平无事，可我们大伙儿呢？这气味实在叫人受不了。谁高兴住在一个满是臭蛋气味的谷仓里啊？”

“别担心，多闻闻就会习惯的。”坦普尔顿说。它坐起来，拉拉它的长胡子，摆出一副圣哲模样，然后爬开，上垃圾场去了。

中饭时间，勒维给威尔伯送来一桶饲料，可离开猪圈还有几步远就一下子站住了。他闻闻空气，做了个鬼脸。

“真是碰到雷打了！”他说。他把桶子放下来，捡起艾弗里丢下的树枝，把食槽重新翻过来。“都是那些老鼠干的！”他说，“呸！我早知道老鼠在食槽下面不会安分。我真厌恶这些老鼠。”

勒维把威尔伯的食槽拖过猪栏，踢了点土到老鼠洞里，把破蛋连同坦普尔顿其他所有财产全部埋了。然后他捡起桶子。威尔伯站在食槽里，饿得流口水。勒维把饲料倒进去。泔脚黏糊糊地泼在小猪的眼里甚至耳朵上。威尔伯呕呕地叫。它大口大口地吃，大口大口地喝，大口大口地吃，大口大口地喝，发出稀哩哗啦、呼噜哗啦的声音，急着要一口气吃个精光。这是一顿美食——脱脂牛奶、麦麸、吃剩的煎饼、半个炸面圈、西葫芦皮、两片隔夜吐司、三分之一个姜味小甜饼、一条鱼尾巴、一块橘子皮、面条汤里的几根面条、一杯榨过汁后的椰子渣、一个不知什么时候的啫喱卷筒蛋糕、垃圾桶的一张衬纸、一勺子悬钩子果冻。

威尔伯闷头大吃。它打算留下半根面条和几滴牛奶给坦普尔顿。

接着它想起老鼠救了夏洛的命，夏洛正在想办法救它的命。于是它留下了整根面条而不是半根。

现在破蛋已经埋掉，臭气没有了，谷仓的气味又好起来。下午过去，傍晚来临。影子拉长。傍晚凉爽可爱的空气透进门窗。夏洛蹲在它的网上，闷着头吃一只苍蝇，想着未来的事。过了一会儿，它忙碌了起来。

它爬下来到网中央，在那里开始咬断几根丝。它缓慢却又不停地结网，这时候其他动物都打盹了。没有一个，甚至包括母鹅，注意到它在工作。威尔伯深深陷在它软绵绵的床上呼呼大睡。那些小鹅在另一头它们心爱的角落里希哩希哩地吹着夜曲。

夏洛把它原来的网拉掉一大片，网当中开了天窗。然后它开始织起什么东西来，代替它拉掉的丝。当老鼠半夜从垃圾场回来时，蜘蛛还在织个不停。

11.

奇迹

第二天有雾。农场里什么东西都湿嗒嗒的。草地看上去像一张魔毯。那片芦笋地像一片银光闪闪的森林。

在雾天的早晨，夏洛的网真是一件美丽的东西。这天早晨，每一根细丝点缀着几十颗小水珠。网在阳光中闪闪烁烁，组成一个神秘可爱的图案，像一块纤细的面纱。连对美不太感兴趣的勒维来给小猪送早饭时，也不由得注意到这张网。他注意到它有多么显眼，他注意到它有多么大，织得有多么精细。他再看一眼时，看到了一样东西让他不觉放下桶子。瞧，在网中央，整整齐齐地织着几个大字，这是一句话。它写的是：

王牌猪

勒维都要瘫下来了。他用手擦擦眼睛，更加一个劲地盯住夏洛的网看。

"我看到了什么啦，"他喃喃地说。他跪下来祷告了两句。接着他压根儿忘了威尔伯的早饭，快步跑回屋里去叫朱克曼先生。

“我想你最好到猪圈去一下。”他说。

“出什么事了？”朱克曼先生问道，“小猪出事啦？”

“不不不是，”勒维说，“你还是自己去看看吧。”

两个人默默地走到威尔伯的猪栏边。勒维指着门上的蜘蛛网。“你看到我看到的东西了吗？”他问道。

朱克曼先生看着网上的字。接着他读出来“王牌猪”。接着他看勒维。接着他们两个开始发抖。夏洛干了一个通宵，瞌睡沉沉，看到这番情景微笑起来。威尔伯过来，就站在网下。

“王牌猪！”勒维低声嘟囔说。

“王牌猪！”朱克曼先生悄悄地说。他们把威尔伯看了又看，看了又看，看了半天。接着他们看夏洛。

“你想，不会是那蜘蛛……”朱克曼先生开口说——可他摇摇头，没把话说完。相反，他庄重地回到屋里去对他太太说了。“伊迪丝，出怪事了。”他有气无力地说。他走进起居室，坐下来，朱克曼太太跟着进来。

“我有事要告诉你，伊迪丝，”他说，“你最好坐下。”

朱克曼太太跌坐在椅子上。她看上去面色苍白，怕得不得了。

“伊迪丝，”他拼命保持着平静，说，“我想，你必须得说，我们有一只极不寻常的小猪。”

朱克曼太太脸上露出完全困惑不解的神情。“霍默·朱克曼，天啊，你到底在说什么啊？”她说。

“这是一件非常严重的事情，伊迪丝，”他回答说，“我们的小猪根本不是一只普通的猪。”

“这小猪有什么不寻常啊？”朱克曼太太问道，她正开始从惊吓中恢复过来。

“这个嘛，我还没真正弄明白，”朱克曼先生说，“不过我们已经得到一个信号，伊迪丝——一个神秘的信号。这农场已经出现了一个奇迹。谷仓底的门口有个大蜘蛛网，就在猪圈上面，今天早晨勒维去喂小猪，他注意到了这个网，因为有雾，你也知道，在雾里蜘蛛网是很醒目的。就在网的正当中有这样三个大字：‘王牌猪’。这几个字是织在网上的。它们真真切切是网的一部分，伊迪丝。我知道这件事，因为我亲自到那里去看了。这几个字是‘王牌猪’，再清楚不过。一点也错不了。一个奇迹已经出现，一个信号已经降落人间，就降落在这里，就降落在我们的农场，我们有一只非比寻常的猪。”

“得了，”朱克曼太太说，“看来你有点不正常。我觉得我们有一只非比寻常的蜘蛛。”

“噢，不对，”朱克曼先生说，“非比寻常的是小猪。网当中的大字是这么说的。”

“也许是这样，”朱克曼太太说，“反正我一定得去看看那只蜘蛛。”

“它只是一只普普通通的灰色蜘蛛，”朱克曼先生说。

他们站起来，一起到威尔伯的猪栏去。“你看到了吗，伊迪丝？它只是一只普普通通的灰色蜘蛛。”

威尔伯很高兴得到那么多关注。勒维还站在那里，加上朱克曼先生和太太，他们三个站在那里近一个小时了，翻来覆去读网上的字，看威尔伯。

夏洛很高兴它的把戏奏效。它坐在那里一动不动，听这几个人说话。当一只小苍蝇撞到网上，就撞在“猪”字旁边时，夏洛连忙下来，把它捆好带走了。

过了一会儿雾散了，网干了，那几个字不那么清楚了。朱克曼夫妇和勒维回家。就在他们离开猪圈前，朱克曼先生最后看了威尔伯一眼。

“你们知道，”他用郑重其事的声音说，“我已经想通了，我们这只小猪是一只特级好猪。它是一只王牌猪。这猪是天字第一号的。你看到它的肩膀多么棒吗，勒维？”

“当然。我当然看到了，”勒维说，“我一直注意这小猪。它真是只王牌猪。”

“它个子长，皮光滑，”朱克曼先生说。

“一点没错，”勒维同意，“它光滑到了极点。它是一只王牌猪。”

朱克曼先生回到家，脱下工作服，穿上最好的衣服。然后他上了汽车，开到牧师家。他在那里待了一个小时，向牧师解释，说他的农场出现了奇迹。

“到现在为止，”朱克曼先生说，“这个奇迹世界上一共只有四个人知道——我一个，我太太伊迪丝一个，我的雇工勒维一个，还有一个就是你。”

“不要再告诉任何人，”牧师说，“我们还不知道这是什么意思，不过我也许会领悟出来，如果我领悟出来了，在下一个星期日布道时，我会作出解释。毫无疑问，你是有一只最不寻常的猪。我打算在我的布道中提到它，指出这个社区有一只珍奇动物光临了。对了，这猪有名字吗？”

“当然有，”朱克曼先生说，“我的小外甥女叫它威尔伯。我这小外甥女是个十分古怪的孩子——满脑子怪念头。她用奶瓶喂养过这小猪，小猪一个月大的时候，我从她那里把小猪买了下来。”

他同牧师握握手，离开了。

要保密是很难的。离星期日还有好几天，消息却已经在全县传开了。朱克曼家的一个蜘蛛网出现了征兆这件事，简直无人不晓。个个都知道了朱克曼家有只王牌猪。周围多少英里的人赶来看威尔伯，读夏洛的网上那几个大字。朱克曼家的车道上，从早到晚满是小汽车大卡车——福特车、雪佛莱汽车、别克车、通用小卡车、普利茅斯汽车、史蒂倍克汽车、帕卡德汽车、带螺旋转动装置的德索托、带火箭发动机的奥尔兹汽车、吉普旅行车、庞蒂亚克汽车。王牌猪的消息一直传到山里，农民乘轻便马车和平板马车嗒嗒嗒地赶来，在威尔伯的猪圈

前站上一个小时又一个小时，瞻仰这只奇迹般的小猪。大家异口同声地说，他们一辈子都没见过这样一只小猪。

当弗恩告诉妈妈，说艾弗里曾经想用树枝打朱克曼家的蜘蛛时，阿拉布尔太太非常吃惊，不让艾弗里吃饭就勒令他去睡觉，以此作为惩罚。

接下来几天，朱克曼先生为接待来访的人忙得不可开交，连他的农场上的活都忘了。现在他一直穿着他最好的衣服——早晨一起床就穿上。朱克曼太太给威尔伯准备特殊的伙食。勒维修了脸剪了发，他的主要任务就是当人们参观时喂小猪吃东西。

朱克曼先生吩咐勒维给威尔伯加餐，从一天三顿改为一天四顿。

朱克曼家接待来客太忙，忘掉了农场上其他的事情。黑刺莓熟了，朱克曼太太来不及做黑刺莓酱。玉米地需要锄草了，勒维找不到工夫锄草。

星期日教堂坐满了人。牧师向大家解释那个奇迹。他说蜘蛛网上的字证明，人类必须时刻注意奇迹的降临。

一句话，朱克曼家的猪圈成了吸引人的中心。弗恩很高兴，因为她觉得夏洛的把戏起了作用，威尔伯的性命可能保得住。不过她发现谷仓现在一点也不那么讨人喜欢——人太多了。她更喜欢她能够独自一个人跟她那些动物在一起的日子。

12.

会议

在夏洛的网上出现大字几天以后的一个傍晚，蜘蛛召集仓底的所有动物开会。

“我现在点名了。威尔伯？”

“到！”小猪说。

“公鹅？”

“到，到，到！”公鹅说。

“你这样叫，听上去像是三只公鹅，”夏洛咕噜说，“你为什么不能只说一声‘到’呢？你为什么说什么都要重复呢？”

“这是我的习——习——习惯。”公鹅回答。

“母鹅？”夏洛说。

“到，到，到！”母鹅回答。夏洛瞪了瞪它。

“小鹅，一到七？”

“哔——哔——哔！”“哔——哔——哔！”“哔——哔——哔！”“哔——哔——哔！”“哔——哔——哔！”“哔——哔——哔！”“哔——哔——哔！”七只小鹅一只只地说。

“这倒有点像开大会了，”夏洛说，“谁听了都会以为，我们有三只公鹅，三只母鹅，二十一只小鹅。羊？”

“到——噢——噢！”所有的羊同时回答。

“小羊羔？”

“到——噢——噢！”所有的小羊羔同时回答。

“坦普尔顿？”

没有回答。

“坦普尔顿？”

没有回答。

“好，除了老鼠，我们全到齐了，”夏洛说，“我想没有它，我们也可以把这个会开起来。现在，你们大家一定都注意到了我们这里这几天发生的事。我在网上赞美威尔伯的字大家看到了。朱克曼家的人相信了，其他的人也相信了。朱克曼先生认为威尔伯是一只不寻常的猪，因此他不会想要杀它吃它。我想我的把戏大概会奏效，威尔伯的性命可以保住。”

“万岁！”全场欢呼。

“非常感谢你们，”夏洛说，“现在我请大家来开会，是要听听大家的建议。我要让这个网有新花样。人们一个劲儿地老读着‘**王牌猪**’这三个字都读厌了。如果谁想得出另一句话，我很高兴把它织在网上。对于这个新横幅，谁有什么建议吗？”

“‘细皮肥猪’怎么样？”一只小羊问道。

"不好，"夏洛说，"这听上去像油腻的菜名。"

"'了不起，了不起，了不起'怎么样？"那母鹅说。

"去掉两个'了不起'，只留下一个'了不起'倒很不错，"夏洛说，"我想'了不起'会给朱克曼先生留下深刻的印象。"

"不过夏洛，"威尔伯说，"可我并不了不起。"

"这一点儿也没关系，"夏洛回答说，"一丁点也没关系。看到印出来的东西，发表出来的东西，人们都会相信的。这里有谁知道'了不起'这个字眼怎么写吗？"

"依我想，"公鹅说，"'了'字是一横一钩一竖一钩，最后这个钩要长，然后跳过去到'不'——'不'——'不'……"

"怎么，你以为我是个什么蹦蹦跳跳的杂技演员吗？"夏洛愤慨地说，"在我的网上织这样一个字眼，那我就得害上圣维特斯舞蹈病。"

"对不起，对不起，对不起。"公鹅说。

接着最老的那只羊发言了："要救威尔伯的命，我赞成在网上要有新花样。如果夏洛找新字眼需要帮忙，我想从我们的朋友坦普尔顿那里可以找到。这老鼠经常去垃圾场，有机会接触到旧杂志。它可以啃下一点广告，叼到仓底这儿来，夏洛就有点什么字眼可以抄抄了。"

"好主意，"夏洛说，"不过我说不准坦普尔顿肯不肯帮忙。你们知道它是怎么个家伙……它一向只顾自己，从来不想别人。"

"我打赌我能让它帮忙，"老羊说，"我会引诱它卑劣的本能，这种卑劣的本能，它多的是。瞧它来了。我跟它说话时，大家不要响！。"

老鼠照它的老样子走进谷仓——贴着墙边爬。

“什么事？”看到所有的动物聚在一起，它问道。

“我们在开头头会议，”老羊回答说。

“好了，散会吧！”坦普尔顿说，“开会让我心烦。”老鼠开始爬墙边挂着的绳子。

“听我说，”老羊说，“下一回你上垃圾场去，坦普尔顿，你啃点杂志带回来好吗？夏洛需要新字眼织在网上，好救威尔伯的命。”

“让它死掉算了，”老鼠说，“我才不在乎呢。”

“到冬天你就在乎了，”老羊说，“到一月，早晨只有零度，你就在乎了，那时候威尔伯不在了，没有人会再送来一桶热乎乎的泔脚倒在食槽里。威尔伯吃剩的东西是你的主要食物来源，坦普尔顿。这一点你是知道的。威尔伯的食物就是你的食物，因此，威尔伯的命运和你的命运息息相关。要是威尔伯给杀了，它的食槽会天天都是空空的，你就要瘦而又瘦，肚子瘪得我们可以穿过它看到另一边的东西。”

坦普尔顿听了，胡子抖了起来。

“你的话也许对，”它粗声说，“明天下午我上垃圾场去一趟。要是能找到杂志，我啃点纸片带回来。”

“谢谢你，”夏洛说，“现在散会。我要忙一个晚上了。我得把网拆散。织上‘**了不起**’几个字。”

威尔伯脸都红了。“可我并不了不起，夏洛。我只是普普通通一只猪。”

“可我觉得你很了不起，”夏洛甜甜地回答说，“这就行了。你是我最好的朋友，我觉得你了不起。现在别争了，去睡你的觉吧！”

13.

进展顺利

深夜，当其他动物睡觉时，夏洛还在它的网上干活。它首先拆掉靠近中心的几根圆线，留下辐线支撑整张网。它这样工作，八条腿帮了大忙。它的牙齿也帮了忙。它爱结网，是结网的专家。等到它把不要的线拆掉，它的网就成了这个样子：

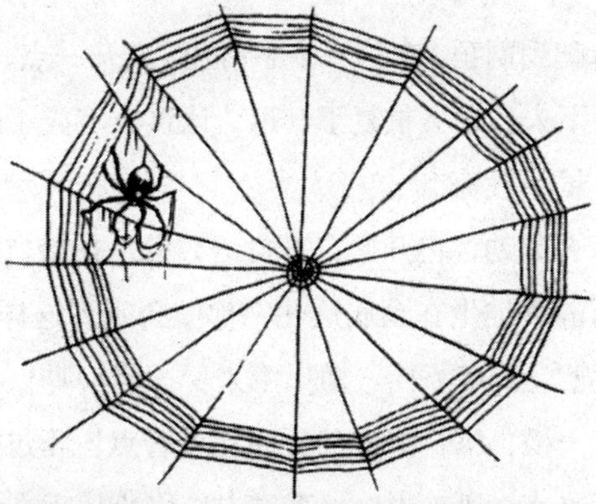

一只蜘蛛能吐好几种丝。它用粗的干丝做底线，用有黏性的丝做捕捉昆虫的线——它们会粘住昆虫，把它们捉住。夏洛决定用它的干

丝织出新的字。

"如果我用有黏性的丝织'**了不起**'这几个字，"它想，"甲虫来了就会粘在上面，把字弄坏。"

"现在让我想想，第一个字是'**了**'。"

夏洛爬上网顶左边。它把它的吐丝器晃到位，吐出丝来，横着过去，然后向左斜下来，到一半的地方往下直落，到了底下，又向左回上去一点。这就织出了一个"了"字。不过夏洛还不满意。它爬到上面去再吐丝，就吐在第一次织的字旁边，把整个字从头再来一遍。这么一来，这个字就不是单线而是双线了。"我把几个字都织成双线，它们就更醒目了。"

"现在来写'不'字。"

于是它重新爬到网顶，在第一个字右边，离开一点，开始吐丝，横过去，向左角斜下去。它又重复了一遍，让这个字成了双线……它的八条腿帮着忙，忙个没完。

夏洛干得那么起劲，它开始自言自语，像是在给自己打气。如果那天晚上你碰巧静静地坐在仓底这儿，你就会听到这样的话：

"现在轮到织'起'字了！一横！下来！一竖！哔！接上！很好！再一横！下去！一横！哔！好样的！现在稳着点！爬过去！接上！一撇下去！现在上来点，到右边！一直过去！停止！现在向右边翘起一点！好！现在回上去！一横！一竖！现在到左边！再一横！爬过去！好了！别急，保持那些线连在一起！现在织出'起'字最后一笔！下来！哔！横过去！翘上去一点！整个字再来一次！好样的！”

就这样，蜘蛛自言自语地干它辛苦的工作。等到全部完工，它觉得饿了，吃了一只原先留着的小甲虫。最后它睡觉了。

第二天早晨威尔伯起来，站在那个网底下。它呼吸着早晨的空气。一滴滴露水对着太阳光，使得蜘蛛网十分显眼，让人看得清清楚楚。当勒维送来早饭时，漂亮的小猪站在那里，在它头顶上，几个大字一笔一画织得整整齐齐，写的是：**了不起**。又是一个奇迹。

勒维连忙奔过去叫朱克曼先生。朱克曼先生连忙奔过去叫朱克曼太太。朱克曼太太连忙奔过去打电话叫阿拉布尔先生和太太。阿拉布尔先生和太太连忙爬上他们的卡车开着赶来。他们全都站在猪圈前面，抬头看着蜘蛛网，读那几个字，读了又读，这时威尔伯真正觉得了不起，静静地站着，挺起它的胸，把猪鼻子晃过来晃过去。

“了不起！”朱克曼先生满心欢喜，低声赞美说，“伊迪丝，你最好给《周报》记者打个电话，告诉他出了什么大事。他会想知道这件事的。他会把摄影师带来。整个州没有一只猪有我们这只猪这样了不起。”

消息一下子传开。如今威尔伯“了不起”了。当初它是“王牌猪”时来看过它的那些人又回来看它了。

那天下午，朱克曼先生去挤牛奶和打扫牛棚的时候还在想，我有了一只多么了不起的猪啊。

“勒维！”他叫道，“不要再把牛粪扔到猪圈去了。我有的是只了不起的猪。我要这只猪天天睡干净发亮的干麦草。你明白吗？”

“明白，老板，”勒维说。

“还有，”朱克曼先生说，“我要你给威尔伯做一个板条箱。我决定九月六号带这猪去赶我们县的集市。板条箱要做得大，漆成绿色，写上金色大字。

“写上什么呢？”勒维问道。

“应该写上朱克曼的名猪。”

勒维捡起一把叉子，就去弄来干净的麦草。有那么只了不起的名猪，这等于说，额外的工作自然就多，这一点他明白。

在苹果园下面的那条小路的尽头就是那个垃圾场。朱克曼先生把所有垃圾和不要的东西都扔在那里。就在这儿，在小桤木和野悬钩子丛遮住的一小块空地上，是好大好大一堆旧瓶子、空罐子、脏布头、碎铁片、破瓶子、破铰链、破弹簧、废电池、上个月的过期杂志、扔掉的刷碗碟小抹布、破套靴、锈钉子、漏水的桶子、给忘掉的塞子、各种各样没用的垃圾，包括破冰淇淋桶尺寸不对的曲柄。

这垃圾场坦普尔顿最熟悉最喜欢。那里有可以躲藏的好地方——对老鼠来说是呱呱叫的藏身之处。那里总是有里面还粘着点食物的罐子。

坦普尔顿这会儿就在这个地方挖来挖去。等到它回谷仓，它嘴里叼着从一本卷起来的杂志上啃下来的一小片广告。

“这个怎么样？”它把广告给夏洛看，问它说，“是‘**松脆**’。在你的网上织上‘松脆’这个字眼挺好的。”

“这正好是个馊主意，”夏洛回答说，“馊得不能再馊了。我们不要朱克曼先生想到威尔伯松脆。他会想到松脆煎熏肉，这一来，又会想到美味的火腿。这个字眼只会引起他想到这些东西。我们必须宣传威尔伯的高尚品质而不是它的味道。请你去另找一个，坦普尔顿，谢谢你！”

老鼠似乎很厌烦。不过它还是溜回到垃圾场去了。过了一会儿，叼着一块布条回来。“这个怎么样？”它说，“是从一件旧衬衫上咬下来的标签。”

夏洛把那标签仔细看了看。上面写着：**防缩**。

“很抱歉，坦普尔顿，”它说，“‘**防缩**’根本不能用。我们要朱克

曼先生想的是威尔伯好好长大而不是缩小。我只好求你再去找找。”

“你把我当什么了，一个差来遣去的听差吗？”老鼠抱怨说，“我可不要把我的时间花到跑垃圾场找广告上面去。”

“就再去一次吧……谢谢你！”夏洛说。

“我来告诉你我怎么办，”坦普尔顿说，“我知道那板棚里有一盒肥皂。盒子上有字。我去啃两个字给你叼来就是了。”

它爬上墙边的绳子，钻过天花板上的一个窟窿，不见了。它回来时，牙齿间叼着一小片蓝白相间的纸板。

“给你！”它得意地说，“这个怎么样？”

夏洛读着上面的字：“勿失时机，行动起来，包你光彩照人。”

“这是什么意思？”夏洛问道，它一辈子都没用过肥皂。

“这我怎么知道？”坦普尔顿说，“你要字，我就把它们带来了。我想你接下来该是要我去给你弄一本字典了。”

它们一起研究这个肥皂广告。“‘勿失时机，行动起来，包你光彩照人’，”夏洛慢慢地再读一遍。“威尔伯！”它叫道。

在麦草上睡大觉的威尔伯跳了起来。

“勿失时机，行动起来！你团团转地跑！”夏洛命令它，“我要看看你行动起来的样子，看看你是不是光彩照人。”

威尔伯飞快地跑到猪栏尽头。

“现在跑回来，跑得更快点！”夏洛说。

威尔伯又飞快地跑回来。它的皮发亮。它的尾巴尖卷成一个很漂亮的小圈。

“跳高！”夏洛大叫。

威尔伯能跳多高就跳多高。

“膝盖挺直，把你的耳朵碰到地面！”夏洛叫道。

威尔伯乖乖地照办。

“半转身后空翻！”夏洛又叫。

威尔伯一个后空翻，空翻时转动它的身体。

“好了，威尔伯，”夏洛说，“你可以回去睡你的大觉了。行，坦普尔顿，我想这肥皂广告合用。我说不准威尔伯的行动是不是百分之百地让它光彩照人，不过很好玩。”

“真的，”威尔伯说，“我觉得眼睛都发光了。”

“是吗？”夏洛说，充满爱意地看着它，“说实在的，你是只好小猪，你会光彩照人的。这件事我现在越陷越深，一不做二不休，我要把它做到底。”

威尔伯又跑又跳，忙了一通，累了，在干净的麦草上躺下来。它闭上眼睛。麦草像是有点扎肉——没有牛粪舒服。躺在牛粪上面总是觉得松软可爱。因此它推开麦草，在肥料上伸开手脚。威尔伯叹了口气。这一天——它变得了不起的第一天—够忙的。这个下午几十人几十人地来参观它，它只好站着摆姿势，尽可能让人看到它了不起。这会儿它累了。弗恩来过，静静地坐在角落里她那张凳子上。

“给我讲个故事吧，夏洛！”威尔伯躺在那里等睡着时说，“给我

讲个故事吧！”

于是，尽管夏洛也很累，它还是做威尔伯要它做的事。

“从前，”它讲起来，“我有一个漂亮的堂姐，它能把它的网从小溪这边结到小溪那边，横跨在小溪上面。有一天，一条小鱼腾空跳起，缠在网上。我的堂姐自然十分吃惊。鱼拼命扑腾。我的堂姐简直不敢对付它。可它还是干了。它扑下去，吐了许多丝捆那小鱼，勇敢地搏斗，要把它捉住。”

“它成功了吗？”威尔伯问道。

“这是一场让人永远忘不了的战斗，”夏洛说，“先说那小鱼吧，它只给捆住了一个鱼鳍，它的尾巴拼命地拍打，在阳光下闪闪发亮。再说那张网，它在鱼的重压下岌岌可危地晃来晃去，越坠越长。”

“那条鱼有多重？”威尔伯问道。

“不知道，”夏洛说，“再回过来说我堂姐，它滑进滑出，头被那拼命挣扎的鱼无情地拍打，跳进跳出，吐出丝来，顽强抵抗。它先在鱼尾巴上一个左手拳，鱼打回来。接着它在鱼尾巴上又一个左手拳，在鱼身上一个右手拳。鱼又打回来，接着它闪到一边，在鱼鳍上一个右手拳，又一个右手拳。接着在鱼头上狠狠一个左手拳，这时网晃来晃去，坠得很低了。”

“接下来怎么样？”威尔伯问道。

“没怎么样，”夏洛说，“鱼打败了。我的堂姐把它裹得严严实实，它动也没法动。”

“接下来怎么样？”威尔伯又问。

“没怎么样，”夏洛说，“我的堂姐让鱼这样过了一阵，等到好了，吃得下，就把鱼吃了。”

“再给我讲一个故事吧！”威尔伯求它。

于是夏洛给它讲另一个堂姐的故事，这堂姐是只飞天蜘蛛。

“怎么叫飞天蜘蛛？”威尔伯问它。

“它乘气球飞天，”夏洛说，“我这堂姐经常倒过头来竖蜻蜓站着，吐出足够的丝做成一个气球。然后，它把气球放飞，温暖的风把气球连同它一起吹上了空中。”

“这是真的吗？”威尔伯问道，“是你编出来的吧？”

“这是真的，”夏洛回答说，“我有几个非常出色的堂姐。好了，威尔伯，你该睡觉了。”

“那么唱点什么吧！”威尔伯闭上眼睛求它。

于是夏洛便唱起催眠曲，同时蟋蟀在草丛里唧唧叫，谷仓黑下来了。夏洛这样唱着：

睡吧，睡吧，我的好宝宝，
在肥料里，在黑暗中，美美地睡觉，
不用害怕，不要觉得孤独苦恼！
就在这时候，青蛙和鸫鸟，
在林中，在灯心草丛里，赞美这个世界多么好。
抛开一切心事吧，我的好宝宝，
在肥料里，在黑暗中，美美地睡觉！

可威尔伯早就睡着了。等到歌唱完，弗恩便站起来回家了。

14.

多里安医生

第二天是星期六。弗恩站在厨房水池旁边，把妈妈洗干净的早餐盘子擦干。阿拉布尔太太默默地干活。她希望弗恩出去和别的孩子玩，而不要上朱克曼家的谷仓，坐在那里一个劲儿地看着那些动物。

“我听到过那么多人讲故事，夏洛是讲得最棒的。”弗恩一面用抹布擦碗一面说。

“弗恩，”她妈妈严厉地说，“你再也不可以胡编乱造了。你知道蜘蛛不会讲故事。蜘蛛根本不会说话。”

“可夏洛会，”弗恩回答说，“它说话不很响，可它会说话。”

“它讲什么故事啦？”阿拉布尔太太问她。

“哦，”弗恩说起来，“它告诉我们，它的一个堂姐用它的网捉住了一条鱼，你不觉得这个故事很动人吗？”

“弗恩，亲爱的，鱼怎么会落到蜘蛛网里呢？”阿拉布尔太太说，“你知道的，这种事不可能发生。这是你编出来的。”

“噢，这件事的确发生了，”弗恩回答说，“夏洛从来不说谎。它这个堂姐结了一张网，横过一条小溪。有一天它在网上，一条小鱼跳上半空，缠到网里了。小鱼的一个鱼鳍给缠住了，妈妈，可它的尾巴拼命拍打，在阳光中闪闪发亮。你看不出来吗，那蜘蛛网在鱼的重压下岌岌可危地晃来晃去？夏洛的堂姐一个劲儿地滑进滑出，头被那拼命挣扎的鱼狠狠地拍打，可它跳进跳出，吐出……”

“弗恩！”妈妈厉声叫住她，“住口！别胡编这些鬼话了！”

“我没胡编，”弗恩说，“我只是告诉你一件真事。”

“那最后怎么样呢？”她妈妈问道，她的好奇心开始占上风。

“最后夏洛的堂姐赢了。它把鱼裹了起来，然后等它好了，想吃了，就把鱼吃掉了。蜘蛛也得吃东西啊，就跟我们人一样。”

“是的，我想它们是得吃东西，”阿拉布尔太太含糊地说了一声。

“夏洛还有一个堂姐是飞天蜘蛛，就是乘气球飞天的蜘蛛。它倒过头来竖蜻蜓站着，吐出许多许多丝，给风带到天上去了。妈妈，你不想那样做吗？”

“是的，想到这样的事，我也会想那样做，”阿拉布尔太太回答说，“不过，弗恩，小宝贝，我希望你今天在外面玩，不要上霍默舅舅的谷仓去了。在外面找两个小伙伴，做点有意义的事吧。你在谷仓那里花的时间太多了——老这样孤孤单单的，这对你不好。”

“孤孤单单？”弗恩说，“孤孤单单？我最好的朋友都在仓底。那地方可热闹了，一点也不孤单。”

弗恩转眼就不见了，一路上朱克曼家去。她妈妈在起居室做清洁。

她一面打扫一面还在想着弗恩。一个小姑娘家的，对动物这么着迷，似乎不正常。最后阿拉布尔太太拿定主意去看多里安医生，要向他请教请教。她坐上汽车，开到村子里他的诊所那儿。

多里安医生有把大胡子。他看到阿拉布尔太太时很高兴，端了一把舒适的椅子请她坐下。

"是弗恩的事，"阿拉布尔太太开门见山说明来意，"弗恩把太多的时间花在朱克曼家的谷仓了。这似乎不正常。她总是坐在仓底靠近猪圈的角落里的一把挤牛奶的凳子上，看那些动物，看一个钟头又一个钟头。她就这样在那里坐着听着。"

多里安医生靠在椅背上，闭上眼睛。

"多么迷人啊！"他说，"那里一定是个真正安静的好地方。霍默有好些羊，对吗？"

“对，”阿拉布尔太太说，“不过一切是从我们让弗恩用奶瓶喂小猪开始的。她给小猪取了个名字叫威尔伯。霍默把这头小猪买去了，自从小猪离开我们家后，弗恩就一直上她舅舅家去待在它身边。“

“关于那只小猪，我听到了好些新闻，”多里安医生一下子睁开眼睛说，“他们说这小猪了不起。”

“你也听说蜘蛛网上出现的字了？”阿拉布尔太太紧张地问道。

“对，”医生回答说。

“那么，你明白了？”阿拉布尔太太问道。

“明白什么？”

“明白蜘蛛网上怎么会有字。”

“噢，不，”多里安医生说，“我不明白。可说到这件事，我首先就不明白，蜘蛛是怎么学会结网的。那些字的出现，大家说是奇迹。不过没有人指出，蜘蛛网本身就是一个奇迹。”

“蜘蛛网有什么奇迹呢？”阿拉布尔太太说，“我不明白你为什么说蜘蛛网是个奇迹——就是一张蜘蛛网罢了。”

“你试过结网吗？”多里安医生问道。

阿拉布尔太太在她的椅子上不自在地动着身子。“没有，”她回答说，“不过我会编织小餐巾，也会编织短袜子。”

“不错，”医生说，“不过你是有人教的，对吗？”

“是我妈妈教的。”

“那么蜘蛛是谁教的呢？蜘蛛很小就会结网，没有任何人教。你不觉得这是个奇迹吗？”

“我想是的，”阿拉布尔太太说，“可我以前从来没有这样看待过这件事。只是我还是不明白，那些字怎么会出现在蜘蛛网上。这件事我不明白，我不喜欢自己不明白的事。”

“我们没有人喜欢，”多里安医生叹气说，“我是一个医生，人们以为医生什么都明白，可我不是什么都明白，我也不打算为这件事苦恼。”

阿拉布尔太太坐立不安。“弗恩说那些动物互相交谈。多里安医生，你相信动物会说话吗？”

“我从来没听说过动物会说话，”多里安医生说，“不过这不证明什么。很可能有只动物曾经私底下对我说过话，可我没听到，只因为我没在意。孩子们比大人更在意。如果弗恩说朱克曼家谷仓的动物说话，我很乐意相信她的话。也许如果人少说话，动物就会多说些。人是喋喋不休地在说话的——我可以向你保证。”

“很好，我对弗恩觉得放心些了，”阿拉布尔太太说，“你不觉得我该为她担心吗？”

“她看上去好不好？”医生问。

“哦，很好。”

“胃口也好？”

“哦，是的，她老觉得肚子饿。”

“夜里睡得好吗？”

“噢，很好。”

“那你就不用担心，”医生说。

“你认为她除了猪、羊、鹅、蜘蛛，还会想些什么东西吗？”

“弗恩多大了？”

“八岁。”

“那么，”多里安医生说，“我想她会一直爱动物。不过我不相信她一辈子待在霍默·朱克曼的谷仓底。男孩呢——她认识什么男孩子吗？”

“她认识亨利·富西。”阿拉布尔太太一下子欢快地说。

多里安医生又闭上眼睛沉思。“亨利·富西，”他喃喃地说，“嗯嗯嗯。好极了。好，我认为你没什么可担心的。如果弗恩高兴，你就让她和她谷仓里的那些朋友打交道吧。我可以不假思索地说，蜘蛛和猪完全与亨利·富西一样有趣。不过我说在前面，有一天连亨利也会偶然说出些吸引弗恩注意的话来。真叫人惊奇，孩子们一年一年变样。艾弗里怎么样？”他睁大眼睛问。

“噢，艾弗里，”阿拉布尔太太格格笑，“艾弗里一直很好。当然，他碰上过毒漆，被黄蜂和蜜蜂蜇过，把青蛙和蛇带回家。而且手碰到什么打破什么。不过他很好。”

“那就好！”医生说。

阿拉布尔太太跟多里安医生告别，非常感谢他的指点。她大大放了心。

15.

蟋蟀

蟋蟀在草丛里唱歌。它们唱夏季收场之歌，一支忧伤单调的歌。“夏天完了，结束了，”它们唱，“完了，结束了，完了，结束了。夏天在死亡，在死亡。”

蟋蟀觉得这是它们的责任，警告大家夏日不能持久。就算是在一年中最美丽的日子——在夏天进入秋天的日子——蟋蟀还是向大家传布这个哀伤和变化的消息。

人人都听到了蟋蟀的歌。阿拉布尔家的艾弗里和弗恩走在泥路上时听到它，知道快要开学了；那些小鹅听到它，知道它们再也不是鹅宝宝；夏洛听到它，知道自己时间不多了；在厨房干活的阿拉布尔太太听到它，心中也不由得一阵伤感。“又是一个夏天过去了，”她叹气说；在给威尔伯做板条箱的勒维听到它，知道该挖土豆了。

“夏天完了，结束了，”蟋蟀反复唱，“到冷天还有多少夜啊？”蟋蟀唱道，“再见了，夏天，再见了，再见了！”

羊听到蟋蟀的歌声，觉得浑身不自在，在牧场板墙上撞出洞来，走到大路那边的田野上去。公鹅发现了这个洞，带领它一家大小钻出去，到果园吃落在地上的苹果；沼泽地上一棵小槭树听到蟋蟀的歌声，急得叶子红了。

威尔伯如今在农场里是吸引力的中心、关注的焦点。定时吃好东西显示出了效果：威尔伯成了一只人见人爱的猪。每天来到它的猪栏边，站在那里欣赏它的超过一百人。夏洛已经在网上织出了**光彩照人**四个大字，威尔伯站在金色的阳光里，真是光彩照人。自从蜘蛛开始扶助它，它就尽力活得跟它的名声相衬。夏洛的网说它是**王牌猪**，威尔伯尽力让自己看上去是只王牌猪；夏洛的网说它**了不起**，威尔伯尽力让自己看上去了不起；现在网上说它**光彩照人**，它尽力让自己光彩照人。

让自己看上去光彩照人很不容易，可威尔伯决心来一下。它微微转动它的头，眨动它的长睫毛。然后它深呼吸。等到观众看厌了，它又跳高来个转半身后空翻。观众看到这一招，全不由得哇哇欢呼起来。"一只猪怎么能做出这样的动作啊？"朱克曼先生心里太高兴了，问道，"那猪真是光彩照人。"

威尔伯在谷仓的有些朋友担心所有这些捧场会冲昏它的头脑，害得它骄傲自大。可没这回事。威尔伯始终十分谦虚，名气并没有害了它。它还是对未来有点担心，因为它很难相信，小小一只蜘蛛就能挽救它的性命。有时候它夜里会做噩梦。它梦见人们拿着刀枪来捉它。但这只是梦。白天威尔伯通常觉得快活和放心。没有哪只猪能比它有更忠实的朋友了，它感觉到友谊是天底下最使人称心的东西。甚至蟋蟀的歌也没有让威尔伯太难过。它知道县里举办集市的时间快到了，它在等着上那儿去。只要它能在集市上出人头地，也许还赢得点奖金，它相信这样一来，朱克曼先生就会让它活下去。

夏洛也有它自己担心的事，不过它闭口不言。一天早晨，威尔伯问它集市的事。

“你和我一起去，对吗，夏洛？“它说。

“这个嘛，我不知道，”夏洛回答说，“对我来说，集市来得不是时候。这时候，我不便离开家，哪怕只去几天。”

“为什么呢？”威尔伯问它。

“噢，我就是觉得不想离开我这张网。这里事情太多了。”

“请和我一起去吧！”威尔伯求它，“我需要你，夏洛。不和你一起上集市去，我要受不了的。你就是得去。”

“不，”夏洛说，“我想我最好留在家里，看能不能把活儿做好。”

“什么活儿呢？”威尔伯问道。

“产卵。是我该做一个卵袋，在里面装满卵的时候了。”

“我不知道你会产卵。”威尔伯惊讶地说。

“噢，当然，”蜘蛛说，“我是多才多艺的。”

“‘多才多艺’是什么意思——是满是卵吗？”威尔伯问道。

“当然不是，”夏洛说，“‘多才多艺’是指我能很轻松地做很多事情，多才多艺意味着我并不是只会结网、捉昆虫这些绝活。”

“你为什么不和我一起到集市，在那里产你的卵呢？”威尔伯恳求着它，“那会非常好玩的。”

夏洛拉拉它的网，忧郁地看着它晃动。“我怕不行，”它说，“你不知道产卵最要紧的是什么，威尔伯。我不能让我的家庭责任迁就集市的安排。我该产卵就得产卵，不管集市不集市的。不过我不要你为这件事担心——担心你就会瘦下来。我们就这么讲定了：我有可能上集市去我就去。”

“噢，好！”威尔伯说，“我知道，在我最需要你的时候，你是不会丢下我的。”

那一整天威尔伯待在里面，在麦草上过得舒舒服服。夏洛也休息下来，吃了一只蚱蜢。它知道再不能给威尔伯帮什么忙了。几天之内它就得丢下一切事情，做那个美丽的小袋来装它的卵。

16.

上集市去

上县里集市去的前夜，大家都早早休息了。弗恩和艾弗里八点钟就上床。艾弗里做了个梦，梦到费里斯转轮一下子停了，他正坐在转轮最顶上的一个厢子里。弗恩也做了梦，梦到自己在高空的秋千上作呕。

勒维八点半上床。他梦到自己向一只布猫投球，赢来一条货真价实的纳瓦霍毯子。朱克曼先生和太太九点上床。朱克曼太太梦到深冻冰箱。朱克曼先生梦到威尔伯。他梦到威尔伯已经长到一百一十六英尺长、九十二英尺高，赢得了集市上所有的奖项，身上披着蓝绸带，连尾巴尖都结着一条蓝绸带。

在下面谷仓底，动物也睡得很早，只除了夏洛。第二天就是赶集市的日子。所有动物都打算早起，欢送威尔伯去碰它的大运气。

第二天早晨，大家天一亮就起来。这一天很热。在那头的阿拉布尔太太家，弗恩费力地提着一桶热水到她的房间洗了个澡，用海绵擦了身子。然后她穿上自己最漂亮的连衣裙，因为她知道在集市里会看到男孩子。阿拉布尔太太把艾弗里的后颈擦干净，弄湿他的头发，把

头发分开，狠狠地刷，直刷到头发平贴在头顶上为止——头发基本上服帖，只有六根左右还是翘起来。艾弗里穿上干净内衣、干净牛仔裤、干净衬衫。阿拉布尔先生穿好了衣服，吃过早饭，然后出来擦他的卡车。他已经答应用车送大家去集市，包括威尔伯。

这边，勒维已经早早在威尔伯的板条箱里铺上干净麦草，拿进猪圈。板条箱漆成绿色，上面写着金色大字：

朱克曼的名猪

夏洛从它的网上可以清楚地看到一切。威尔伯慢慢地吃着它的早饭。它要尽量不让食物粘在耳朵上，好让自己看起来光彩照人。

在厨房里，朱克曼太太突然宣布一件事。

"霍默，"她对她的丈夫说，"我要去给那猪洗个脱脂牛奶澡。"

"什么澡？"朱克曼先生问道。

"脱脂牛奶澡。当年我奶奶的猪脏了，她总是用脱脂牛奶给它洗澡——我这才想起来。"

"可威尔伯不脏，"朱克曼先生自豪地说。

"它耳朵后面脏，"朱克曼太太说，"每次勒维给它倒泔脚时，泔脚都从它耳朵那儿落下去。泔脚水干了就结块。它侧身躺在肥料上的那一边也有肥料的污迹。"

"可它如今躺在干净的麦草上，"朱克曼先生纠正她的话。

"总而言之，统而言之，它脏了，该洗个澡。"

朱克曼先生无力地坐下，吃他的炸面圈。他的太太到板棚去了，回来时穿着橡胶靴子和旧雨衣，拎了一桶脱脂牛奶，拿着一根搅拌用的小木桨。

"伊迪丝，你疯了。"朱克曼先生嘀咕说。

可她没理他。他们一起来到猪圈。朱克曼太太一点不浪费时间。她爬进猪圈来到威尔伯那里，马上就动手。她把木桨放进牛奶里浸湿，擦威尔伯的全身。那些鹅围上来看热闹，大羊小羊也是。连坦普尔顿也小心翼翼地探出头来看威尔伯洗牛奶澡。夏洛太感兴趣了，用一条丝挂下来好看得清楚些。威尔伯闭上眼睛，站着不动。它感觉到牛奶流下它的身体。它张开嘴，一些牛奶流到嘴里。味道太好了。它觉得光彩照人，觉得快活。等到朱克曼太太洗完，把它擦干，它真是一只你见也没见过的最干净最漂亮的猪。它全身雪白，耳朵和鼻子粉红，毛像丝一样光滑。

朱克曼夫妇回去换上最好的衣服。勒维刮干净胡子，穿上他的格子衬衫，打上紫色领带。牲口留在谷仓里。

七只小鹅围着它们的妈妈。

“谢谢你，谢谢你，谢谢你带我们上集市去！”一只小鹅求它。接着七只小鹅全吵着要去。

“谢谢你，谢谢你，谢谢你，谢谢你，谢谢你，谢谢你……”它们吵得昏天黑地。

“孩子们！”母鹅厉声说，“我们不去，安安静静——安安静静——安安静静留在家里。只有威尔伯——威尔伯——威尔伯上集市去。”

就在这时候，夏洛插话了。

“我也去，”它轻轻地说，“我拿定主意了，要和威尔伯一起去。它也许需要我。我们说不准在集市会发生什么事。得有个会写字的和它一起去。我想坦普尔顿最好也去——我可能要个帮手跑来跑去做点事。”

“我不去，我就留在这里，”老鼠咕哝说，“我对集市一点兴趣也没有。”

“那是因为你从来没有去过，”老羊说，“集市是老鼠的乐园。集市里人人扔食物。老鼠夜里可以出来大吃特吃。在马棚里，你会找到马洒落的燕麦；在场地上践踏过的草丛中，你会找到扔下的旧饭盒，里面有吃剩的花生酱三明治、煮鸡蛋、饼干屑、炸面圈屑、干酪屑；在游艺场的硬泥地上，等到闪亮的灯关了，人们回家睡觉去了，你会找到真正的宝贝：累坏的孩子们扔下的爆米花、一滴滴奶油冰淇淋、冰糖苹果，还有棉花糖、盐水杏仁、冰棍、咬剩的冰淇淋蛋卷筒、棒棒糖棍。到处都是老鼠的好东西——在帐篷里，在货亭里，在干草阁楼上——这还用说，集市上留下了足够的让人恶心的食物，够大队老鼠吃个痛快。”

坦普尔顿听得眼睛都发亮了。

“这是真的吗？”它问道，“你说的这些吊胃口的故事奇谈是真的吗？我喜欢高档生活，你说的东西引得我直流口水。”

“这是真的，”老羊说，“上集市去吧，坦普尔顿。你会发现集市的东西好得你连做最疯狂的乱梦时也梦不到。桶子沾着酸麦芽糖浆，罐头装着剩下的金枪鱼，还有些油腻的纸袋装着臭了的……”

“够了够了！”坦普尔顿叫道，“不要再说下去了。我要到那里去。”

“很好，”夏洛对老羊眨眨眼睛说，“现在——时间不等人。威尔伯很快就要装箱出发。坦普尔顿和我必须这就进板条箱里躲起来。”

老鼠一分钟也不耽搁。它爬到板条箱那里，从板条间钻了进去，用麦草把身体盖住不让人看见。

“好，”夏洛说，“我接着来。”它吐出一根长丝，飞过去，轻轻落到地上。然后它爬上箱子，躲到顶板上的一个节孔里。

老羊点点头。“一箱多妙的货物啊！”它说，“那个横幅应该写成：

‘朱克曼的名猪加两名偷乘者’。”

“小心，人们来了——来了——来了！”公鹅叫道，“安静——安静——安静！”

阿拉布尔先生握住大卡车的方向盘，慢慢地倒车，朝谷仓院子开来。勒维和朱克曼先生走在车旁边。弗恩和艾弗里站在车厢里，靠着侧板。

“听我说，”老羊悄悄对威尔伯说，“当他们打开板条箱让你进去的时候，你要挣扎！不要乖乖地去。猪给装上车时总是要反抗的。”

“我一挣扎身子就会弄脏的。”威尔伯说。

“别管这个——你照我说的做！要挣扎！如果你毫不反抗，乖乖地进板条箱，朱克曼先生会以为你中邪了。他会不敢上集市去的。”

坦普尔顿从麦草里探出头来。“该挣扎你就得挣扎，”它说，“不过请好心记住，我躺在木箱下面这里，我不想给踩着或者给踢脸，或者给压了，或者给撞了，或者给踏扁，或者给顶了，或者给挤伤，或者给弄破皮，或者给吓着了，或者给蹬了。就是他们把你推进去的时候请动作小心些，光彩照人先生，拜托拜托！”

“别响了，坦普尔顿！”老羊说，“把你的脑袋缩进去——他们来了。做出光彩照人的样子，威尔伯！躺低，夏洛！欢呼捧场，你们这些鹅！”

卡车慢慢地倒过来，开到猪圈旁边停下。阿拉布尔先生关掉发动机，下车绕到后面，放下尾板。那些鹅发出欢呼声。阿拉布尔太太下了车。弗恩和艾弗里跳到地上。朱克曼太太从家里走过来。人人排在围栏边，等待着欣赏威尔伯和那漂亮的绿板条箱的时刻到来。没有人知道板条箱里已经装着一只老鼠和一只蜘蛛。

“那是王牌猪！”阿拉布尔太太说。

“它了不起。”勒维说。

“它光彩照人。”弗恩说着，想起它出生的那一天。

“真好，”朱克曼太太说，“它到底干干净净、光光亮亮了。脱脂牛奶的确有效。”

阿拉布尔先生仔细看威尔伯。“不错，它真是只了不起的王牌猪，”他说，“真难相信，它是一窝猪里的落脚猪。到杀这猪的时候，你就有特别好的火腿和熏咸肉了，霍默。”

威尔伯一听这话，心脏都几乎停止跳动了。“我想我要昏倒了，”它悄悄地对站在旁边看着的老羊说。

“跪下来！”老羊悄悄地回答它说，“让血冲到你的头上！”

威尔伯跪下来，所有的光彩全没了。它的眼睛闭上。

“瞧！”弗恩尖叫，“它在昏过去！”

“嘿，看我！”艾弗里大叫一声，趴下来爬进板条箱。“我是猪，我是猪！”

艾弗里的脚碰到了麦草下面的坦普尔顿。“真是乱七八糟！”老鼠心里说，“男孩子都是神经病！我干吗自投罗网进来受这份罪呢？”

那些鹅看到艾弗里在板条箱里，尽情地欢呼起来。

“艾弗里，你马上从板条箱里出来！”他妈妈命令他说，“你以为你是什么？”

“我是猪！”艾弗里大叫，把大把大把的麦草撒向空中。“呼噜，呼噜，呼噜！”

“卡车滑走了，爸爸。”弗恩说。

没人驾驶的卡车开始朝山下滑去。阿拉布尔先生连忙冲上驾驶座，紧急刹车。卡车停下了。那些鹅又欢呼起来。夏洛蹲在节孔里，让身子缩到最小，因此艾弗里没看见它。

“马上出来！”阿拉布尔太太大叫。艾弗里趴下身子爬出板条箱，对威尔伯做怪脸。威尔伯昏过去了。

“猪昏倒了，”朱克曼太太说，“快用水浇它！”

“用牛奶！”艾弗里出主意说。

那些鹅又欢呼起来。

勒维跑去拿水。弗恩爬进猪圈，跪在威尔伯身边。

“是中暑了，”朱克曼先生说，“对它来说，天太热了。”

“它也许死了。”艾弗里说。

“你马上从猪圈出来！”阿拉布尔太太叫道。艾弗里听从妈妈的话，爬到卡车车厢里，好看得清楚些。勒维把冷水拿来了，泼在威尔伯身上。

“泼一点到我身上！”艾弗里大叫，“我也热。”

“噢，别响！”弗恩大叫，“别响！”她已经热泪盈眶了。

威尔伯感受到身上的冷水，醒了过来。在那些鹅的欢呼声中，它慢慢地站起身子。

“它起来了！”阿拉布尔先生说，“我想它没事。”

“我饿了，”艾弗里说，“我要个冰糖苹果。”

“威尔伯现在好了，”弗恩说，“我们可以动身了。我要去坐费里斯转轮！”

朱克曼先生、阿拉布尔先生和勒维把猪抱起来，头朝前推进板条箱。威尔伯开始挣扎。人们越是用力推，它越是向后撑。艾弗里跳下车帮大人推。威尔伯又踢又扭又呼噜叫。“这猪没事，”朱克曼先生用膝盖顶威尔伯的屁股，兴高采烈地说，“现在大家一起上，伙伴们！推！”

最后一推，他们总算把威尔伯推进了板条箱。那些鹅又欢呼起来。勒维在箱头上钉上几块板条，威尔伯出不来了。然后他们用足力气，把板条箱抬起来，装上卡车。他们不知道麦草下面还有一只老鼠，节孔里有一只灰色大蜘蛛。他们只看到了猪。

“大家上车！”阿拉布尔先生叫道。他开动汽车。太太们上了驾驶室坐到他旁边。朱克曼先生、勒维、弗恩和艾弗里坐到后面，靠着侧板。卡车开始前进。那些鹅发出欢呼。两个孩子也欢呼着回应它们。大伙儿就这样上集市去了。

17.

叔叔

车子开进集市场地时，他们听到音乐声，看到费里斯转轮在空中旋转。他们闻到被洒水车洒湿了的跑道的灰尘气味，闻到煎牛肉饼的香味，看到气球飘在空中。他们听到羊在羊栏里咩咩叫。扩音器里有人大声说："请注意！那辆庞蒂亚克的车主，牌照号码是H—2439的，请把你的汽车开走，不要停在烟火棚前面！"

"可以给我点钱吗？"弗恩问道。

"也给我一点吗？"艾弗里问道。

"我要去转轮盘赢一个洋娃娃，它一定会停在我押的号码上面。"弗恩说。

"我要去开喷气式飞机，让它撞另外一架。"

"可以给我买个气球吗？"弗恩问道。

"可以给我买奶油冰淇淋、干酪三明治、悬钩子汽水吗？"艾弗里问道。

"你们孩子别吵，先等我们把猪搬下车。"阿拉布尔太太说。

"还是让我们先把孩子们打发走吧，"阿拉布尔先生建议，"集市每年只来一次。”阿拉布尔先生说着给了弗恩两个25分的硬币和两个10分的硬币，又给了艾弗里五个10分的硬币和四个5分的硬币。“现在快去吧！”他说，“不过记住，这钱要用一整天。别几分钟不到就把它们花光了。中午回到卡车这里来，我们一起吃中饭。别乱吃一通肚子疼。”

“要是去荡高空秋千，”阿拉布尔太太说，“可要抓紧了！你们要抓得十分紧。我的话听进去没有？”

“别走丢了！”朱克曼太太说。

“别弄脏了！”

“别热坏了！”他们的妈妈说。

“提防扒手！”他们的爸爸叮嘱说。

“马来了不要过跑道！”朱克曼太太在后面叫。

两个孩子手拉手，朝着旋转木马，朝着美妙的音乐，朝着惊人的冒险，朝着奇妙的兴奋地，蹦蹦跳跳地跑去，跑进那神奇的游艺场。那里没有爸爸妈妈保护他们，指点他们，他们可以快快活活、自由自在，爱干什么就干。阿拉布尔太太静静地看着他们走开。接着她叹了口气。接着她擤擤鼻子。

“你真认为这样做好吗？”她问道。

“得了，他们总要长大的，”阿拉布尔先生说，“我想集市是个很好的起点。”

当威尔伯给搬下车，从板条箱里出来，放进它的新猪圈时，一群又一群人围上来看。他们看着那几个大字：**朱克曼的名猪**。威尔伯回看他们，尽力显出特别棒的样子。它很喜欢它的新家。圈里长着青草，有棚顶挡住太阳。

夏洛看到它的机会来了，从板条箱里爬出来，爬上棚顶下面的一根柱子上。没有人注意到它。

坦普尔顿不想在大白天出来，它静静地待在箱底的麦草下面。朱克曼先生在威尔伯的食槽里倒进一些脱脂牛奶，叉了些干净麦草放进它的猪圈里，然后和朱克曼太太以及阿拉布尔夫妇一起走开，去牛棚看纯种母牛，去看各种东西。朱克曼先生特别想看拖拉机。朱克曼太太想看深冻冰箱。勒维自个儿走开，希望碰到个朋友，到游艺场去玩玩。

人们一走，夏洛就对威尔伯说：

“我在上面看到的东西是你在下面看不到的。”它说。

“你看到什么了？”威尔伯问道。

“隔壁猪圈有只猪，很大很大。我怕它比你大多了。”

“也许它的岁数比我大，活得比我长。”威尔伯说。它的眼里流出了泪水。

“让我吊下去靠近些好好看看它。”夏洛说。于是它顺着横梁爬到隔壁猪圈上面。它吐出一根长丝，一直落到那大猪的鼻子前面。

“能请问一下，你叫什么名字吗？”夏洛彬彬有礼地问道。

那猪看着它。“我没有名字，”它响亮地大声说。“那就叫我‘叔叔’吧。”

“很好，‘叔叔’，”夏洛回答说，“你是哪一天出生的？你是春猪吗？”

“我当然是春猪，”“叔叔”回答说，“你以为我是什么，一只春鸡吗？哈，哈——这笑话不错吧，对吗，小妹妹？”

“相当滑稽，”夏洛说，“不过我听到过更滑稽的。很高兴碰到你，现在我得走了。”

夏洛慢慢地爬上去，回到威尔伯的猪圈。

“它说它是只春猪，”夏洛禀报说，“也许是的。有一件事可以肯定，它太不讨人喜欢了。它太放肆，太吵闹，还叽叽呱呱地说些蹩脚的笑话。还有，它一点没你干净，也不及你讨人喜欢。我和它就谈了两句，已经觉得很不喜欢它。不过由于它个子大，有分量，赢这只猪可不容易，威尔伯。可是有我相助，这件事做得到。”

“你什么时候开始结网呢？”威尔伯问道。

“要是不太累，今天下午，”夏洛说，“这几天最小的事也会把我累坏。我似乎没有以前那种精力了。我想是岁数的关系。”

威尔伯看着它的朋友。夏洛看上去肿胀得厉害，像是很累的样子。

“听你说觉得不舒服，我特别难过，夏洛，”它说，“也许你结出网来，捉上两只苍蝇会感到好些。”

“也许吧，”夏洛有气无力地说，“不过我感觉到像是漫长一天到了尽头。”它倒过来挂在天花板上，开始打盹，留下威尔伯十分担心。

整个上午人们走过威尔伯的猪圈。几十几百个陌生人停下来看它，赞美它一身丝一样细柔的白毛，它卷曲的尾巴，它善良的表情和光彩照人。接下来他们到隔壁猪圈去看躺在那里的更大的猪。威尔伯听到有几个人称赞“叔叔”的大个子。它没法不听到这些评语，没法不担心。“现在，加上夏洛感觉不舒服……”它想，“噢，天啊！”

整个上午坦普尔顿在麦草底下静静地安睡。天气越来越热，热坏了。下午朱克曼夫妇和阿拉布尔夫妇回到猪圈来。过了几分钟，弗恩和艾弗里也露脸了。弗恩抱着一只玩具猴子，吃着爆米花胶糖。艾弗里把一个气球拴在他的一只耳朵上，啃着冰糖苹果。孩子们又热又脏。

“真是热啊！”朱克曼太太说。

“热死人了！”阿拉布尔太太说，拿着一张深冻冰箱的广告拼命扇风。

他们一个个爬上卡车，打开饭盒。太阳无处不晒。似乎没有人觉得肚子饿。

“评判员什么时候评定威尔伯呢？”朱克曼太太问道。

“至少要到明天。”朱克曼先生说。

勒维回来了，拿着赢来的一条印第安毯子。

“这正是我们需要的，”艾弗里说，“一条毯子。”

“当然需要。”勒维说。他把毯子搭在卡车两边的侧板上，就像一个小帐篷。孩子们坐在毯子下的阴影里，觉得好多了。

吃过中饭，他们伸展手脚，睡着了。

18.

凉爽的晚上

在暮色笼罩了集市场地，傍晚凉爽下来以后，坦普尔顿从板条箱里爬出来朝四下里看。威尔伯在麦草上睡着了，夏洛在结网。坦普尔顿那个尖鼻子闻到了空气中的许多美味。老鼠这时又饥又渴。它决定去探察一番。也没对谁说一声，它就走了。

“给我带个字眼回来！”夏洛在它后面叫道，“我今天夜里最后一次织字。”

老鼠管自咕噜了一声，就钻到阴影里不见了。它不喜欢让人当听差似的差来差去。

热了一天，傍晚到来正合心意，大家松了口气。费里斯转轮这时候灯火辉煌。它在空中转啊转，好像比白天高了一倍。游艺场里到处都是灯，可以听到吃角子老虎机的嘎啦声、旋转木马的音乐声、摇彩摊的喊号码声。

两个孩子睡了一觉，觉得精神了。弗恩碰到她的朋友亨利·富西，他请她一道去坐费里斯转轮。他甚至请客，这样弗恩就一分钱也没花。阿拉布尔太太碰巧抬头看星空，一眼看到女儿和亨利·富西坐在一起，朝空中越升越高，她看到弗恩非常开心，不禁摇头。“天啊，天啊！”她说，“亨利·富西。想想看吧！”

坦普尔顿悄悄地躲开人们。在牛棚后面的高草丛里，它找到一张折叠的报纸。报纸里是什么人中饭吃剩的东西：一块辣味火腿三明治、一片瑞士干酪、一点煮鸡蛋、一个虫蛀过的苹果的芯子。老鼠钻进去把它们吃光了。接着它从报纸上啃下一个字眼，卷起来，动身回到威尔伯的猪圈去。

当坦普尔顿叼着报纸纸片回来时，夏洛的网差不多织好了，只在网当中留下一个大空当。这时间猪圈四周没有人，只有老鼠、蜘蛛和猪三个。

“我希望你带回来一个好字眼，”夏洛说，“这是我写的最后的字眼了。”

“给你。”坦普尔顿把卷起来的纸片打开。

“上面写的是什么啊？”夏洛问道，“你得读给我听。”

“写的是‘**谦卑**’。”老鼠说。

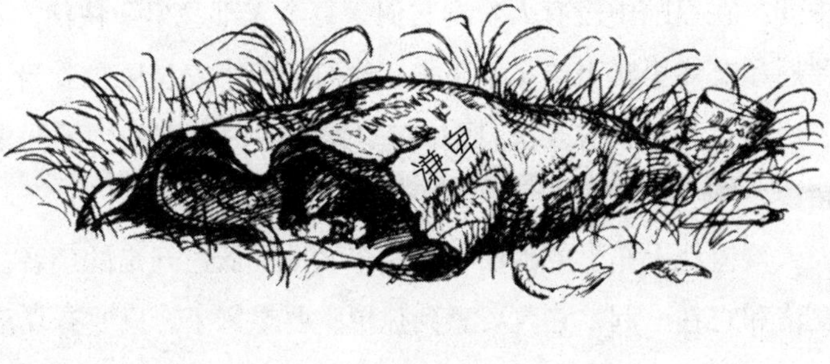

“谦卑？”夏洛说，“‘谦卑’有两重意思。‘谦’是‘不自高自大’，‘卑’又有‘低下’的意思。这全合乎威尔伯。它不自高自大，它也总是在地面上，位置低下。”

“好，我希望你满意了，”老鼠回答说，“我可不想把我的时间都花在跑来跑去拿东西上面。我到这集市来是要享受享受，而不是当听差把纸送来送去。”

“你已经帮了大忙，”夏洛说，“你想多看看集市，那你去吧。”

老鼠龇着牙齿笑。“我要来个欢乐今宵，”老鼠说，“老羊说得对——这集市是老鼠的乐园。多好吃的食物啊！多好喝的饮料啊！到处是躲藏的好地方，找到东西的好地方。再见，我谦卑的威尔伯！祝你好运，夏洛，你这老滑头！这将是一只老鼠终身难忘的一夜。”

它钻进阴影中不见了。

夏洛回过来干它的活。现在漆黑一片了。远处开始放烟火——天上满是火箭式大烟火、散开的火球。等阿拉布尔和朱克曼两家人和勒维从大看台回来，夏洛已经织完它的网，**谦卑**两个大字整整齐齐地织在网中间。在黑暗中没有人看到它们。每个人都又累又快活。

弗恩和艾弗里爬上卡车躺下来。他们把印第安毯子拉到身上。勒维给了威尔伯一叉新鲜麦草。阿拉布尔先生拍拍它。“我们要回家了，”他对猪说，“明天见。”

大人慢慢地上车，威尔伯听到汽车发动、低速开走的声音。要不是有夏洛和它在一起，它真要感到孤单，要想家了。只要有夏洛在身边，它从不感到孤单。在远处，它还能听到旋转木马的音乐声。

当它要睡觉的时候，它跟夏洛说话了。

“再把那支歌唱一遍给我听吧，关于肥料和黑暗什么的。”它恳求夏洛说。

“今天不唱了，”夏洛低声说，“我太累了。”它的声音听上去不像是从它的网那边传来的。

“你在哪里啊？”威尔伯问道，“我看不见你。你在你的网上吗？”

“我在后面这儿，”夏洛回答说，“在后面墙角上头。”

“你为什么不在网上？”威尔伯问道，“你几乎是从来不离开你那张网的。”

“今天晚上我离开了。”

威尔伯闭上眼睛。“夏洛，”过了一小会儿它又说，“你真认为朱克曼先生会让我活下去，天气冷了以后不杀我吗？你真这样想吗？”

“当然，”夏洛说，“你是一只大名鼎鼎的猪，你是一只好猪。明天你可能得奖。全世界都会知道你。朱克曼先生会因为有你这样一只猪而自豪得意。你不用怕，威尔伯——什么都不用担心。你也许会永远活下去——谁知道呢？而现在，你睡觉吧。”

有一会儿寂静无声。接下来又是威尔伯的说话声：

“你在那上面干什么啊，夏洛？”

“哦，我在做一样东西，”它说，“跟平常一样在做东西。”

“这东西是为我做的吗？”威尔伯问道。

“不，”夏洛说，“这东西是为我自己做的。为了变化。”

“谢谢你告诉我，这是什么东西啊？”威尔伯求它说。

“明天早晨我再告诉你，”它说，“只等天空出现第一道光线，麻雀活动，牛震动它们的链子；只等公鸡啼叫，星星隐退；只等公路响起最早的汽车声音，你抬头朝上面这里看，我会让你看到一样东西。我会让你看到我的杰作。”

它话没说完，威尔伯已经睡着了。从它的呼吸声可以听出来，它埋在麦草里睡得很安宁。

在许多英里之外的阿拉布尔家，男人们围坐在厨房桌子旁边吃着一盘罐头桃子，谈一天的事情。在楼上，艾弗里准备上床睡觉。阿拉布尔太太给床上的弗恩塞好被单。

“你在集市上玩得开心吗？”她吻她的女儿说。

弗恩点点头。“我这一辈子里，在任何地方任何时间都没有这样开心过。”

“是吗？”阿拉布尔太太说，“这样就太好了。”

19.

卵袋

第二天早晨，当天空一出现光线，麻雀开始在树上活动，牛震响它们的链子，公鸡啼叫，最早的汽车在路上呜呜开过，威尔伯醒了过来，睁开眼睛寻找夏洛。它看到夏洛在头顶上，靠近猪圈后面的墙角。夏洛很安静，八条腿张开。它好像在夜里一下子缩小了。威尔伯看到，在它旁边有一样古怪的东西贴在天花板上。这是个袋子，或者茧。它是粉红色的，看上去像是用棉花糖做的。

"你醒了吗，夏洛？"威尔伯轻轻地说。

"是的。"回答声传过来。

"那个漂亮的小东西是什么啊？是你做的吗？"

"当然是我做的。"夏洛用有气无力的声音说。

"是做来玩的吗？"

"做来玩？当然不是。这是我的卵袋，我的 magnum opus。"

"我不知道这话是什么意思。"威尔伯说。

"那是拉丁语，"夏洛解释说，"它的意思是'伟大的作品'。这卵袋是我的杰作——是我做过的东西中最好的。"

"它里面都是什么啊？"威尔伯问道，"是卵吗？"

"五百十四个卵。"夏洛回答说。

"五百十四？"威尔伯说，"你在开玩笑。"

"不，我不开玩笑。我把它们都数过了。我一直数了又数——只为了让我的心不闲着。"

"这卵袋漂亮极了。"威尔伯说，高兴得好像是它自己做的一般。

"不错，它是漂亮，"夏洛用它两条前腿拍拍它。"至少我可以保证它很结实。它是用我最有韧性的材料做的。而且它还防水。里面又温暖又干爽。"

"夏洛，"威尔伯做梦似的说，"你真的要有五百十四个孩子吗？"

"要是不出事，是的，"夏洛说，"当然，它们要到来年春天才出生。"威尔伯注意到夏洛的声音很伤感。

"是什么让你的声音那么伤感呢？我以为这件喜事会让你快乐无比。"

"噢，别管我，"夏洛说，"我只是再没有力气了。我想我觉得难过，是因为我将看不到我这些孩子。"

"你看不到你的孩子，这是什么意思？你当然看得到。我们全都看得到它们。这简直是了不起，来年春天谷仓底有五百十四只蜘蛛宝宝到处奔来跑去。那些鹅要有新一代鹅宝宝，那些羊又有它们的小羊羔……"

"也许吧，"夏洛安静地说，"不过我有一种感觉，我不会看到昨天夜里辛苦工作的成果。我一点不觉得舒服。对你说实话，我想我在衰竭。”

威尔伯不明白“衰竭”是什么意思，但不想问夏洛，免得麻烦它解释。不过它实在太担心，觉得又只好问它。

“‘衰竭’是什么意思？”

“就是感到老了，越来越没有力气了。我不再年轻啦，威尔伯。不过我不要你为我担心。今天是你的大好日子。你看看我的网——上面有露水，它看上去不是很漂亮吗？”

夏洛的网从来没有像今天早上这样漂亮过。每一条丝上停着几十颗清晨闪亮的小露珠。东方的晨光照着它，让它看得清清楚楚。这是一幅设计精巧的完美的织品。再过一两个钟头，川流不息的人将要经过这里，他们会赞美它，读它，然后低头看威尔伯，惊叹这个奇迹。

当威尔伯在细看这张网的时候，两撇长胡子和一张尖脸出现了。坦普尔顿慢慢地拖着身子走过猪圈，在角落里扑躺下来。

“我回来了，”它用粗哑的声音说，“多么美好的一夜啊！”

老鼠的个子比原先膨胀了一倍。它的肚子有啫喱瓶那么大。

“多么美好的一夜啊！”它沙哑地再说一遍，“多么丰盛的大餐和酒席啊！真正是大吃大喝了一通！我一准吃了三十顿饭菜剩下来的东西。我从来没见过这样的残羹剩饭，样样东西经过天长日晒，都十分成熟了。噢，太丰盛了，我的朋友们，太丰盛了。”

“你该为自己感到害羞，”夏洛不以为然地说，“如果你消化不了，闹肚子痛，这是你活该。”

“不用为我肚子担心，”坦普尔顿咆哮说，“它什么都能受用。不过我有个坏消息。我回来的时候经过隔壁那只猪的猪圈——那只自称什么‘叔叔’的猪——看到它那猪圈前面有一个蓝色的牌牌。这是说，它得头奖了。我想你落选了，威尔伯。你也可以死了这条心啦——没有人会在你的脖子上挂个什么奖章了。而且，如果朱克曼先生对你改变了主意，我也不会觉得奇怪。等着他来想吃新鲜猪肉、烟熏火腿和松脆熏咸肉吧！他会拿着刀向你走来，我的伙计。”

“住口，坦普尔顿！”夏洛说，“你撑饱了，都不知道自己在说什么。别去理它，威尔伯！”

威尔伯尝试不去想老鼠刚才说过的话。它决定改变话题。

“坦普尔顿，”威尔伯说，“你要是不那么昏头昏脑，你就会注意到夏洛刚做了一个卵袋。它要做妈妈了。告诉你，在那粉红色小袋里有五百十四个卵呢。”

“这是真的吗？”老鼠怀疑地看那个袋，问道。

“对，这是真的。”夏洛叹了口气。

“恭喜你！”坦普尔顿咕噜说，“这真是个美妙的夜！”它闭上眼睛，拉了点麦草盖住身体，就死死地睡过去了。威尔伯和夏洛很高兴，能摆脱它一会儿了。

九点钟，阿拉布尔先生的卡车开进集市市场，停在威尔伯的猪圈那里。大家爬下车。

“看！”弗恩叫道，“看夏洛的网！看它上面说什么啦！”

大人和孩子手拉手站在那里，看新织的大字。

“‘**谦卑**’，”朱克曼先生读出来，“我说，这对威尔伯来说不是再贴切不过的字眼吗？”

大家很高兴看到又出现了蜘蛛网的奇迹。威尔伯深情地抬头看他们的脸。它的样子非常谦卑，满含感激。弗恩对夏洛眨眨眼。勒维很快就忙起来。他在食槽里倒进一桶热泔脚。当威尔伯吃它的早饭时，勒维用一根光滑的树枝搔它的背。

“等一等！”艾弗里说，“看这个！”他指着“叔叔”猪圈的蓝牌子。“这只猪已经得头奖了。”

朱克曼和阿拉布尔两家人看着那牌子。朱克曼太太哭了起来。没有人开口说句话。他们只是盯住牌子看。然后他们看“叔叔”。然后他们又看牌子。勒维掏出一条手帕大声擤鼻子——声音实在太响了，连那边马棚的马童都听见了。

“可以给我点钱吗？”弗恩问道，“我要到游艺场去。”

“你就得待在这里！”她妈妈说。弗恩眼泪都流出来了。

“大家哭什么？”朱克曼先生说，“让我们把事情赶紧做起来！伊迪丝，你去拿脱脂牛奶来！”

朱克曼太太用手帕擦擦眼睛。她到卡车那里拿过来一加仑罐的脱脂牛奶。

“是洗澡时间了！”朱克曼先生快活地说。他和朱克曼太太跟艾弗里爬进威尔伯的猪圈。艾弗里把牛奶慢慢地浇在威尔伯的头上和背上，当牛奶流下它的两边身体和脸颊时，朱克曼先生和太太把牛奶揉进它的毛里和皮肤上面。路过的人停下来看。很快就围上来一大群人。威尔伯变得雪白漂亮，浑身光滑。朝阳透过它粉红色的耳朵。

“它没有隔壁那只猪大，”一个参观的人说，“可是它更干净可爱。我就喜欢这样。”

“我也是。”另一个男人说。

“而且它谦卑。”一个女人读着网上的字说。

来参观猪圈的人个个说威尔伯的好话。个个赞赏蜘蛛网。当然，没有人注意到夏洛。

忽然传来扩音器的声音。

“请注意！”它说，“现在请霍默·朱克曼先生把他的名猪带到大看台前面的评判员席那儿去。过二十分钟要颁发给它一个特别奖。请所有人出席。朱克曼先生，请把你的猪放进板条箱，赶快到评判员席报到！”

广播一完，阿拉布尔和朱克曼两家人简直说不出话来，动也没法动。最后艾弗里抓起一把麦草，高高地撒向天空，高声欢呼。麦草像婚礼上撒的五彩纸屑一样纷纷扬扬落到弗恩的头发上。朱克曼先生拥抱朱克曼太太。阿拉布尔先生亲吻阿拉布尔太太。艾弗里亲吻威尔伯。勒维向每个人招手。弗恩拥抱她的妈妈。艾弗里拥抱弗恩。阿拉布尔太太拥抱朱克曼太太。

在头顶上，夏洛蹲在天花板的阴影里，前腿抱着卵袋，没人看见。它的心跳不如往常有力，它感到疲惫老弱，不过它最后确信，它已经救了威尔伯的命，感到安宁，心满意足。

“我们不能再耽搁时间了！”朱克曼先生叫道，“勒维，帮忙装箱吧。”

“能给我点钱吗？”弗恩问道。

“你等一等！”阿拉布尔太太说，“你没看到大家忙着吗？”

“把空牛奶罐放到车上去！”阿拉布尔先生吩咐说。艾弗里抓住牛奶罐就往卡车奔去。

“我的头发看上去好吗？”朱克曼太太问道。

“很好！”朱克曼先生狠狠地回答一声，和勒维一起把板条箱放在威尔伯面前。

“你连看都没看！”朱克曼太太说。

“你很好，伊迪丝，”阿拉布尔太太说，“你别响。”

在麦草里睡觉的坦普尔顿听到吵嚷声，醒了过来。它没弄清楚是怎么一回事，只看到人们把威尔伯推进板条箱，决定好好看个究竟。它看准机会，趁没有人看到，爬进了板条箱，钻到箱底的麦草里躲起来。

“好了，伙计们！”朱克曼先生叫道，“走吧！”他和阿拉布尔先生、勒维、艾弗里抓住箱子，把它抬出猪圈栅栏，抬上卡车。弗恩跳上车，坐在板条箱顶上。她头发上仍然粘着麦草，看上去十分漂亮，十分兴奋。阿拉布尔先生发动汽车。大家爬上车，开到大看台前面的评判员席前。

他们经过费里斯转轮的时候，弗恩抬起头去看，真希望这时候正在顶上那个厢子里，亨利·富西在她身边。

20.

胜利时刻

“现在郑重宣布！”扩音器用庄严的声音说，“集市主办人十分荣幸地向大家介绍霍默·L·朱克曼先生和他的大名猪。装着这非同寻常的大名猪的卡车正在开进内场。请大家向后退一退，让路给卡车开过来！过几分钟，这只猪将放到大看台前面专门的评选围栏里，要颁发一个特别奖给它。请大家让一让，让卡车开过来。谢谢。”

威尔伯听到这番话，浑身都发抖了。它觉得快活，但头有点晕乎乎。卡车慢慢地低速开行。人群围着它，阿拉布尔先生开得非常小心，免得撞了人。最后他总算开到评奖员席前。艾弗里跳下车，放下尾板。

“我吓得要死，”朱克曼先生悄悄说，“几百几千人在看着我们。”

“鼓起劲来，”阿拉布尔太太说，“这很好玩。”

“请把你的猪放下来！”扩音器里说。

“大家一起来，上，伙计们！”朱克曼先生说。人群中有几个人上前帮忙抬起板条箱。帮手的人当中，数艾弗里最忙了。

“把你的衬衫塞塞好，艾弗里！”朱克曼太太叫道，“束紧皮带。你的裤子要掉下来了。”

“你没看见我正忙着吗？”艾弗里不耐烦地回答说。

“瞧！”弗恩指点说，“亨利在那里！”

“别叫，弗恩！”她妈妈说，“别指指点点！”

“谢谢你，能给我点钱吗？”弗恩问道，“亨利又请我去坐费里斯转轮，不过我想他没钱了。他钱用光了。”

阿拉布尔太太打开她的钱包。“给你，”她说，“这里一共四毛钱。小心别弄丢了！早点回猪圈到我们固定集合的地方！”

弗恩跑开了，在人群里左钻右钻，寻找她的亨利。

“现在朱克曼先生的猪从它的板条箱里出来了，”扩音器的声音隆隆响，“请听候宣布！”

坦普尔顿蜷伏在板条箱底的麦草下面。“真是胡闹！”老鼠嘟哝说，“真是无事瞎忙乎！”

在那边猪圈里，夏洛独自一个在静静地休息。它的两条前腿抱住卵袋。夏洛听到了扩音器说的每一句话。这些话给了它勇气。这是它的胜利时刻。

威尔伯一出板条箱，人群就鼓掌欢呼起来。朱克曼先生摘下帽子鞠躬。勒维从口袋里掏出条大手帕擦脖子后面的汗水。艾弗里跪在威尔伯身边的泥地上，忙着抚摩它和卖弄自己。朱克曼太太和阿拉布尔太太站在卡车的脚蹬板上。

“女士们，先生们，”扩音器说话了，“我们现在来介绍霍默·L·朱克曼先生杰出的猪。这独一无二的猪已经遐迩闻名，吸引了许多贵客来我们这个伟大的州参观。你们许多人一定记得夏天那个让人永远忘不了的日子，朱克曼先生的谷仓里的蜘蛛网神秘地出现几个大字，呼吁大家注意这样一个事实，就是这只猪是完完全全与众不同的。这个奇迹始终无法得到充分的解释，虽然许多学者纷纷前来参观了朱克曼家的猪圈，研究和观察了这个现象。最后分析下来，我们只知道我们碰到的这件事乃是天意，我们只应该感到自豪，多谢老天爷。蜘蛛网上写的是，女士们和先生们，这是一只王牌猪。”

威尔伯脸红了。它站着完全一动不动，尽力做出最棒的样子。

“这一只出色的猪，”扩音器说下去，“的确是了不起。看看它吧，女士们和先生们！注意它全身雪白光滑，请注意，它的皮肤上一点瑕疵也没有，耳朵和鼻子上透着健康的粉红色。”

“这都多亏了脱脂牛奶。”阿拉布尔太太悄悄对朱克曼太太说。

“还请注意，这猪光彩照人！请记住，那天网上又清清楚楚出现了‘光彩照人’四个字。这些神秘的字是从哪里来的呢？它们不是蜘蛛织出来的，我们可以认为蜘蛛在结网方面聪明透顶，可是不用说，蜘蛛是不会织字的。”

“噢，它们不会吗？它们不会吗？”夏洛自言自语嘟哝说。

“女士们，先生们，”扩音器说下去，“我们绝不能再占用诸位宝贵的时间了。我谨代表集市的主办人，荣幸地颁给朱克曼先生一个特别奖，奖金二十五元，还有一个刻了字的美丽的铜奖章，表示我们对这猪——这光彩照人的、这了不起的、这谦卑的王牌猪——所做出的贡献的奖赏，它吸引了那么多贵客来到我们这个伟大的县集市来。”

威尔伯听着这番长篇大论的颂词，头越来越晕，越来越晕。当它听到人群又开始欢呼鼓掌时，忽然晕过去了。它的腿瘫痪下来，它的脑子一片空白，倒在地上不省人事。

“出什么事了？”扩音器里问道，“怎么回事，朱克曼先生？你的猪有什么不舒服吗？”

艾弗里跪在威尔伯的头边，不住地抚摩它。朱克曼先生跳来跳去用他的帽子扇它。

“它没事，”朱克曼先生叫道，“它有这种毛病，它谦卑，它受不了称赞。”

"这个嘛，我们不能把奖颁给一只死猪，"扩音器说，"从来没有过先例。"

"它没有死，"朱克曼先生大叫，"它只是晕过去了。它很容易紧张。快跑去拿水来，勒维！"

勒维跳出评判围栏，一路跑去了。

坦普尔顿从麦草里探出头来。它看见威尔伯的尾巴尖就在它够得到的地方。坦普尔顿咧开了嘴笑。"我来照顾照顾你吧。"它格格笑着说。它张开嘴去咬威尔伯的尾巴，用尽力气狠狠一咬。威尔伯一下子痛醒了。转眼间它已经站起来。

"唉哟！"它尖叫道。

"万岁万岁万万岁！"人群欢呼起来，"它起来了！这猪起来了！干得好，朱克曼！这真是只王牌猪！"人人兴高采烈。最高兴的要数朱克曼先生。他松了一大口气。没有人看到坦普尔顿，这老鼠干得好，立了大功。

现在一位评判员拿着那些奖品跨过栅栏走进圆围栏。他递给朱克曼先生两张十元钞票和一张五元钞票。接着他把奖章挂在威尔伯的脖子上。接着他跟朱克曼先生握手，这时威尔伯害羞得脸都红了。艾弗里伸出他的手，评判员也跟他握了手。人群欢声雷动。一位摄影师给威尔伯拍了照。

一种极大的幸福感掠过朱克曼和阿拉布尔两家人的心头。在朱克曼先生的一生中，这是一个最伟大的时刻。当着那么多人的面赢得一个奖，再没有比这更让人心满意足的了。

当威尔伯重新给推回板条箱的时候，勒维提着一桶水挤过人群。他的眼睛有一种狂野的目光。他毫不迟疑地把水泼到威尔伯身上。他太激动了，没泼中猪，倒泼到朱克曼先生和艾弗里的身上。他们给淋成了落汤鸡。

"我的天啊！"朱克曼先生大叫，他全身水淋淋的，"你吃错什么药了，勒维，你没看到猪好好的吗？"

"都是你叫我拿水来的。"勒维逆来顺受地说。

"我可没叫你给我冲凉。"朱克曼先生说。周围的人群哈哈大笑。最后朱克曼先生也只好笑。当然，艾弗里看到自己给淋得湿透，只有高兴的份，马上手舞足蹈扮小丑。他装作冲凉，做鬼脸，跳来跳去，在胳肢窝里假装擦肥皂，接着又装作用毛巾擦干身子。

"艾弗里，你停下来，别这样！"他妈妈大叫，"别出洋相了。"

可是众人爱看这个。艾弗里别的听不见，只听到拍手喝彩声。他就爱在众目睽睽之下，在大看台前面的圆围栏里扮小丑。他发现桶底还剩有一点水，干脆把桶举高，把水浇在自己身上，做怪脸。大看台上的小朋友们看得尖声高叫，满意得不得了。

最后，一切平静下来。威尔伯给装上了卡车。艾弗里让他妈妈从圆围栏里给拉了出来，坐到卡车座位上让身子干透。卡车由阿拉布尔先生慢慢地开回猪圈。艾弗里的湿裤子把车上的座位弄湿了一大片。

21.

最后一天

夏洛和威尔伯单独待着。那两家人去找弗恩了。坦普尔顿在睡大觉。威尔伯躺在那里，经过颁奖典礼上兴奋了一通，紧张了一番以后，正在休息。它的奖章仍旧挂在脖子上；用眼角它能看到它。

"夏洛，"过了一会儿，威尔伯说，"你为什么这样安静啊？"

"我喜欢一动不动地坐着，"它说，"我一向就是十分安静的。"

"对，不过你今天好像特别安静。你没事吧？"

"也许有点累。不过我觉得很平静。你今天上午在圆围栏里的成功，在很小的程度上也是我的成功。你的未来有保证了。你会活下去，安然无恙，威尔伯。现在没有什么能伤害你了。秋天的白昼要变短，天气要变冷。树叶要从树上飘落。圣诞节于是到了，接下来就下冬雪。你将活下来欣赏冰天雪地的美景，因为你对朱克曼先生来说太重要了，他怎么也不会伤害你。冬天会过去，白昼又变长，牧场池塘的冰要融化。北美歌雀将回来唱歌，青蛙将醒来，和暖的风又会吹起。所有这些景物、声音和香气都是供你享受的。威尔伯……噢，这个美好的世界，这些珍贵的日子……”

夏洛停了下来。过了一会儿，威尔伯的眼睛里涌出了泪水。“噢，夏洛，”它说，“想到第一次见到你，我还以为你嗜血，很残酷！”

等它从情感激动中恢复过来，它又说了。

“你为什么为我做这一切呢？”它问道，“我不配。我没有为你做过任何事情。”

“你一直是我的朋友，”夏洛回答说，“这件事本身就是一件了不起的事。我为你结网，因为我喜欢你。再说，生命到底是什么啊？我们出生，我们活上一阵子，我们死去。一只蜘蛛，一生只忙着捕捉和吃苍蝇是毫无意义的，通过帮助你，也许可以提升一点我生命的价值。谁都知道人活着该做一点有意义的事情。”

“唉，”威尔伯说，“我不会说话。我也不能像你一样说得那么好。不过你救了我，夏洛，我很高兴为你献出生命——我真心愿意。”

“我断定你会的。我感谢你这种慷慨之心。”

“夏洛，”威尔伯说，“我们今天都要回家了。这集市差不多结束了。重新回到谷仓，又和那些羊和鹅聚在一起，这不是好极了吗？你不盼着回家吗？”

夏洛半晌不语。接着它用那么轻的声音说话，威尔伯好不容易才听出来它在说什么。

“我不回谷仓去了。”它说。

威尔伯跳起来。“不回去？”它叫道，“夏洛，你在说什么？”

"我不行了，"它回答说，"我一两天之内就会死。我甚至没有力气爬到下面板条箱里。我怀疑我的吐丝器里是不是还有足够的丝可以吊到地面。"

威尔伯一听这话，悲痛万分，扑倒下来。它大声抽嗒，浑身哆嗦。它喘着气悲伤地哼哼叫。"夏洛，我忠实的朋友。"

"好了，我们不要婆婆妈妈了，"蜘蛛说，"安静下来，威尔伯。不要折腾自己了！"

"可我受不了，"威尔伯大叫，"我不能让你单独留下来等死。你留下来我也要留下来。"

"别胡说了，"夏洛说，"你不能留在这里。现在，朱克曼先生、约翰·阿拉布尔和其他人随时都会回来，他们把你推进那板条箱，你们就走了。再说，你留在这里也毫无意义。这里没人养你。集市场地很快就要空掉，人都走光。"

威尔伯惊恐万状。它在猪圈里团团转地跑着。它忽然有了一个主意——它想到了那卵袋和五百十四只要在春天孵出来的小蜘蛛。万一夏洛自己不能回到谷仓，至少可以把它这些孩子带回去。

威尔伯冲到猪圈前面。它把它的前脚扑到最上面一块栏板上朝四下里看。它看到远处阿拉布尔和朱克曼两家人正在走来。它知道事不宜迟，得赶快干。

"坦普尔顿在哪里？"它问道。

"它在那角落的麦草底下睡觉。"夏洛说。

威尔伯冲过去，把它有力的鼻子钻到老鼠底下，把它挑上半空。

"坦普尔顿！"威尔伯尖叫，"你听我说！"

老鼠本来睡得熟熟的，一下子给吓醒了，它看上去先是昏头昏脑，然后是大不高兴。

"这是什么恶作剧？"它咆哮说，"老鼠不能睡一会儿，不这样粗暴地给挑到半空去吗？"

"听我说！"威尔伯大叫，"夏洛生了重病。它只能活很短的时间了。由于身体不好，它不能和我们一起回家。因此，我绝对必须把它的卵袋带回去。我够不着，又爬不上去。只有你能把它拿下来。现在一秒钟也不能再耽搁了。人们在往这儿赶——随时就到这里。谢谢你，谢谢你，谢谢你，坦普尔顿，爬上去把那个卵袋拿下来吧。"

老鼠打哈欠。它拉拉胡子。接着它抬头看那卵袋。

"是这么回事！"它厌恶地说，"又是要老坦普尔顿去救助，对不对？坦普尔顿，你干这个；坦普尔顿，你干那个；坦普尔顿，谢谢你跑到垃圾场去啃一片杂志带回来；坦普尔顿，谢谢你借给我一根绳子，我好结网。"

"噢，赶快啊！"威尔伯说，"赶快啊，坦普尔顿！"

可是老鼠不急不忙。它开始学威尔伯的口气说话。

"又是'赶快啊，坦普尔顿，'对吗？"它说，"嗬，嗬，嗬。我倒想知道，我帮了这么多忙，我得到过什么感谢呢？对老坦普尔顿一句好话也没有，只有毁谤、讥讽和冷言冷语。对老鼠一句好话也没有。"

"坦普尔顿，"威尔伯真是没辙了，"你再不停止叽叽咕咕，赶快一点，那就全完了，我就要心碎而死。谢谢你，爬上去吧！"

坦普尔顿躺回麦草上去。它懒洋洋地把前爪伸上去搁在头底下，交叉双膝，一副完完全全休息的样子。

"心碎而死，"它学口学舌说，"多么感动人！唉呀，唉呀！我注意到了，一有麻烦你总是来找我。可我从来没听说有什么人为了我心碎。噢，没有。谁关心老坦普尔顿呢？"

"起来！"威尔伯尖叫，"别再像个惯坏的孩子了！"

坦普尔顿咧开嘴笑，躺着不动。"是谁一次又一次上垃圾场去？"它问道，"还用说，是老坦普尔顿！是谁用臭鹅蛋吓走阿拉布尔家那个男孩救了夏洛的命？我的天啊，我相信又是老坦普尔顿。今天上午你在观众面前昏过去，是谁咬你的尾巴让你重新站起来？是老坦普尔顿。你想到过，我这样给差来差去，做这做那，我已经厌烦了吗？你以为我是什么，是只有活就差去干的老鼠吗？"

威尔伯真是绝望了。那些人正在走来。老鼠却不听它的话。它忽然想起坦普尔顿贪吃。

"坦普尔顿，"它说，"我对你庄严保证，只要你把夏洛的卵袋拿下来，从今以后，当勒维给我喂食的时候，我一定让你先吃。我让你食槽里爱吃什么挑什么吃，在你吃够之前，我绝不碰食物。"

老鼠一听就坐起来了。"你这话当真？"它说。

"我保证，我在心口画十字。"

“好吧，成交！”老鼠说。它走到墙边，开始向上爬。由于隔夜吃得太饱，它的肚子还涨鼓鼓的。它哼哼哈哈抱怨着，慢慢爬上天花板。它爬过去，一直爬到卵袋那里。夏洛缩到一边让它。它快死了，不过还有点力气动一动。这时候，坦普尔顿龇起它难看的长牙齿，开始咬断把卵袋挂在天花板上的丝。威尔伯在下面看着。

“要极其小心！”它说，“我不希望有一个卵受伤。”

“我满嘴都是丝，”老鼠抱怨说，“这比拔丝糖还粘嘴。”

可是坦普尔顿的嘴不停地动，终于把卵袋的丝都咬断，把卵袋带

到地面上来，扔到威尔伯面前。威尔伯大大松了口气。

“谢谢你，坦普尔顿，”它说，“我一天活着，一天不会忘记这件事。”

“我也不会，”老鼠剔着它的牙齿说，“我觉得好像吃了一团丝。好了，我们要回家了！”

坦普尔顿爬进板条箱，钻到麦草里去。它正好及时不见。就在这时候，勒维、约翰·阿拉布尔和朱克曼先生回来了，后面跟着阿拉布尔太太和朱克曼太太、艾弗里和弗恩。威尔伯已经决定该如何带走卵袋——也仅有一种办法可行。它小心翼翼地把这卵袋放到嘴里，用舌头托住。它记得夏洛告诉过它——这卵袋是防水的，很结实。卵袋在舌头上让威尔伯觉得异样，有点流口水。威尔伯当然不能说话。不过在它被推进板条箱时，它抬起头去看夏洛，向它眨眨眼睛。夏洛知道，威尔伯这是用它惟一的办法跟它说再见。夏洛也知道，它的孩子们平安无事了。

“再见！”夏洛悄悄地说。接着它鼓起全身力气向威尔伯挥挥它的一条前腿。

它再也没有动过。第二天，当费里斯转轮被拆下来、赛马被装上装运车、艺人们收拾好东西把他们带活动房屋的拖车开走时，夏洛死了。集市场面很快就空无一人。棚子和建筑物空了，被遗弃了。场地上满是瓶子和垃圾。在来过集市的数以千计的人中，没有一个知道，一只灰蜘蛛曾经起过最重要的作用。在它死的时候，没有任何一个谁陪在它身边。

22.

温暖的风

就这样，威尔伯回到了谷仓底下它心爱的肥料堆上。它这次回来非常特别。它的脖子上挂着荣誉奖章，它的嘴里含着一个蜘蛛卵袋。当威尔伯把夏洛那五百十四个还没出生的孩子小心地放在安全角落时，它想，没有比家更好的地方了。谷仓闻上去真是好。它的老朋友，羊和鹅，很高兴看到它回来。

那些鹅热热闹闹地欢迎它。

“恭喜——恭喜——恭喜你！”它们叫道，“干得好。”

朱克曼先生把奖章从威尔伯的脖子上拿下来，挂在猪圈墙上的一颗钉子上面，让参观的人可以仔细看它。威尔伯自己要看，也随时可以看到。

在接下来的日子里它非常快活。它长得又肥又大。它不用再担心被杀掉了，因为它知道朱克曼先生要养它一辈子。威尔伯经常想到夏洛。它那个旧网的几根丝还挂在门口。每天威尔伯会站在那里，看着那张破了的空网，喉咙一阵哽塞。没有人有过这样一个朋友——那么深情，那么忠诚，那么有本事。

秋天的白昼越来越短，勒维从菜园把南瓜什么的收进来，堆在谷仓地板上，它们在这里，严寒的夜晚也不会冻坏。槭树和桦树变成鲜亮的颜色，风吹得它们摇来摇去，叶子一片一片落到地上。在牧场的野苹果树下，红色的小苹果厚厚地铺了一地，羊啃它们，鹅啃它们，狐狸夜里来闻闻它们。一天晚上，就在圣诞节来临之前，开始下雪了。雪盖住了房子，盖住了谷仓，盖住了田野和林子。威尔伯还没有见过雪。早晨它走出去，踩踏猪栏里的积雪，开出路来，只是为了好玩。弗恩和艾弗里拖着一个雪橇上这儿来。他们滑下小路，滑到牧场上结了冰的池塘里去。

"滑雪最好玩了。"艾弗里说。

"不对，"弗恩顶他说，"最好玩的是费里斯转轮停下来，亨利和我在顶上那厢子里，亨利让厢子晃来晃去，我们在那上面能看到许多英里许多英里许多英里远。"

"天啊，你还在想着那老费里斯转轮？"艾弗里厌恶地说，"集市都不知道是多少多少个星期以前的事了。"

"我一直想着它。"弗恩擦掉耳朵上的雪说。

圣诞节过后，温度表显示温度降到零下十度。天寒地冻。牧场冷得刺骨，样样都冻住了。现在牛一直待在谷仓里，只有阳光明媚的早晨，它们才到外面去，站在谷仓院子里麦草堆挡住风的地方。羊也待在谷仓附近的背风处。它们渴了就吃雪。鹅围着谷仓院子转，就像男孩围着杂货铺转一样，朱克曼先生给它们喂玉米和萝卜，让它们高兴。

“非常，非常，非常感谢！”它们一看到食物来了就这么说。

入冬以后，坦普尔顿一直在户内活动。猪食槽底下的那个老鼠洞太冷了，因此它在谷仓里的粮仓后面给自己做了个舒服的窝。它在窝里垫上肮脏的报纸碎片和破布片，什么时候一找到点小玩意儿或者纪念品，它就把它们拿回家储存在那里。它一天三次去看威尔伯，准时在吃饭时间，威尔伯遵守自己作出的诺言，让老鼠先吃。等到坦普尔顿吃得一口也再吃不下去了，威尔伯才吃。吃得过饱的结果就是，坦普尔顿比你见过的任何老鼠都更大更胖。它庞大无比，像只小旱獭。

有一天，老羊就它的个子对它说：“如果你吃得少一点，你就可以活得长一点。”

“谁需要长生不老呢？”老鼠讥讽说，“我天生是个大食鬼，从大吃大喝的乐趣中得到说不出的满足感。”它拍拍肚子，对老羊龇着牙齿笑笑，爬到上面粮仓去躺下来。

整个冬天，威尔伯一直盯住夏洛的卵袋看，像是护卫它自己的孩子。它在肥料堆里拱出一个专门的地方放这卵袋，就在栅栏旁边。在严寒的夜里，它躺着让自己的呼吸能温暖它。对威尔伯来说，它生活中再没有一样东西比得上这小圆球重要——不管是什么东西。它耐心地等着冬天结束，这些小蜘蛛诞生。当你在等着什么事情发生，等着什么孵出来时，生活总是一段稳定充实的时光。最后，冬天终于到头了。

“今天我听到青蛙叫，”一天傍晚老羊说，“听！现在你能听到它了。”

威尔伯站着不动，竖起了耳朵。从池塘那里传来几百只小青蛙的合叫声。

“春天，”老羊沉思说，“又是一个春天。”它走开时，威尔伯看到一只新的小羊羔跟在它后面。小羊羔才几个钟头大。

雪融化成水流走了。小溪和沟渠流水潺潺。一条胸前有条纹的歌雀飞来，唱起了歌。白昼变长，天亮得更早了。羊棚里几乎每天早晨都会多一只小羊羔。那只母鹅坐在九个蛋上面。天空似乎更加开阔，温暖的风吹了起来。夏洛那张旧网最后剩下的一些蛛丝也飘走了，不见了。

一个大晴天，威尔伯吃过了早饭，站在那里看它的宝贝袋子。它没有多想什么。它就那么站在那里，可忽然之间，它看到有什么东西在动。它走近一点看。一只小蜘蛛正从袋子里爬出来。它不会比一粒沙子大，不比一个针头大。它的身体是灰色的，底下有一道黑条纹。它的腿是灰色和棕色的。它的样子看上去跟夏洛一模一样。

威尔伯一看到它，顿时浑身发抖。这小蜘蛛向它招手。威尔伯再靠近一点看。又有两只小蜘蛛爬出来招手。它们在袋子上绕圈圈，探索它们的新世界。接着又有三只小蜘蛛。接着又是八只小蜘蛛。接着又是十只小蜘蛛。夏洛的孩子们终于都出来了。

威尔伯的心怦怦直跳。它开始呜呜尖叫。接着它绕着圈圈跑，把肥料踢上半空。接着它一个后空翻。接着它用前腿猛地站稳，在夏洛的孩子们面前停住。

“喂，你们好！”它说。

第一只小蜘蛛说：“你好。”不过它的声音小得威尔伯听不见。

“我是你们妈妈的老朋友，”威尔伯说，“我很高兴看到你们。你们都好吗？一切平安吗？”

那些小蜘蛛向它挥动前腿。威尔伯从它们的举动能看出来，它们很高兴看到它。

“有什么东西我能给你们吗？你们需要什么东西吗？”

那些小蜘蛛只是招手。有好几天好几夜，它们爬来爬去，爬上爬下，绕过来绕过去，向威尔伯招手，在它们身后拖着细丝，探索它们的家。它们几十只几十只。威尔伯不会数数，不过它知道，它有了许多新朋友。它们长得很快。没多久，每一只都有BB猎枪弹①那么大了。它们在袋子附近结出些一丁点儿大的网。

接着到了一个安静的早晨，朱克曼先生把北边的一扇门打开。一股温暖的气流轻轻地穿过谷仓底。空气中有潮湿的泥土香味，有云杉树的香味，有甜蜜的春天气息。蜘蛛娃娃们感觉到温暖的上升气流。一只小蜘蛛爬到栅栏的顶上。接着它做出一件让威尔伯大为吃惊的事。那小蜘蛛倒过头来竖蜻蜓站着，把吐丝器指向天空，吐出一蓬漂亮的丝。这些丝成了一个气球。威尔伯就那么眼巴巴地看着它离开栅栏，飞到空中去了。

“再见！”小蜘蛛飞出门时，说了一声。

“等一等！”威尔伯尖叫，“你这是上哪儿去啊？”

可是小蜘蛛已经飞得没影了。接着又是一只小蜘蛛爬到栅栏顶上，用头倒立，吐出一个气球，也飞走了。接着又是一只小蜘蛛。接着又是一只。空中很快飞满了小气球，每个小气球带走一只小蜘蛛。

威尔伯简直要发疯了。夏洛的小宝宝们很快都不见了。

“回来，孩子们！”威尔伯大叫。

“再见！”它们纷纷叫道，“再见，再见！”

最后有一只小蜘蛛在吐出气球前，停了足够时间能跟威尔伯说两

① BB猎枪弹的直径是0.18英寸。

句话。

“我们在乘着这温暖的上升气流离开这里。这是我们动身的时刻。我们是飞天蜘蛛，我们正在到世界上去结我们的网。”

“可是到哪儿去呢？”威尔伯问道。

“风把我们吹到哪儿就到哪儿。高处，低处。近处，远处。东，南，西，北。我们乘着微风飞走，要上哪儿就上哪儿。”

“你们全都去吗？”威尔伯问，“你们不能全都去。这样就只剩我一个了，没有朋友。我断定你们的妈妈不会希望这样的。”

空中这时满是气球，谷仓底看上去简直是起了雾一般。几十个几十个气球飞起来，打转，飞出门，乘着微风飞走。“再见，再见，再见！”的叫声微弱地传到威尔伯耳朵里。它再也看不下去了，难过地扑倒在地，闭上眼睛。被夏洛的孩子们抛弃，这近乎世界的末日。威尔伯哭着哭着，睡着了。

等到它醒来，已经是下午后半晌。它看着那卵袋，已经空了。它抬头看空中。气球全都没有了。于是它垂头丧气地走到门口，夏洛的网过去一直在那里。威尔伯站在那里，想着夏洛，这时它猛然听到一个很小的声音。

“你好！”那声音说，“我在你头顶呢。”

“我也是。”另一个很小的声音说。

“我也是，”第三个声音说，“我们三个留下来。我们喜欢这个地方，我们喜欢你。”

威尔伯抬起头看。门梁上结了三个小蜘蛛网。每个网上都有一个夏洛的女儿忙着工作。

“我能够这样看这件事吗？”威尔伯问道，“这表示你们已经拿定主意，在这谷仓底住下来了，我要有三个朋友了？”

“你当然能够这样认为。”那些小蜘蛛说。

“请问你们叫什么名字？”威尔伯问，快乐得直发抖。

“我会告诉你我的名字的，”第一只小蜘蛛回答说，“如果你告诉我你为什么发抖。”

“我是快乐得发抖。”威尔伯说。

“那么我的名字就叫快乐。”第一只小蜘蛛说。

“那么我妈妈中间名字的缩写是什么？”第二只小蜘蛛问。

“阿。”威尔伯说。

“那么我的名字叫阿拉妮。”这只小蜘蛛说。

“那么我呢？”第三只小蜘蛛问，“你可以给我取一个又好听，又有意思的名字吗——不要太长，不要太花哨，也不要太傻。”

威尔伯埋头拼命地想。

“内莉？”威尔伯想出了一个。

“很好，我非常喜欢，”第三只小蜘蛛说，“你就叫我内莉吧。”它轻巧地把它的环线接到网的下一根辐线上去。

威尔伯的心里洋溢着快乐。它觉得自己该对这无比重要的时刻发表一篇简短的讲话。

“快乐！阿拉妮！内莉！”它开口说，“欢迎你们来到谷仓底。你们选中了一个神圣的门口结你们的网。我想我应该告诉你们，我一向全心全意爱你们的妈妈。我的性命是它救回来的。它卓越，漂亮，一直到死都忠心耿耿。我永远珍藏着对它的回忆。对于你们，它的女儿们，我发誓和你们友好下去，直到永远。”

“我也发誓和你友好下去。”快乐说。

“我也是。”阿拉妮说。

“我也是。”内莉说，它正好捉住了一只小蚊蚋。

对威尔伯来说，这是一个快乐的日子。接下来是更多快乐安宁的日子。

时间流逝着，一个月又一个月，一年又一年，来了又去了，可威尔伯从来不缺少朋友。弗恩不再那么经常来谷仓。她在长大，小心地避开孩子气的事，例如端张挤奶凳子坐在猪圈旁边。可是年复一年，夏洛的子女、孙子女、曾孙子女一直住在门口那儿。每年夏天都有新的小蜘蛛出世代替老的。它们绝大多数都乘气球飞走了。可总是有两三只留下来，在门口安家。

朱克曼先生很好地照顾着威尔伯的一生。经常有朋友和慕名而来的人来看望威尔伯，因为没有人会忘记它的峥嵘岁月和网上奇迹。谷仓里的生活非常好——不管白天还是黑夜，冬天还是夏天，春天还是秋天，阴沉日子还是晴朗日子。威尔伯想，这真是个最好的地方，这温馨可爱的仓底，有嘎嘎不休的鹅，有变换不同的季节，有太阳的温暖，有燕子来去，有老鼠在附近，有单调没变化的羊，有蜘蛛的爱，有肥料的气味，有所有值得称赞的东西。

威尔伯永远忘不了夏洛。它虽然热爱它的子女、孙子女、曾孙子女，可是这些新蜘蛛没有一只能取代夏洛在它心中的位置。夏洛是无可比拟的。这样的人物不是经常能够碰到的：既是忠实朋友，又是写作好手。夏洛两者都是。

译后记

E · B · 怀特，也就是埃尔温 · 布鲁克斯 · 怀特(Elwyn Brooks White, 1899 — 1985)，他本来就是美国一位大作家，优秀的散文家，后来他兴之所至，又写起了儿童文学作品，成了一位著名的儿童文学作家。看来，从国际范围说，他作为儿童文学作家的名声反而更大，因为他的儿童文学作品被介绍到许多国家，受到各国小读者欢迎。

E · B · 怀特一八九九年生于美国纽约州的芒特弗农市，一九二一年毕业于康奈尔大学。一九二六年起，他和《纽约客》杂志长期合作，担任特约编辑和作者。《纽约客》以其幽默风格驰名，E · B · 怀特这位幽默散文大家对奠定这杂志的独特风格起了重大作用。一九三九年，他搬到了缅因州的一个农场，在那里从事写作。

E · B · 怀特在世界儿童文学上如此有名，其实他一共只写了三部童话，这就是《精灵鼠小弟》(1945)、《夏洛的网》(1952) 和《吹小号的天鹅》(1970)。这三部童话全都被改编拍成了电影。《精灵鼠小弟》因为受到热烈欢迎，还拍了续集。《夏洛的网》拍了不止一次，就在我写这篇文章的时候，新拍的一部电影要跟大家见面了。在E · B · 怀特的三部童话中，《夏洛的网》被公认为他的代表作，在美国《出版人周刊》的读者调查中，它位居“美国十佳儿童文学名著”的首位。它如今已经成为世界儿童文学的一部经典作品。

《夏洛的网》这个童话从一只小猪讲起。

说来这只小猪也真不幸，生下来就是一只落脚猪。你们知道落脚猪是什么吗？母猪一胎生下好多只小猪，最后生下来的一只总是又弱又小，它那些壮实的猪兄猪姐们争夺母猪乳汁最多的奶头时，它总给挤开，这样下去，它是很难养活的。反正这样的落脚猪活不下去，养猪的人家往往提早把它“解决”掉。这只小猪生下来就是如此不幸。

正当这小猪的主人从家里拿着斧子要去杀它的时候，他的女儿弗恩看到了，认为小猪生下来小，它自己也没有办法，只因为它生下来小就把它杀掉，这太不公平了。她紧紧抓住爸爸的斧子，又哭又叫，爸爸爱女儿，只好答应不杀它，把它带回家让女儿用牛奶喂养。弗恩拿到了小猪，高兴极了，还给它取了一个名字，叫威尔伯。

小猪威尔伯吃得好，还跟弗恩的洋娃娃一起坐婴儿车去兜风，快快活活的，长得很好。可过了个把月，弗恩的爸爸又要把它卖掉，其他小猪也都卖掉了。弗恩当然又是大哭挽留，可是这回爸爸说不能老把小猪当小宝宝养下去。还是弗恩的妈妈出的主意，让弗恩的舅舅买了这小猪，他家离得近，弗恩空了可以去看它。于是威尔伯便住到了舅舅家谷仓底下的肥料堆里。

尽管吃得好，谷仓里也有许多动物，可是它们各忙各的，谁也不肯跟威尔伯玩，弗恩也只能放了学才来看它。威尔伯感到孤独，它需要朋友，需要爱。在一个黑暗的夜里，正当威尔伯十分伤心的时候，黑暗中传来一个很细很好听的声音："我可以做你的朋友，我喜欢你。"

到第二天他才看到这个朋友——蜘蛛夏洛。

威尔伯如今除了弗恩，又有了可以谈心的朋友夏洛，吃得又好，养得白白胖胖。正在它很开心的时候，谷仓里最老的那只羊告诉它，到了圣诞节，它就要给杀掉做熏肉火腿。这个消息像晴天霹雳，让威尔伯号啕大哭，扑倒在地尖叫："我不要死！救救我！"

"你不会死，"夏洛轻轻地说，"我救你。"

夏洛为了救威尔伯，动足了脑筋，最后出了奇迹，它的网上织出了"王牌猪"三个字。夏洛的网这个奇迹轰动了四乡，大家走的走来，坐车的坐车来，就为了一睹"王牌猪"的尊容。这是怎么回事啊，谁也说不明白，但王牌猪就是王牌猪，威尔伯是王牌猪，王牌猪的主人更是高兴得不得了。为了继续加热，夏洛在网上又织出了"了不起"、"光彩照人"。于是"光彩照人"、"了不起"的"王牌猪"威尔伯成了大新闻。

秋天到了，集市举行赛猪的日子到了，也就是说，最后关头到了，只要威尔伯获奖，它的性命就能保住。然而这时候夏洛到了产卵季节，应该待在家里。然而到了赶车上集市时，夏洛还是毅然决然去了。

比赛对威尔伯有点不利，因为来了一只特大肥猪。夏洛为了产卵，已经有气无力，但它还是拼了最后的力气，织了一个新网，上面织着“谦卑”两个字，这件事再次轰动了全场，威尔伯获得了特别奖！

可是夏洛留下它装着五百十四个卵的卵袋，它回不去了。它只能和威尔伯诀别。它为威尔伯能活下去享受这个美好的世界而感到高兴。因为它一直是威尔伯的朋友。它因为能在一生做这件好事而觉得活得有价值。它鼓起全身力气向威尔伯挥手告别，悄悄地说了声：“再见！”

威尔伯用嘴衔着夏洛那有五百十四个卵的防水卵袋回家。到了时候，看到一只一只小蜘蛛爬出来，它们又织出气球飞走，只留下了三只。威尔伯对它们说：“我全心全意爱你们的妈妈，我的性命是它救回来的。我永远珍藏着对它的回忆。我发誓和你们友好下去，直到永远。”

威尔伯一直活下去，看到了夏洛的子女、孙子女、曾孙子女……但它永远忘不了夏洛。

《夏洛的网》是一部好看的童话，故事生动，情节有趣，充满悬念，小朋友一定爱读。但E · B · 怀特这位散文大师又用他幽默的文笔，深入浅出地讲了些很有意义的哲理，关于爱，关于友情，关于生死……正因为这个缘故，这本书也受到成人读者的喜爱。

作者长期生活在农村，在这本书里他亲切地写了农村的生活，生动地刻画了农村的人和动物。甚至那只很讨人和动物嫌的老鼠也发挥了很大的作用，它帮忙到垃圾场里啃来杂志广告的碎片，夏洛挑选它要织的字眼，让这老鼠也感到，为救威尔伯，它也有一部分功劳的。

对威尔伯第一位救命恩人弗恩的描写也很有道理。她本来天天去看威尔伯，能听懂威尔伯和夏洛的对话，回家讲给大人听，弄得大人担心她脑子是不是出了毛病，去请教医生。医生说得好，这小女孩会长大的，到时候她会被其他事吸引。后来在集市上，当大家为威尔伯的成功欢乐时，她不是被一个男生吸引，只想着和他去游乐场坐转轮吗？孩子就是这样长大的。

作者还借蜘蛛夏洛的口说出了好些很有意思的话。当夏洛要织上“了不起”这话时，威尔伯很谦虚地说：“可我并不了不起。”夏洛说：“一丁点也没关系。看到印出来的东西，发表出来的东西，人们都会相信的。”这真正是E·B·怀特式的讽刺性的话。尤其叫人感动的，是夏洛和威尔伯诀别时说的话：“生命到底是什么啊？我们出生，我们活上一辈子，我们死去。一只蜘蛛，一生只忙着捕捉和吃苍蝇是毫无意义的，通过帮助你，也许可以提升一点我生命的价值。谁都知道，人活着该做一点有意义的事情。”

对于我们这些写作的人，全书最后那句话很值得深思：“这样的人物不是经常能够碰到的，既是忠实朋友，又是写作好手。夏洛两者都是。”

任溶溶

二〇〇六年十二月

图书在版编目（CIP）数据
夏洛的网/ Charlotte's Web：英汉双语珍藏本/（美）怀特（White，E. B.）著；任溶溶译.—上海：上海译文出版社，2008.8（2012.3 重印）
ISBN 978-7-5327-4609-5

Ⅰ. 夏…　Ⅱ. ①怀…②任…　Ⅲ. ①英语—汉语—双语读物②童话—美国—现代　Ⅳ. H391.4：I
中国版本图书馆 CIP 数据核字（2008）第 096746 号

图字：09-2003-269 号

夏洛的网
〔美〕E. B. 怀特／著　**任溶溶**／译
责任编辑／张　颖　装帧设计／张志全

上海世纪出版股份有限公司
译文出版社出版、发行　www. yiwen. com. cn
上海福建中路 193 号
200001　易文网：www. ewen. cc
全国新华书店经销
上海译文印刷厂印刷

开本 890×1240　1/32　印张 10　插页 3　字数 200，000
2008 年 8 月第 1 版　2012 年 3 月第 9 次印刷
印数：64,001－74,000 册
ISBN 978-7-5327-4609-5/I・2606
定价：22.00 元

E·B·怀特随笔

如同宪法第一修正案一样，E·B·怀特的原则与风范长存。

——《纽约时报》一九八五年十月四日讣告

E·B·怀特是一位伟大的文体家，一位超绝的文体家，他的文学风格之纯净，在我们的语言中较之任何人都不遑多让。它是独特的、口语化的、清晰的、自然的、完全美国式的，极美的，他的人长生不老，他的文字超越时空。

——《纽约客》前总编威廉·肖恩

E·B·怀特（E. B. White，1899—1985），“二十世纪最伟大的美国随笔作家”。作为《纽约客》主要撰稿人的怀特一手奠定了影响深远的“《纽约客》文风”。怀特对这个世界上的一切都充满关爱，他的道德与他的文章一样山高水长。除了他终生挚爱的随笔之外，他还为孩子们写了三本书：《斯图尔特鼠小弟》（又译《精灵鼠小弟》）、《夏洛的网》与《吹小号的天鹅》，同样成为儿童与成人共同喜爱的文学经典。

“E·B·怀特随笔”由作者本人选定，囊括了这位最伟大的随笔作家最重要的随笔作品，中文版分为两卷出版，名曰：《这就是纽约》与《重游缅湖》。